GEORGE BUSH SPEAKS OUT

BUSH & REAGAN—"There was never a hint of negative feeling left over from our fight for the presidential nomination because Reagan's instinct, I learned, is to think the best of the people he works with. It was clear that once he'd made his decision on the vice presidency, he viewed the Reagan-Bush ticket not simply as a convenient political alliance but as a partnership. We would run and serve together as a team."

BUSH AT WAR—"Suddenly there was a jolt, as if a massive fist had crunched into the belly of the plane. Smoke poured into the cockpit, and I could see flames rippling across the wing. . . . I homed in on the target, unloaded our four 500-pound bombs and pulled away. Once over water, I leveled off and told [my two crew members] to bail out. Neither one of them survived."

BUSH & NIXON—August 7, 1974: "Dear Mr. President . . . It is my considered judgment that you should now resign . . . This letter is much more difficult because of the gratitude I will always feel toward you. If you do leave office, history will properly record your achievements with lasting respect."

BUSH IN CHINA—[As Ambassador, I] was provided a Chrysler sedan. But by the time my mother arrived for a Christmas holiday visit, Barbara and I were known among the Chinese staff members as "Busher, who ride the bicycle, just as the Chinese do."

ABOUT THE CO-AUTHOR

VICTOR GOLD is a Washington journalist and author who served
as a senior consultant on Vice President Bush's staff during the
1980 and 1984 presidential campaigns.

LOOKING FORWARD

George Bush
with Victor Gold

BANTAM BOOKS
TORONTO · NEW YORK · LONDON · SYDNEY · AUCKLAND

The Vice President's share of profits from the sale of this book will be divided equally between the M. D. Anderson Hospital in Houston, for its work in the field of leukemia, and the United Negro College Fund.

This edition contains the complete text
of the original hardcover edition.
NOT ONE WORD HAS BEEN OMITTED.

LOOKING FORWARD

A Bantam Book / published by arrangement with Doubleday

PRINTING HISTORY
Doubleday edition published September 1987
Bantam edition / July 1988

PHOTO CREDITS

We gratefully acknowledge the following sources of photographs appearing in this book:

George and Barbara Bush: numbers 1, 2, 3, 4, 5, 6, 7, 9, 12, 14, and 15
Dave Valdez, The White House: numbers 16, 17, 18, 19, 20, 21, 22, 23, and 24
International Communication NYC: number 10
Time-Life Picture Agency: number 11
Benjamin Brink, *Journal Tribune,* Biddeford, Maine: number 13

Excerpts from *Legacy: The Story of the Permian Basin Region of West Texas and Southwest New Mexico* by Gus Clemens, copyright © 1983 by The Nita Stewart Haley Memorial Library, published by Mulberry Avenue Books, 1983, are reprinted by permission of the author.

Permission is gratefully acknowledged to reprint lines from "The Gambler." Written by Don Schlitz, copyright © 1978, Writer's Night Music.

ISBN 0-553-27791-X

Published simultaneously in the United States and Canada

Bantam Books are published by Bantam Books, a division of Bantam Doubleday Dell Publishing Group, Inc. Its trademark, consisting of the words "Bantam Books" and the portrayal of a rooster, is Registered in U.S. Patent and Trademark Office and in other countries. Marca Registrada. Bantam Books, 666 Fifth Avenue, New York, New York 10103

PRINTED IN THE UNITED STATES OF AMERICA

KR   0 9 8 7 6 5 4 3 2 1

To my mother and father,
whose values lit the way

Acknowledgments

My appreciation to the following friends for their help in furnishing information and material in the preparation of this book: Jack and Valta Casselman; C. Fred Chambers; Earle Craig; Tom Fowler; Roy Goodearle; Governor Hugh Gregg; Gary Laughlin; my first boss, Bill Nelson; John Overbey; Don Rhodes; and Chase Untermeyer. Special thanks to Dr. William K. (Sandy) Muir of the University of California for encouraging me to proceed with this project, and to my editor, Patrick Filley, for his constructive criticism and helpful suggestions as the book progressed.

GB

Contents

Introduction

It was in January 1977 that I was first bitten by the bug that often bites people who pass the age of fifty: I wanted to tell my story, to relate my experience to others, after a decade that had taken me, my wife Barbara, and our family, from Houston, to Washington, t ew York, to Beijing, then to Washington again.

The timing couldn't have been better. In January 1967, I'd begun my public career as a congressman. In January 1977, I'd ended it—at least, put it on hold—after serving a year as Director of the Central Intelligence Agency. All that was needed was a publisher to suggest, "Have you considered writing a book?" and I was on my way, taking notes and talking into my tape recorder.

Then, as often occurs in the life of a book, a funny thing happened on the way to the printer. In July 1980, I became Ronald Reagan's running mate on the Republican national ticket. In January 1981, I was sworn in as Vice President.

Still, I like to finish what I start, whether it's political or autobiographical. The idea of completing the book stayed with me. In fact, it expanded over the years to include not only 1967–77 but the years that had gone before—the early experiences that shaped my life, my values, and my philosophy.

. . .

A few weeks after this autobiography was first published, I became a candidate for President; not exactly the political surprise of the year, since five of our previous vice presidents have, under various circumstances, done the same thing.

Lyndon Johnson and Jerry Ford, of course, ran as presidential incumbents, after succeeding to the office. Walter Mondale ran as former vice president in 1984, as did Richard Nixon when he defeated Hubert Humphrey—then the incumbent vice president—in 1968.

All of which led to one of the first questions asked by reporters after I entered the presidential race last fall. It concerned the effect the Van Buren Hex might have on my candidacy.

Martin Van Buren served as Andrew Jackson's vice president from 1833 to 1837. When Jackson left the White House, Van Buren succeeded him, defeating William Henry Harrison in the election of 1836. Since that time, reporters reminded me, no incumbent vice president has ever been elected to the presidency.

Question: *How did I plan to do what no incumbent vice president since Van Buren has been able to do?*

My answer came in two parts. First, I said that the circumstances that applied to past campaigns have little or no bearing on the presidential campaign of 1988. Second, even if they did, I have an ace-in-the-hole: Shirley MacLaine —so I've been told—thinks I was Martin Van Buren in a former life.

So much for hexes. On a more serious note, I was asked how a Bush presidency would differ from the Reagan presidency.

Again, my answer came in two parts. First, I pointed out that Ronald Reagan and I fundamentally agree on the major issues facing our country. Second, the biggest difference between the Reagan presidency and a Bush presidency, right from the start, will be the state of the nation, compared to what it was when Ronald Reagan came to Washington in 1981.

This year's first-time voters were teenagers back then. At home, our economy was stagnant, weighed down by inflation and high interest rates. Overseas, American prestige was at a post–World War Two low. The new President's challenge was to revitalize the economy and strengthen America's role as a world leader.

The Reagan presidency has done that, and more. We're now in the midst of the longest peacetime economic expansion on record. Overseas, the Western alliance is again on firm footing and there's hope for a major breakthrough in arms-reduction talks with the Soviets.

As Vice President these past seven years, I'm proud to have been part of the administration that built this record. Now, as a candidate for President, I'm campaigning on my own agenda for leadership, beginning with the Number One priority for any American President in the nuclear age—safeguarding freedom and securing peace.

The INF treaty President Reagan signed with Mikhail Gorbachev last December broke new ground in U.S.–Soviet relations. It provided for arms verification and openness. We've begun a test—a test of whether Soviet talk about openness is backed by action. There's reason for hope. But experience tells us that in dealing with the Soviets optimism is best tempered with realism.

Let's not forget, after all, what finally brought the Soviets to the INF treaty table. President Reagan first proposed the so-called "zero option" seven years ago, when the Soviets had a monopoly on intermediate-range missiles in Europe. They said "Nyet." We countered their missiles with our own buildup. They tried to back us down, but the President stood firm. Only then did they change their minds.

There's a lesson in that, one that follows a pattern going back to the early years of the post–World War Two era. In negotiating with the Soviets, we must deal from strength, not weakness. That's why it's critical that we continue funding on the Strategic Defense Initiative—SDI. The Soviets have been working on SDI technology much longer than we have. They hoped to maintain a monopoly in space defense,

George Bush

which is why Gorbachev tried to make the elimination of our SDI program a precondition for an INF agreement.

He didn't succeed. And he won't succeed if he makes the same demand in arms negotiations with a Bush administration. I strongly support SDI funding because it provides a defensive shield that puts weapons, not people at risk.

Watchful optimism will be the byword of the Bush administration in dealing with the Soviet Union in the years ahead. If Soviet talk about "openness" is matched by Soviet action allowing strict verification, progress can be made in both ICBM and conventional force reduction.

We can also work to eliminate chemical and biological weapons. I put a proposal for a chemical-biological weapons ban on the negotiating table in Geneva in 1984. The Soviets turned it down. But given the history of INF negotiations, we can hope for a change in their position in this area as well. A verifiable ban on chemical-biological weapons will be a top priority in my administration.

U.S.–Soviet negotiations are only one aspect of arms control, however. We can't overlook the danger posed by nuclear proliferation.

The possibility that nuclear weapons might be used in a regional conflict or in a terrorist attack poses enormous danger to world peace. What only a handful of nations could accomplish twenty years ago can be duplicated by many today. But the situation isn't hopeless, given a sound strategy for nuclear restraint.

Bilaterally, we have the power to screen and restrict the export of American technology for nuclear-related projects. Some businessmen argue that this policy is too restrictive. I disagree. As President, I'll insist that these provisions be rigorously enforced. A Bush administration will also launch a major effort to commit every nation to the Nuclear Non-Proliferation Treaty and to strengthen the International Atomic Energy Agency—one U.N. agency that works effectively in carrying out its job.

International drug traffic poses a different but no less dangerous threat to our national security. Last year seventy tons of cocaine—a drug that retails for well over $1,000 an

ounce—were seized by federal, state, and local age........
the past seven years hundreds of tons of cocaine and tens of
thousands of tons of marijuana have been confiscated, as our
national campaign against illegal drugs has grown into a
major domestic war.

To fight this war, we've appointed tougher judges and
tougher prosecutors—the conviction rate has increased from
75 to 84 percent and sentences in drug cases are now one-
third longer than they were in 1980.

Still, the flow of illegal drugs into the country continues, turning sections of our major cities into combat zones,
ruining young lives, corrupting our system. Clearly,
stronger action is needed—more must be done—if we're to
win this war.

A multinational antidrug effort is needed, since drug
traffickers respect no borders. The Bush administration will
step up aid to source countries to fight these traffickers by
furnishing boats, planes, and helicopters and training their
antidrug enforcement personnel.

Domestically, I'll seek stronger penalties for drug of-
fenses, not simply for drug traffickers but drug users. Our
goal should be to send them a message—not just to punish
but to deter.

Not that this war can be won by law enforcement
alone. We'll need a renewed commitment to drug prevention
and treatment programs. But most of all, we'll need a
change in public attitudes regarding drug use and users. At
the community level, this means supporting programs to
keep order in our schools and get drug violence out. It
means setting clear boundaries that provide the guidance
and discipline young people need—and our society needs—
if we're to turn back this threat to our nation's health and
safety.

The 1990s will also find America involved in a global
rivalry of another kind, not only with our adversaries, but
with our friends and allies. Japan, Europe, and the emerging
industrial nations will pose a growing challenge in the decade ahead, one that will test our competitive mettle.

To meet this challenge, some would have us look elsewhere for inspiration—to other countries and other ways of life. As one who built a business from the ground up, I don't buy that theory. I think the best way—the only way—we can meet foreign competition in the international marketplace is by taking a hard look at ourselves—by seeking an American solution.

An American solution to the economic challenge of the '90s means renewing our emphasis on product quality—by setting production standards that are, not 95 percent error-free, but 100 percent error-free. It means better education and training for Americans as we approach a new century.

Consider: the United States now spends more on education than any nation on earth—yet 13 percent of our seventeen-year-olds are functionally illiterate. They lack the reading skills needed to work and compete in today's world.

Education is the great lifting mechanism of a free society. It lifts not simply the individual but the society itself. But to do this, education has to be rigorous, demanding, and geared to the needs of a technological age.

American kids won't succeed—and our economic system won't be able to compete—if our educational system doesn't instill in its students the basic values of hard work, respect for learning, and self-discipline. These are the values that underlie an American solution, not simply to competing, but to prevailing in a modern world.

Beyond education, an American solution to the challenge of the '90s means stripping away corporate fat in our industrial community—creating companies that are lean, trim, and ready to compete for their share of the global market.

—It means breaking down the barriers to the movement of goods and services, not putting up new ones.

—It means eliminating government red tape that impairs our ability to compete.

Summed up, it means relying on the incentives of the free market—not the largesse of the federal government—to fuel a growing economy.

The federal deficit: On Day One of the Bush presidency I intend to name a team of negotiators to represent the executive branch in top-level budget sessions with the Congress. I'm talking about a Deficit and Budget-Balancing Summit. As President, I'll head the executive branch negotiating team, and I'll go to the table with an agenda that calls for (1) a freeze on government spending; (2) giving the President the line-item veto; (3) no increase in taxes.

Repeat: No increase in taxes. The basic philosophy of the Bush administration will be that the answer to the country's budget and deficit problem lies in restrained government spending—making better use of the money we've already got.

We've made progress toward reducing waste in government these past seven years, but more is needed if we're going to solve the nation's fiscal problem. The Bush administration will continue to cut wasteful spending on all fronts —including the Pentagon. Our byword in reducing federal expenditures will be, *No Sacred Cows.* Keeping America strong doesn't mean closing our eyes to bureaucratic bloat, whether it be in the Department of Health and Human Sevices or in wasteful defense procurement.

Jobs, continued growth, a prosperity that touches every citizen—these would be the economic goals of a Bush administration. But prosperity means little in the long run unless it is used to good purpose. Greed on Wall Street, influence-peddling in Washington . . . we diminish not only our achievements but ourselves when we view wealth as an end in itself.

Prosperity-with-purpose means giving something back to the country that has given us so much. It means working for a just society, a free society, in a world at peace. It means turning the American ideal into reality by making life better not only for ourselves but for those less fortunate.

These past seven years I've learned, firsthand, that the Presidency is like no other office. It provides an incomparable opportunity for moral leadership. A President can set a tone, an atmosphere, a standard for the nation. As President, I mean to work toward a new harmony, a greater tolerance, an understanding that this country is a partnership—a partnership bound together not for the mere pursuit of material gain but in the shared faith that, in the words of Herman Melville, "we bear the ark of liberties of the world."

GEORGE BUSH
Washington, D.C.
April 1988

Look up and not down; look out and not in; look forward and not back; and lend a hand.

EDWARD EVERETT HALE, Chaplain
United States Senate, 1903–9

One

HELLO,
GEORGE . . .

Detroit/Summer 1980

Politics is supposed to be about people and running—running for office, running to the next event—but sooner or later it comes around to sitting in hotel rooms, waiting. On the humid night of July 16, 1980, I was doing just that at the Pontchartrain Hotel, overlooking the Detroit River and the distant lights of Windsor, Ontario: sitting with Barbara, our kids, and a few friends, sipping a beer, eating popcorn, watching television, and waiting.

Waiting for the other shoe to drop.

The first shoe had dropped six weeks earlier and 1,100 miles away in the living room of my home in Houston. Jim Baker, my campaign manager, had brought together a group of political advisers from around the country to discuss the future of my presidential campaign. The meeting began at 10 A.M. over midmorning coffee. By 10:05 a consensus was reached—the campaign had no future: Ronald Reagan would win the nomination on the first ballot. There was only one dissenting voice. Mine.

"We've got the primaries coming up in California, New Jersey, and Ohio," I argued. "We still have a shot at it."

Now a good campaign manager has to have a multitude of virtues. He has to be an efficient administrator. He has to know the players in the field, not only on his own team but on the other side. He has to stay cool when the campaign gets heated. But most important of all, he has to be able to tell his candidate what the candidate doesn't want to hear.

Jim Baker was a good campaign manager. That spring morning in Houston he'd brought some hard evidence with him—the unofficial delegate count. "George," he said, "you've got to know when to hold 'em and know when to fold 'em. Take a look at these numbers."

3

He spread his papers across the coffee table, but I
didn't care to see them. My feeling was that if we'd played
percentages I wouldn't have entered the race in the first
place. "Jim," I replied, "I've never quit anything until it was
finished. This is no time to start."

Jim shook his head. "But the campaign *is* finished,
George." He pointed to the numbers. "You're the only one
who doesn't seem to know it. Besides," he added, spreading
another set of numbers across the table, "we're running out
of money."

So much for making a contest out of it in California,
New Jersey, and Ohio. And so much for my presidential
campaign. That night Barbara, our out-of-town guests, and
I went to Molina's, one of my favorite Mexican restaurants,
for a dinner of frijoles, tortillas, tamales, and chili. My appetite was good. It always is once a decision is made, whether I
like it or not.

I'm an early riser, usually up at around six or six-thirty.
By seven the next morning, after going over my congratula-
tory telegram to Governor Ronald Reagan and sending it
off, I got to work calling friends across the country, thank-
ing them for the long days and nights they'd put into the
campaign.

I don't remember who mentioned it first, but it seemed
as if two out of every three people asked what the chances
were for a Reagan-Bush ticket. The question came up again
at a midmorning news conference at the Galleria Hotel. I
brushed it off. After nearly three years running full throttle
for the presidency, my inner machinery wasn't ready to shift
gears that fast. I needed to get away for a while. A cooling-
off period. Time to sort things out.

Besides, I knew that you don't campaign for the vice
presidency, because it's a calling. And the caller is whoever
happens to be the presidential nominee.

At Miami Beach in 1968, Congressman Bill Steiger of
Wisconsin and some well-meaning friends, along with a few
party elders like Tom Dewey and John Bricker, had floated
my name as a possible running mate for Richard Nixon.

With his own nomination sewed up, Nixon was going through the ritual of soliciting advice on a vice presidential nominee. As we learned later, he'd already settled on Maryland Governor Spiro T. Agnew. But Nixon knew that a little suspense is needed to keep the convention press happy and the television audience interested.

Mayor John Lindsay of New York City had been mentioned by some media observers as a possible Nixon choice. The case for Lindsay was that he was a rising political star who could appeal to young voters. But Lindsay was considered too liberal by most delegates. With the call out for a new, young Republican face, and as a forty-four-year-old Republican congressman from Texas with family ties in the East, I was viewed as a possibility.

That sort of mention can't hurt a young politician, even when it's a trial balloon that runs out of air—which it did in my case that year. In a receiving line after the convention, Nixon took time to explain why he had passed me over.

"You had a nice little campaign going, George, very well orchestrated," he said, in the clinical tone of an old political pro. "But you understand . . . I really couldn't pick a one-term congressman." He was right. I couldn't have brought anything more than a new, young face to the ticket, and that isn't enough in a national campaign.

In 1974, after Nixon resigned and Jerry Ford was mulling over vice presidential possibilities, my name came up again. By then my credentials were a little stronger. I was chairman of the Republican National Committee, had served as U.S. ambassador to the United Nations, and ran first in a vice presidential preference poll of Republican governors and national committee members. I did get a call that time, straight from a White House operator.

"Mr. Bush?"

"Yes?"

"One second, sir . . . Mr. President, Mr. Bush is on the line."

"Hello, George . . ."

"Mr. President, how are you?"

"Fine, George, fine. I'm just calling to let you know that in a few minutes I'm going to announce that Nelson

Rockefeller's name is being sent to the Hill for confirmation as Vice President. . . ."

"Yes . . . Well, Mr. President, you've made a fine choice, and I appreciate your taking the time to call. You really didn't have to. . . ."

And he didn't, but it was typical of Jerry Ford, who was as thoughtful a President as he was a party leader in the House.

The interesting thing about Rockefeller getting the call in 1974 was that he'd always insisted he didn't want the job. He said he couldn't see himself as "back-up machinery." It was the same sort of putdown of the office of Vice President made by people—including some Vice Presidents—dating back to the beginning of the Republic.

John Adams claimed he was miserable in the job. Then he became President and did his best to make *his* Vice President, Thomas Jefferson, miserable. A century later Teddy Roosevelt liked to repeat Mark Twain's joke about the two brothers: one went to sea and the other became Vice President. Neither was ever heard from again.

More recently, John Nance Garner of Texas, Franklin D. Roosevelt's first Vice President, was euphemistically quoted describing the vice presidency as not worth "a bucket of warm spit." Garner had bitterly fought FDR for the presidential nomination in 1932, but when Roosevelt offered him the VP spot, "Cactus Jack" picked up the bucket—even though he had to quit his post as the House Speaker to do it.

Twenty-eight years later another Texan, Lyndon Johnson, lost the presidential nomination to another Northeasterner, John Kennedy. Johnson had also said he didn't want to be Vice President, and his personal antipathy to Kennedy was even greater than Garner's toward Roosevelt. But after the smoke cleared, Johnson gave up his powerful position as Senate majority leader to become Kennedy's running mate.

The message is clear: Although everybody belittles the office of the Vice President, not many people turn it down. There's the obvious reason—the one summed up succinctly (if morbidly) by our first Vice President. "Today I am noth-

ing," wrote John Adams, "but tomorrow I may
thing."

But beyond the morbid, the modern vice presidency
holds out other possibilities. The prestige, if not the power,
of the office has grown since the end of World War Two.
When Harry Truman succeeded FDR, he didn't know about
the A-bomb and needed a crash course to deal with the
major decisions facing him in the final days of World War
Two. That experience led later Presidents to keep their Vice
Presidents informed about the White House decision-making process. Given the right President, it's possible for the
right Vice President to have an impact on administration
policy.

All this went through my mind in the next six weeks, as
Barbara and I prepared to go to the national convention.
Was I interested in becoming Ronald Reagan's running
mate? Yes. Could I do anything about it? No more than had
already been done in eighteen years of political life. Either
the call would come or it wouldn't.

Meanwhile there was still some unfinished business left
over from my presidential race—a $400,000 campaign debt.
A round of fund-raisers kept me on the road to mid-July,
when the debt was settled in full.

Then it was on to Detroit.

Choosing vice presidential candidates has always been
one of the most unpredictable rituals of modern American
politics. What took place at the Republican National Convention of 1980 would be no exception.

Dick Wirthlin, the Reagan campaign pollster, had
taken a nationwide survey in June to single out the strongest
possible running mate for a Reagan-led ticket. The results of
the poll were picked up by the press from insiders in the
Reagan camp. Jerry Ford ran first; I came in second; Howard Baker was third. Other names trial-tested on the list
Wirthlin drew up for his field interviewers included Paul
Laxalt and Jack Kemp.

As Republican leader in the Senate, Howard Baker was
widely respected in Washington, but his support of the Pan-

ama Canal and SALT II treaties had antagonized many Reagan followers. As a senator from Nevada, Paul Laxalt, one of Ronald Reagan's closest friends, couldn't provide the ticket with the geographical balance every national ticket needs. Jack Kemp, a strong supporter of the supply-side theory, wasn't well known outside his New York congressional district.

That seemed to bring the vice presidential choice down to either Jerry Ford or me. Because it didn't seem likely that an ex-President would run for Vice President, Jim Baker felt that chances for a Reagan-Bush ticket were good.

Jim had maintained friendly contacts with Reagan's campaign manager, Bill Casey, and other Reagan insiders like Ed Meese, during the course of the campaign. The race for the Republican presidential nomination hadn't been acrimonious. Still, it had been heated enough in some areas to raise certain questions in the media if a Reagan-Bush ticket came out of the convention.

First there was the matter of "voodoo economics," a phrase I'd used during the Pennsylvania primary in April. Aimed at one facet of Reagan's proposed economic program, it went largely unnoticed at the time but had since been picked up by both the media and the Democrats. Could any differences we had over economic policy be reconciled?

Despite the rhetoric of the campaign, I felt the answer was yes, because Reagan and I basically shared a similar free-enterprise philosophy. We both favored tax cuts and opposed excessive government interference in the operation of the marketplace. When we got together in Los Angeles after the convention to plan campaign strategy, "voodoo economics" pointedly never entered into our conversations. We agreed that economic issues would dominate the race and discussed specific areas where the Carter administration record was vulnerable: double-digit inflation, high interest rates, and industrial stagnation.

The bottom line—both politically and economically— was that Reagan and I agreed that solving the country's economic problems would require not only tax cuts but massive cuts in government spending, along with a whole-sale reduction in federal red tape and overregulation.

If there was an obstacle in the way of a Reagan-Bush ticket, it wasn't any basic disagreement over economic or political philosophy. It was simply that Ronald Reagan and I didn't know each other very well. We'd met several times when I headed the Republican National Committee and he was governor of California, but had never talked at any great length. In 1978 I'd paid a courtesy call at his Los Angeles office to let him know I planned to enter the presidential race; but that, too, was a *pro forma* meeting—cordial, but arm's length.

After the race got underway, what meetings we had came through face-to-face confrontations, in public debate —not the sort of setting calculated to build bridges of understanding.

News of Wirthlin's poll on possible vice presidential prospects seemed to point to a Reagan-Bush ticket. But other reports coming out of the Reagan camp indicated that Reagan was far from decided on his choice of a running mate—that the vice presidential nomination was still wide open.

At midafternoon on the sixteenth—the presidential balloting and vice presidential choice would be made that night —Dean Burch, who was in charge of my convention itinerary, came by the room to say he'd heard that a group of former Ford administration officials, including Henry Kissinger, Alan Greenspan, Bill Brock, and Jack Marsh were meeting with top-level Reagan staffers. They were supposed to be working out a plan that could put together a Reagan-Ford "Dream Ticket."

"It's only a rumor," said Dean, "but I wouldn't discount it." He was right. Most convention rumors have a brief life cycle, then disappear. But as the afternoon wore into the evening and the delegates started filling the floor of the Joe Louis Arena for the evening session, the Reagan-Ford rumor wouldn't go away. In fact, it kept building.

I had a light snack about six o'clock and started to get ready to go to the arena to address the convention. My speech preceded the beginning of the presidential nominat-

ing process. Technically it would serve the purpose of with-
drawing my name as a presidential candidate. Actually it
was scheduled as a party-unification speech, aimed at rallying all Bush delegates at the convention behind the choice of
the convention, Ronald Reagan.

It was an important speech—the most important
speech I'd ever been called on to make. A strong presentation could tip the balance in the vice presidential selection
process. A poor showing might also tip the balance, toward
someone else.

I was knotting my tie when Walter Cronkite and Jerry
Ford came on screen, talking about Reagan's options in
choosing a running mate. A few blocks away, as I was to
learn, Ronald Reagan was also watching the interview.
When he heard Ford tell Cronkite his ideas about how a
President and Vice President could divide the powers of the
presidential office—a clear sign that some kind of negotiations were going on—Reagan, according to later reports,
was stunned. He didn't know Ford would go public with the
news. I was stunned for my own reasons. What Ford was
describing amounted to a copresidency.

Dean Burch went with me to the convention hall. A
native Arizonan, Dean began his political career as Barry
Goldwater's top aide and later became a White House counselor in both the Nixon and Ford administrations. Soft-spoken and seldom ruffled, he could always be counted on to
take a cool, analytical view of the political scene. When I
asked whether he had watched the Ford interview, he
looked bemused. Yes, he said, he'd seen it, but it didn't add
up, either politically or in terms of the way the White House
really operated.

What Ford seemed to be outlining in his interview with
Cronkite—and what Kissinger and others were trying to
work out at a meeting with Reagan's representatives—was
an arrangement where Reagan would be in charge of domestic and economic policy; while Ford, presumably with Kissinger's help, would be responsible for foreign and defense
policy.

"Put it out of your mind, George," Dean urged as we

moved through the crowd and headed backstage. "Just concentrate on your speech."

I was trying to do just that, reviewing the text five minutes before walking up the long ramp to the convention podium, when a backstage worker came by, patted me on the back, and said, "I'm sorry, Mr. Bush, really sorry. I was pulling for you."

"Sorry about what?" I asked, as we shook hands.

"You mean you haven't heard? It's all over. Reagan's picked Ford as his running mate."

Waiting for the other shoe to drop . . .

Back at the hotel I changed into a sports shirt and slacks, certain there wouldn't be any more public appearances that evening. I felt good about my reception at the arena. After New York Congressman Barber Conable introduced me, there'd been a long ovation—the Bush delegates, getting in their last hurrah. The speech itself had about ten to twelve interruptions for cheers and applause. Not entirely unexpected, since I'd made a case against the Carter administration—a sure way to get a Republican audience to its feet —then outlined the country's future under a Reagan administration.

Now, except for a possible cameo appearance on the podium the next night, after the acceptance speeches by the presidential and vice presidential nominees, my convention duties were over. No brass rings, no cigars. But for the moment, no regrets, no agonizing, either.

Do your best and don't look back. That was a lesson I hadn't learned until my early thirties, when I was working eighteen hours a day to build a company from the ground up. I was a chronic worrier back then, and on a hectic business trip to London I woke up one morning, started to get dressed, then suddenly found myself on the hotel-room floor. No pain, just dizziness. I tried getting to my feet, couldn't make it, and wound up crawling to the bedside and pushing the buzzer for help.

Scared? No, jolted is a better description. When you've always enjoyed good health and your body caves in for no apparent reason, it gives you an immediate sense of priorities. I had no idea what was wrong. The hotel doctor's quick examination reassured me. He said it was nothing more than mild food poisoning, wrote out a routine prescription, and advised me to rest.

Some food poisoning! After staggering through a day, I cut my visit short, boarded an all-night trans-Atlantic flight, and headed back to Houston. There at the Texas Medical Center, my friend and physician, Dr. Lillo Crain, told me I had a bleeding ulcer. Luckily, the bleeding had stopped spontaneously.

A bleeding ulcer? Other people got bleeding ulcers. Nervous wrecks, not me.

Dr. Crain quickly disabused me of that stereotype. "George, you're a classic ulcer case," he said. "A young businessman with only one speed, all-out. You try to do too much and you worry too much."

I told him that was the way I'd always been. There wasn't much I could do to remodel myself at that late date.

"There'd better be, or you won't be around in ten years, maybe five," he replied, writing out a short-term prescription.

At that point he had my undivided attention. "I'm putting you on some temporary medicine and a strict diet," he continued. "But that can only control the damage you've already done to yourself. If you want to keep this from happening again, it's up to you."

His long-term prescription wasn't medicine or diet but went to the source of my ailment. All my life I'd worked at channeling my emotions, trying not to let anger or frustration influence my thinking. But I'd never given much thought to channeling my energies. That would change, however, after I took in what Dr. Crain had to say. In time, my ulcer was healed completely. I've never suffered a relapse.

All the doctor recommended was a common-sense approach to work; but it took a bleeding ulcer to bring me around to it. "You have to accept the fact that you can't do everything," he said. "Learn to concentrate your energy on the things you *can* change, and don't worry about the things you *can't*."

If ever a situation fell into the last category, I found myself in it that night in Detroit. Some of our kids were upset that I was being bypassed as the vice presidential nominee. I was taking the news coming over the TV set with Dr. Crain's advice in mind. But the kids weren't quite that philosophical, hearing their father written off by the network analysts. They took it personally. I told them to settle down. There was nothing we could do about it. The boat had sailed, and all that remained, the network pundits were saying, was for Reagan's and Ford's representatives to negotiate a few minor details and the "Dream Ticket" would become a reality.

"Dream Ticket": In theory I could see the benefit that could come from putting Jerry Ford's experience in government and his personal popularity back to work for the country and the Republican Party. Though he lost to Jimmy Carter in 1976, Ford left office with a huge reservoir of public respect and affection. There was something to be said for the idea that the best man Ronald Reagan could find to press the case against Jimmy Carter's administration was the man Carter had defeated four years earlier.

But practically speaking, could someone who had called all the shots at one point in his political career adjust to a number-two role? After all, Jerry Ford had once run his own campaign for President, when he made the decisions and passed the word down to his vice presidential candidate, Bob Dole. Suppose his ideas on campaign strategy differed from Reagan's?

More important, how would the Reagan-Ford team operate after it was elected? Could a copresidency, with one man responsible for domestic-economic policy and another handling foreign-defense policy really work? Like Dean, I had serious doubts. There's only one desk in the Oval Office.

The hotel room phone rang. Jim Baker was talking to someone who had just come from the Reagan-Ford negotiating session. With his hand over the telephone mouthpiece, Jim called across the room. "Hold everything," he said.

"This thing's about to come apart. Somebody's having second thoughts."

There was a stir in the room, but in my own mind the question had already been settled. The hour was late, the long tension of the day and the effort put into preparing and making my convention speech had drained me. Even if a Reagan-Ford ticket couldn't be worked out, there were possibilities other than Reagan-Bush. The unpredictability factor that makes for surprise vice presidential nominations—Bill Miller in 1964, Agnew in 1968—was at work; if Reagan-Ford wasn't the ticket, it might be Reagan-Laxalt, or even somebody who hadn't even been mentioned.

The only thing I knew for certain was that there wasn't much I could do about the situation. The Wirthlin poll and Reagan insiders like Ed Meese and Bill Casey could make the case for my being on the ticket, but in the last analysis the presidential nominee would follow his own instincts.

Another phone call. This time it was the Secret Service to let us know that they were occupying a room two floors below, "in case you need anything."

"Need anything?" someone asked, wondering about the call. "What the hell's that supposed to mean?"

The answer came just seconds later. When the phone rang this time, the call was for me.

The voice couldn't be mistaken, though the tone was different from the one I remembered from our preconvention primary debates.

"Hello, George, this is Ron Reagan." There was a pause. "I'd like to go over to the convention and announce that you're my choice for Vice President . . . if that's all right with you."

The unpredictability factor: Politics is no profession for people who don't like surprises. When I expected the call, it hadn't come; now, when I didn't expect it, it had. The truth is that the flow of events had reversed so quickly that I wasn't completely focused on what was taking place. But I was focused enough to know the answer to Reagan's question:

"I'd be honored, Governor."

There was a momentary pause on the other end of the
line. Then: "George, is there anything at all . . . about the
platform or anything else . . . *anything* that might make
you uncomfortable down the road?"

It seemed an unusual question coming from a presidential nominee to a prospective running mate, but one that
told me something about the difference between Ronald
Reagan and other political leaders. Anything uncomfortable
for *me?* The question generally asked of vice presidential
prospects these days is: "Is there anything about *you* that
might make *me* uncomfortable down the road?"

I told him that I had no serious problem with either the
platform or his position on any of the issues, that I was sure
we could work together, and that the important thing was
that he win the election in November.

"Fine," he said. "I'll head over to the convention, then
we'll get together in the morning."

I thanked him, then slowly put the receiver back into
its cradle. Barbara and the kids rushed across the room and
we exchanged hugs. Jim Baker and Dean Burch shook my
hand. Someone turned up the TV set. *"Not* Ford!" the network reporter was shouting from the convention floor. "It's
Bush!"

Then a hotel room that ten minutes before had been the
scene of a political wake suddenly erupted: friends, staff
members, visitors, Secret Service, were packed wall to wall.
It was eardrum-shattering bedlam. But I couldn't have
cared less. Raucous as it was, it had a sweeter sound than
the thud of another shoe falling.

The next morning Barbara and I joined the Reagans in
the living room of their quarters at the Renaissance Center
Plaza, not far from the Pontchartrain.

Our meeting was later described by the news media as a
strategy session, an opportunity to get our political gears
meshed before leaving Detroit. As is often the case in political meetings like that, there wasn't any firm talk about strat-

egy or issues. Or about any of the hectic events leading up to
my selection as the vice presidential nominee.

All that was history. It was the morning after, and political ritual is that running mates don't look back at past
differences. It didn't concern me that I hadn't been Reagan's
first choice. What was important, as I saw it, was that six
weeks, six months, four years from now, he'd know that
however he came to make it, he'd made the right choice.

The presidential nominee greeted Barbara and me
warmly, with no hint of any tension left over from our primary battles. A few minutes later, Nancy Reagan joined us.
Over coffee, we talked about family, friends, how the convention seemed to be going. Small talk, but every bit as
important, at that moment, as any talk about grand political
strategy. Important because even when Presidents and Vice
Presidents see eye to eye on the issues, their long-term political relationship can only be as strong as their personal relationship. And despite what millions of Americans would
witness that night—the Reagans and Bushes smiling and
waving at the convention's closing session—we still viewed
each other through the narrow lens of political, not personal, experience.

This changed in the next few days, as we went through
the postconvention ritual of joint press conferences and political rallies. The schedule called for launching the campaign in Houston, where the Reagans would visit our home
for lunch and meet our family. There would be a Texas-size
rally at the Galleria—the same hotel I'd used for the news
conference announcing my withdrawal from the presidential
race.

The morning of July 18 we flew to Houston aboard the
Reagan campaign plane, a Boeing 727. There was a VIP
motorcade into town and crowds to greet us wherever we
went . . . a shade more ostentatious, I told Barbara, than
my first arrival in Texas as an Ideco trainee just out of college, some thirty-two years before.

Two

WHATEVER BROUGHT YOU TO TEXAS?

It was hot. But not the humid midsummer heat I remembered from my Navy days at Corpus Christi. This was dry Texas heat, the tumbleweed and bleached-bone kind that can turn asphalt into black quicksand and blister the paint off barns. Three-digit heat that sends field-savvy Texans hustling for the nearest shade tree.

Hugh Evans, one of my coworkers at the Ideco supply store in Odessa, was a field-savvy, laid-back Texan. I liked Hugh personally, but at the same time, calling him a coworker is actually stretching it, because he was one of those people with a gift for fading into the scenery at the slightest hint of physical labor. Every day, while the rest of us downed our morning coffee, Hugh would wait until he heard the boss's Chevy pull into the lot. Then he'd go into his vanishing act.

"Think I'll run over to Nell's and get me a cup," he'd say, heading for the diner down the street. "Tell ol' Bill I'll be right back." By the time Hugh returned, Bill Nelson, our boss at Ideco, had handed out the day's heavy chores, like unloading equipment and stacking tools.

But this particular morning, Hugh's timing failed him. The boss had a special project in mind. "George," he said, just as Hugh reappeared in the doorway, "those pumping units down at the yard look like hell. You and Hugh go over and spruce 'em up."

Spruce 'em up—that meant grabbing some paint cans off the store shelves, getting into the company pickup truck, and heading for the yard where the pumping units were stored. Anyone who's ever traveled through oil country has seen pumping units at work—bulky iron structures that push and pull on a long string of rods. They vary in size,

depending on the depth of the well, but they all look like
iron hobby horses.

The units we were supposed to spruce up were monsters that had been baking in the sun for weeks. That meant
trouble, because the only way to paint a pumping unit is to
move, top to bottom, straddling the main beam as you go.
Imagine riding a hot branding iron without a saddle and
you've got the picture.

Hugh Evans had been down that road before and
wasn't about to make the same mistake twice. So he began
working the base of the largest unit, taking it slow and easy.
After about five minutes, he stopped, lit a cigarette, and
ambled over to a nearby shade tree.

From that point on, I was painting solo.

"Hey, George, you know what the thermometer read
when we left the store?" Hugh bellowed from ten feet below
and twenty-five yards away. "A hundred five degrees. But
out here it's dry heat, so you don't feel it much."

I looked down to see him lighting up another Camel.
He was leaning against the shade tree, blowing smoke, la-
menting the injustice of it all.

"One hell of a day to send folks out to paint a damn
pumping unit, if you ask me," he said. "It just ain't fair."

This was vintage Hugh, figuring if he got someone teed-
off at Bill Nelson, he'd overlook the fact that his coworker
wasn't coworking. From the start Hugh had me pegged as a
young eastern sucker, a college boy who knew the books but
not the angles. And he was right. I still had a lot to learn.

But whether he meant to or not, Hugh was making me
look good. Bill Nelson knew that whatever work was being
done it wasn't Hugh's. I figured that sooner or later Bill
would tell Ideco's Dallas office that this new trainee Bush
was working out okay and deserved more than $375 a
month.

The hours passed, the temperature fell. It couldn't have
been more than ninety-eight degrees by the time the job was
finished. I was wrung out and my rear end was roasted. But
every last pumping unit had a fresh coat of Ideco black and
orange.

"Mighty fine, George," said Hugh Evans, appraising our handiwork. His eyes took in the units, then slowly came around to me, sunburned, and paint-stained. Hugh obviously had something on his mind. "George," he said, "would you mind if I ask a personal question?"

"That depends, Hugh," I replied. "What is it you want to know?"

"Just tell me," he said, "whatever brought you to Texas?"

The question called for a long, drawn-out answer, but all things considered, I settled for a short, simple one. What had brought me to Texas, I told him, was a chance to learn the oil business and make money. Hugh listened, then shook his head. "You've come to the wrong town then," he said. "Midland's where the money is."

He was right. Midland, twenty miles northeast, up Highway 80, was where other newcomers were settling in those postwar Texas oil-rush days. It was the town where the oil deals were made, whereas Odessa was the town where the oil field equipment was sold and the drilling contractors stored their idle rigs.

Midland had the speculators; Odessa had the contractors. Midland had the geologists and engineers; Odessa had the hands-on drillers, roughnecks, and roustabouts. Midland had the money; Odessa had the muscle.

In short, Odessa wasn't the place for a twenty-four-year-old Navy veteran to get rich, quick or otherwise. From a straight economic standpoint, I'd have done better taking my uncle, Herbie Walker, up on an offer to join his stock-brokerage firm.

But money alone wasn't why I'd come to Texas. The full reason had to do with where I came from, where I'd been, and where I hoped to go in life—from Greenwich, Connecticut, to the Bonin Islands, to Yale, and, finally, to what Odessa represented to me and my wife Barbara in that summer of 1948.

• • •

What literally brought me to Texas that summer was a 1947 two-door coupe, one of Studebaker's streamlined post-war models that cost $1,500 during my last year in college. Crimson red, with wraparound windows and a low-slung ultramodern design. A little garish by New Haven standards, but after three years in the Navy, I'd come home with my own ideas about what I wanted out of life.

It wasn't so much that I knew what I wanted as that I knew what I *didn't* want. I didn't want to do anything pat and predictable. I'd come of age in a time of war, seen different people and cultures, known danger, and suffered the loss of close friends. Like a lot of other veterans who'd come home, I was young in years but matured in outlook. The world I'd known before the war didn't interest me. I was looking for a different kind of life, something challenging, outside the established mold. I couldn't see myself being happy commuting into work, then back home, five days a week.

Fortunately I'd married someone who shared these ideas about breaking away. Barbara and I had married in the last year of the war. While I was still majoring in economics at Yale, we talked a lot about doing something different with our lives; and we didn't put any limit on our imagination either.

Once, after reading Louis Bromfield's book, *The Farm*, we seriously considered going into farming. We were attracted by the idea of being self-sufficient, as well as the basic values Bromfield described as being part of farm life. There were Grant Wood visions of golden wheat fields under blue midwestern skies, and bringing up a family in the farm belt.

Then we started looking more deeply into the economics of life on the farm. Not just what it might take to operate a successful farm, but how much was needed for an initial investment in land, stock, and farm equipment. It was more than we could afford: we didn't have the money; we didn't know where to raise it. One thing for certain, it wasn't the sort of business proposition to take up with our families.

My father, Prescott Bush, Sr., was a successful businessman, a partner in the investment banking firm of Brown Brothers, Harriman and Company. He'd made money and our family lived comfortably but not ostentatiously. Dad believed in the old Ben Franklin copybook maxims when it came to earning, saving, and spending. In other ways, too, he and my mother embodied the Puritan ethic, in the best sense of the term. Their children—my brothers Pres, John, and Buck, my sister Nancy, and I—all grew up understanding that life isn't an open-ended checking account. Whatever we wanted, we'd have to earn. From an early age we knew that if an illness or something really serious occurred, our folks would be there to help, but once we left home, we'd make it on our own, in business or whatever we entered in later life.

If I'd really believed there was a solid business prospect to discuss, I wouldn't have hesitated to go to Dad. No matter how we looked at it, though, George and Barbara Farms came off as a high-risk, no-yield investment.

But there was another, even better reason why we never considered going to our families for seed money. Breaking away meant just that—living on our own. I'd saved up three thousand dollars in the Navy. Not much, but enough to get us started independently. We were young, still in our early twenties, and we wanted to make our own way, our own mistakes, and shape our own future.

Actually, I was only doing what my own father and mother had done a generation before. They were Midwesterners who had migrated to New England to make a life for themselves. Dad came from Columbus, Ohio, and Mother, born Dorothy Walker, from St. Louis.

My father first traveled East to go to school. After finishing college at Yale, he enlisted in the Army field artillery when the United States entered World War One. Sent overseas, he rose to the rank of captain, then returned home to begin a career in business management. His father, Samuel P. Bush, was president of Buckeye Steel Casting in Columbus, but Dad wasn't interested in going to work there. He took a job with the Simmons Hardware Company in St. Louis, my mother's hometown.

Dad was a business administrator whose forte was reorganizing failing companies, turning money losers into profit makers. After several years with the Simmons company, he was hired by the creditors of the Hupp Products Company, a floor-covering firm, to straighten out its financial affairs. When Dad pinpointed the problem—in this case, illegal profit skimming—Mr. Hupp took it personally. This led to the kind of crisis management they don't teach in Business Administration 101: my father had to keep a loaded gun in his desk drawer. The situation was finally resolved when Hupp was convicted of swindling. Hupp's creditors asked Dad to stay on and run the small firm. He did, successfully, and after a series of mergers it became part of the United States Rubber Company.

Meanwhile, Dad and Mother had begun bringing up a family of five. My brother Pres, Jr., was born in 1922, when Dad was still with Simmons based in Kingsport, Tennessee. By the time I was born, June 12, 1924, the family had moved to Milton, Massachusetts, where Dad was now working for U.S. Rubber. When that company transferred its headquarters to New York, we finally settled down in nearby Greenwich, Connecticut.

We were a family on the move, at a time when the automobile was uprooting the old nineteenth-century American life-style. Many years later, while on a speaking trip in Kingsport, I met an elderly lady who still remembered Dad's working there during the early 1920s. En route back to Washington I reflected on how much my life would have changed if my parents hadn't moved to New England but had settled down in Kingsport. Would I have migrated to Texas? Joined Howard Baker and Bill Brock in east Tennessee Republican politics?

Texas, probably; that move seemed predestined from the time I was eighteen. Even the aircraft carrier I was as-

signed to during my Navy days was named the *San Jacinto*
and flew the Lone Star flag. But I was a late starter in politics because we weren't much of a political family when I
was growing up. Dad was a Republican and was active in
state party fund raising, but the subject of politics seldom
came up at family gatherings. Once a week he would sit in
as moderator of the Greenwich town meeting, but that was
more of a civic than a political commitment.

It wasn't until 1950, two years after I'd left for Texas,
that Dad entered his first political race, at age fifty-five, as a
candidate for the United States Senate. It didn't surprise me,
because I knew what motivated him. He'd made his mark in
the business world. Now he felt he had a debt to pay.

Newsweek magazine, in a story covering the 1950 Senate campaign, quoted what it called a "hard-boiled political
writer" who was covering Dad's race:

"Pres had an old-fashioned idea that the more advantages a man has, the greater his obligation to do public service. He believes it and damn it, I believe him."

Dad was concerned about the future of the two-party
system, after Harry Truman's upset victory over Tom
Dewey in 1948. By 1950 the Republican Party had been out
of power for eighteen years. In addition to the presidency,
the Democrats had controlled Congress for sixteen of those
years. Five years after Franklin Roosevelt's death, the coalition he created in the 1930s still dominated American politics, and the Republican Party was threatened with permanent minority status.

Republicans at that time were roughly divided along
lines drawn in the years before World War Two. On one side
were the old isolationists who, in the postwar era, were generally opposed to the idea of an American commitment to
Western Europe. On the other side were the Republicans
who supported the North Atlantic Treaty alliance and believed the United States, as leader of the Free World, had to
play an active role in global affairs.

Dad favored NATO and lined up with what, in 1952,
would be known as the Eisenhower wing of the party. He
was a conservative who believed the United States had to

take a strong stand against Communist aggression in Eastern Europe and Asia—an issue that was brought home forcefully in June 1950, when American and allied troops were sent in to prevent a North Korean takeover of South Korea.

My father's 1950 campaign in Connecticut was geared to developing a responsible Republican alternative to the Democrats' New Deal/Fair Deal policies. The Democratic Senate incumbent was Senator William Benton. Dad lost by 1,000 votes out of 862,000 cast—a strong showing for a first-time candidate. When the senior Democratic senator, Brien McMahon, died two years later, Dad was nominated to run in a special election to fill the unexpired term. With Barbara and me cheering him on from Texas, he defeated Abraham Ribicoff for the Senate seat, and in 1956 was re-elected, defeating Thomas Dodd who, like Ribicoff, eventually served in the Senate. He would serve a full decade in the Senate, retiring in 1962—the year I began my own political career in Harris County, Texas.

For the five Bush children growing up in Greenwich, Connecticut—especially the two oldest, Pres Jr. and me—our father had a powerful impact on the way we came to look at the world. But the writer who once described Dad as "the single greatest influence" on my life was only partly right. Our mother's influence and example were equally strong. Dad taught us about duty and service. Mother taught us about dealing with life on a personal basis, relating to other people.

Like Dad (and her own father), Mother was a first-rate athlete. She wasn't big, but she was a match for anyone in tennis, golf, basketball, baseball—for that matter I don't recall a footrace Mother was ever in that she didn't come in first. Even when her teenage sons outgrew her, she could bring us down to size whenever we'd get too full of ourselves.

Fifty years later, Mother still stays on the alert for anything that sounds like "braggadocio" coming from one of her children. "You're talking about yourself too much, George," she told me after reading a news report covering one of my campaign speeches. I pointed out that as a candidate, I was expected to tell voters something about my qualifications. She thought about that a moment, then reluctantly conceded. "Well, I understand that," she said, "but try to restrain yourself."

Even after I became Vice President, Mother called to set me straight on my appearance during one of the President's televised State of the Union messages. She said it didn't look right for me to be reading something while President Reagan was speaking. When I explained that House Speaker "Tip" O'Neill and I were given advance copies of the speech in order to follow the President's remarks, she was less than persuaded. "I really can't see why that's necessary," she said. "Just listen and you'll find out what he has to say."

Sometimes Mother is more subtle in her suggestions about my deportment as Vice President. "George, I've noticed how thoughtful President Reagan is to Nancy," she once called to say. "I've never seen him climb off a plane ahead of her or walk ahead of her. He's so thoughtful!" I got the message.

But Mother's criticism of her children, like Dad's, was always constructive, not negative. They were our biggest boosters, always there when we needed them. They believed in an old-fashioned way of bringing up a family—generous measures of both love and discipline. Religious teaching was also part of our home life. Each morning, as we gathered at the breakfast table, Mother or Dad read a Bible lesson to us. Our family is Episcopalian, and we regularly attended Sunday services at Christ Church in Greenwich.

We were a close, happy family, and never closer or happier than when we crammed into the station wagon each summer—five kids, two dogs, with Mother driving—to visit Walker's Point in Kennebunkport, Maine. It was named after my grandfather, George Herbert Walker, and his father, David, who had bought it jointly as a family vacation home.

Grandfather Walker was born into a devout Catholic

family in St. Louis and named after the seventeenth-century religious poet George Herbert. He was a midwestern businessman, but more of a free-spirited entrepreneur than my Ohio grandfather, Sam Bush. After studying law, he joined his father in the family business, Ely Walker & Company, then the largest dry-goods wholesaler west of the Mississippi. But in time the free spirit moved him to start his own investment firm, G. H. Walker and Company.

An athlete and sportsman, he went in for hard-contact sports in his younger days, becoming amateur heavyweight champion of Missouri. In later life golf was his game. He not only played the game well (a six-to-seven handicap) but served as a member of the International Rules Committee and, from 1921 to 1923, as president of the U.S. Golf Association.

One of Grandfather Walker's closest St. Louis friends, Dwight Davis, had created an amateur championship tournament in tennis—the Davis Cup. He suggested that a similar international competition be created for golf, and in 1923 grandfather took the suggestion and established the Walker Cup, a trophy still awarded each year, with America's best amateur golfers competing against Great Britain's best.

This is the grandfather I was named after, but not without complications. My mother couldn't make up her mind which of her father's names she wanted me to have, first leaning toward George Walker, then toward Herbert Walker. When christening time arrived, she finally decided not to decide, naming me George Herbert Walker Bush.

A few years later, my own father had second thoughts about the name. The way Mother tells the story, Dad drew her aside one day to say they had made an "awful mistake," because Grandfather Walker's sons—my uncles—called him "Pop," and had started calling me "Little Pop" and "Poppy." That was all right for a small boy, said my father, but it just wouldn't do as a nickname that might follow me through life.

Dad usually had a good crystal ball, but this time he was wrong. "Poppy" didn't follow me as far as the Navy or to Texas, and nobody uses it any more, except—since I became Vice President—an occasional "Doonesbury" character.

For the younger members of the Bush family, Maine in the summer was the best of all possible adventures. We'd spend long hours looking for starfish and sea urchins, while brown crabs scurried around our feet. There was the wonder of tidal pools, the smell of cool salt air, the pulsating sound of waves crashing ashore at night, and the natural wonder of storms that suddenly swept across the rocky coastline.

Then there was the adventure of climbing aboard my grandfather's lobster boat, *Tomboy,* to try our luck fishing. In those days the fighting bluefish hadn't yet come to the Maine Coast, and our sights were set on bringing back hauls of small mackerel and pollock. Grandfather believed in the straight-and-simple method of fishing. Just a basic green line wrapped around a wooden rack with cloth from an old shirt or handkerchief used as lure.

Nothing fancy. We didn't need it. If the mackerel were running, they'd bite on anything, and the big ones—big for Pres and me back then meant 1 1/2 or 2 pounds—could strike hard and put up a pretty stiff battle. For pure summertime pleasure, bringing one in, especially a green beauty, ranked right up there with eating ice cream and staying up late.

It was Grandfather Walker who first taught us how to handle and dock a boat. When Pres was eleven and I was nine, we got permission to take the *Tomboy* into the Atlantic by ourselves.

Pres and I still remember that first sea adventure, the exhilaration of doing on our own what we'd watched our grandfather do, of putting into practice what he'd taught us about handling swift currents, waves, and tides.

As I grew older, I graduated from outboard motors to powerboats and could move one at fast speed through fairly rough waters. Handling boats became second nature. I loved the physical sensation of steering a powerful machine, throttle open in a following sea, and the surge that came when the waves lifted the stern and drove the bow down.

When the Japanese bombed Pearl Harbor, December 7,
1941, there wasn't any doubt which branch of the service I'd
join. My thoughts immediately turned to naval aviation.
College was coming up the following fall, but that would
have to wait. The sooner I could enlist, the better.

Six months later I got my diploma from Phillips Acad-
emy Andover. Secretary of War Henry Stimson came from
Washington to deliver the commencement address. He told
members of our graduating class the war would be a long
one, and even though America needed fighting men, we'd
serve our country better by getting more education before
getting into uniform.

After the ceremony, in a crowded hallway outside the
auditorium, my father had one last question about my future plans. Dad was an imposing presence, six feet four,
with deep-set blue-gray eyes and a resonant voice.

"George," he said, "did the Secretary say anything to
change your mind?"

"No, sir," I replied. "I'm going in."

Dad nodded and shook my hand.

On my eighteenth birthday, I went to Boston and was
sworn into the Navy as a Seaman Second Class. Not long
thereafter, I was on a railway coach headed south for Navy
preflight training in North Carolina.

I'd joined up to fly, and like the piano student who
didn't see why he couldn't begin his lessons playing *Rhap-
sody in Blue,* I was gung ho to strap on the leather helmet
and goggles the day I arrived at Chapel Hill. Because of the
pilot shortage, the Navy had trimmed its aviator training
course to ten months, but there weren't any shortcuts. It
would be months before I'd finally climb into a Stearman
N-2S trainer—the Navy's "Yellow Peril," a two-cockpit,
open-air special. Even then I got the impression that my
instructor thought I was still too fuzz-faced to trust with an
expensive piece of Navy equipment.

Looking through old scrapbooks at photos taken at the
time, I can't say I blame him. I was younger than the other

trainees—the youngest aviator in the Navy when I got my wings. To make matters worse, I looked younger than I actually was—enough to make me self-conscious. When Barbara came to visit—she was on her way to school in South Carolina—I even asked her to stretch the calendar, add a few months to her age, and tell anybody who asked that she was eighteen, not seventeen.

We'd met six months before, at a Christmas dance. I'm not much at recalling what people wear, but that particular occasion stands out in my memory. The band was playing Glenn Miller tunes when I approached a friend from Rye, New York, Jack Wozencraft, to ask if he knew a girl across the dance floor, the one wearing the green-and-red holiday dress. He said she was Barbara Pierce, that she lived in Rye and went to school in South Carolina. Would I like an introduction? I told him that was the general idea, and he introduced us, just about the time the bandleader decided to change tempos, from fox trot to waltz. Since I didn't waltz, we sat the dance out. And several more after that, talking and getting to know each other.

It was a storybook meeting, though most couples that got serious about each other in those days could say the same about the first time they met. Young people in the late 1930s and early '40s were living with what modern psychologists call heightened awareness, on the edge. It was a time of uncertainty, when every evening brought dramatic radio newscasts—Edward R. Murrow from London, William L. Shirer from Berlin—reporting a war we knew was headed our way.

In the eight months that passed from that first meeting until her visit to Chapel Hill, Barbara and I had progressed from simply being "serious," to meeting and spending time with each other's families—a fairly important step for teenagers in those days. After I got my wings and went into advanced flight training, we took the next important step. In August of 1943, she joined the Bush summer convocation in Maine where, between boating and fishing excursions, we were secretly engaged. Secret, to the extent that the German and Japanese high commands weren't aware of it. That December we went public with our engagement, though we knew that marriage was years away. My training days were drawing to a close at the Naval Air Station in Charlestown, Rhode Island. In the fall of 1943 I was assigned to VT-51, a torpedo squadron being readied for active duty in the Pacific.

Eight months after V-J Day, *Life* magazine ran a story, "Home to Chichi Jima," telling of the war-crimes trial of two Japanese officers charged with executing American fliers shot down over the Bonin Islands and "even more revolting, of practicing cannibalism on them."

I read the piece as a Yale freshman, not long out of the Navy. It brought back memories of the worst hours I spent during the war.

The date was September 2, 1944. It was the second day of concentrated air strikes on the Bonins by our squadron, VT-51, operating off the *San Jacinto*, one of eight fast carriers in Vice Admiral Marc Mitscher's Task Force 58. My aviator's log book for that day reads: *Crash Landing in Sea —Near Bonin Is.—Enemy action.*

Under the column for *Passengers* were the names *Delaney* and *Lt. (jg) White.* Jack Delaney was the young radioman/tail gunner on my Grumman Avenger torpedo bomber. William G. (Ted) White was the squadron's gunnery officer, filling in that day for Leo Nadeau, our regular turret gunner.

VT-51 had an air complement of twenty-six F6F Hellcats and nine TBM Avengers. The quick, mobile Hellcat fighter kept the skies clear of enemy aircraft. The Avenger had earned a reputation as the biggest, best single-engine bomber around, used for torpedo runs, glide bombing, antisub patrols, and providing air cover during amphibious landings. The TBM carried a three-man crew—aviator, turret gunner, and radioman/tail gunner, or "stinger," along with a 2,000-pound bomb payload.

The target for that day was a radio communications center on Chichi Jima, one of three islands in the Bonin chain. The others were Haha Jima and the best-remembered

Pacific island of World War Two, Iwo Jima. The day before, Delaney, Nadeau, and I had flown a mission targeting gun emplacements on Chichi. We knocked some out, but not enough. The Japanese who were dug in on the island still had a potent antiaircraft reserve.

Delaney, Nadeau, and I had been together since VT-51 was first attached to the *San Jacinto,* back in the States.

We'd flown missions over Wake Island, Palau, Guam, and Saipan, and survived a fair number of close calls, including a ditching operation when our plane sprang a leak while still carrying four depth charges intended for enemy subs. How do you put a TBM Avenger into the water with four 500-pound bombs in its belly? Very carefully, with adrenaline running, a prayer on your lips, and your fingers crossed.

In flight training at Corpus Christi and along the East Coast, we were taught to gauge wind velocity and the height of waves. Given winds at about fifteen knots and a fair chop on the sea, I trimmed the nose of the plane as high as possible without risking a stall. We landed tailfirst and were able to scramble onto the wing, inflate our safety raft, and start paddling, just as the plane went down.

We felt lucky. Within seconds we felt even luckier, when the plane's torpedoes detonated after their safety devices gave way to undersea pressure. Then, about thirty minutes later, came a happy ending: the destroyer U.S.S. *Bronson* sighted our raft and picked us up.

Like most TBM Avenger pilots, I liked the teamwork and camaraderie that went with being part of a three-man crew. I became attached to my plane, nicknaming it "Barbara."

The TBM Avenger wasn't fast—the unofficial Navy line described it as "low and slow." As Leo Nadeau once put it, the TBM "could fall faster than it could fly." Cruising speed was about 140 knots, brought down to less then 95 knots for a carrier landing. But it was sturdy and stable. Sturdy and stable enough to allow for pilot error on even a bad landing. From the start, back during flight training, I liked the challenge the TBM offered, the sensation of diving, getting close down to the water, going full bore.

There's nothing quite like putting a plane down on a carrier. While it was intimidating at first, you quickly got used to it. The *San Jacinto* was a new-model light carrier, with a very narrow flight deck on a converted cruiser hull. It took total concentration to make the tight turn coming into the ship's stern, then follow through on your pattern, watching the signal officer as he waved his paddles to let you know whether you were too high or too low. Screw up the plane's "attitude" and you crashed into the sea or the deck—like the Hellcat pilot I once saw miss the arresting wires on a return flight from Guam.

Our squadron was coming in after a strike, the Avengers first, then the fighter planes. I'd already landed and was standing on deck, watching as the pilot jammed his throttles forward trying to get airborne again, but lost air speed. His plane spun in, ending up by a gun mount. The gun crew was wiped out. Just a few yards away was a crewman's leg, severed and quivering. The shoe was still on. More than forty years later I can still see it.

Two other members of the squadron were alongside me when the accident happened. We were all familiar with combat risks and at one time or another had lost close friends: my first roommate, Jim Wykes, flew out on a routine antisub patrol one day and just disappeared. But none of us had ever seen death come that close, that suddenly. Four seamen who'd been with us seconds before were dead because of a random accident, for no logical reason.

Then, breaking the tension, the chief petty officer in charge of the deck crew moved in, shouting orders. "All right, you bastards," he yelled. "Let's get to work. We still have planes up there and they can't land in this goddamn mess." War, it seemed, has a perverse logic all its own.

A little after 6 A.M., the morning of September 2, I was in the ready room getting briefed for our second day of air strikes against Chichi Jima. Word came that Task Force 58 was heading south to become Task Force 38, under Admiral "Bull" Halsey. The move was scheduled to take place immediately after the Chichi Jima raid. That meant if we were going to knock out the enemy airstrips and communications on the Bonins, today would be the day.

Nobody had to remind us that the going would be rough. The day before, we'd run into strong enemy antiaircraft fire and lost a plane. The Bonins were six hundred miles from Tokyo, a key supply and communications center, and the Japanese had dug in for a protracted fight. We were learning that the closer we got to the enemy's homeland, the fiercer the resistance.

Ted White knew this when he approached me to ask if he could fill in as turret gunner during the raid. Ted was a personal friend. Our families knew each other back home. As gunnery officer, he wanted to check the equipment out under actual combat conditions.

We were due to take off at 0715. "You'll have to hurry it," I told him, looking at my watch. "But if it's okay with the skipper, and Nadeau doesn't mind, it's okay with me."

The skipper in this case was Lieutenant Commander D. J. Melvin, who had headed VT-51 since it was formed. In his early thirties, Don Melvin was a seasoned flier who knew everything there was to know about naval aircraft—a cool, collected leader who inspired confidence in younger members of his squadron. Before the war was over, he'd earned the Navy Cross not once, but twice. That morning, September 2, he cleared Ted White for the Chichi Jima mission. Leo Nadeau also signed off on the request.

We took off on schedule, first the TBMs, then the fighters, some catapulted, others making a full-deck takeoff. After I was harnessed in, my plane was hooked onto the catapult. I ran it up full-throttle, gave the catapult officer my arm-across-the-chest signal, and was launched skyward.

The sky was clear, broken only by a few clouds, not enough to provide cover for an incoming flight. Though it was still early morning, the weather was like every other day in that part of the Pacific, warm and humid. It took us about

an hour to reach the island; climbing along the way to our
attack height of 12,000 feet.

Our squadron attack plan called for three groups of
three torpedo bombers apiece, flying first in V formations,
then shifting to echelons as we prepared to dive. We were
joined by planes from other carriers as we closed in.

The flak was the heaviest I'd ever flown into. The Japanese were ready and waiting; their antiaircraft guns were set
up to nail us as we pushed into our dives. By the time VT-51
was ready to go in, the sky was thick with angry black
clouds of exploding antiaircraft fire.

Don Melvin led the way, scoring direct hits on a radio
tower. I followed, going into a thirty-five-degree dive, an
angle of attack that sounds shallow but in an Avenger felt as
if you were headed straight down. The target map was
strapped to my knee, and as I started into my dive, I'd
already spotted the target area. Coming in, I was aware of
black splotches of gunfire all around.

Suddenly there was a jolt, as if a massive fist had
crunched into the belly of the plane. Smoke poured into the
cockpit, and I could see flames rippling across the crease of
the wing, edging toward the fuel tanks. I stayed with the
dive, homed in on the target, unloaded our four 500-pound
bombs, and pulled away, heading for the sea. Once over
water, I leveled off and told Delaney and White to bail out,
turning the plane starboard to take the slipstream off the
door near Delaney's station.

Up to that point, except for the sting of dense smoke
blurring my vision, I was in fair shape. But when I went to
make my jump, trouble came in pairs.

According to the book, you dive onto the wing; then
the wind pulls you away from the plane. But something
went wrong. The wind was playing tricks, or more likely, I
pulled the rip cord too soon. First my head, then my parachute canopy collided with the tail of the plane. It was a
close one. A fraction of an inch closer, and I'd have been
snagged on the tail assembly. As it was, the only damage
that came out of the collision was a gashed forehead and a
partially torn canopy.

I came down fast—because of the torn canopy, faster than I wanted. That was when all those tedious hours of emergency training paid off. Rule No. 1 in bailing out at sea: Don't get tangled up in your parachute after landing. Still dazed, I instinctively started unbuckling on the way down and easily slipped out of my harness when I hit the water.

I looked around for Delaney and White, but the only thing in sight was my parachute drifting away. My seatback rubber raft was somewhere in the area, but if it hadn't been for Don Melvin swooping down, then up, to signal its location, I'd never have seen, much less swum to it. And while I didn't know it at the time, if it hadn't been for Doug West in his Avenger and a few of our Hellcat escorts, the raft wouldn't have done much good even when I reached it. A couple of Japanese boats had left the island, headed out to pick me up. Doug and the fighter planes drove them back while I swam toward the raft, hoping that it hadn't been damaged by the fall and would inflate. Good news, it did. I scrambled aboard. Bad news, the fall had broken the emergency container and I had no fresh water. Doug didn't know that, but coming in low he'd seen that my head was bleeding and dropped a medical kit. I retrieved it and hand-swabbed my forehead with Mercurochrome.

Then I checked out my regulation .38-caliber pistol to see if it was in working order. It was, for all the good it would do me; I would have traded it and fifty more like it for one small paddle. The wind was playing tricks again. Alone in my raft, my squadron headed back to the carrier, I was slowly drifting toward Chichi Jima.

Where were Delaney and White? There was no sign of other yellow rafts on the horizon. Just cloudless blue sky and choppy green water rolling toward the shoreline. I was hand-paddling furiously just to stay put.

My head still ached. My arm was burning from the sting of an angry Portuguese man-of-war. And to complicate matters, I'd swallowed a few pints of brackish water along the way, which meant I'd occasionally have to stop paddling to lean over the side.

Still, I was alive and had a chance. The question was whether my crew members had survived. Neither had responded after the order to bail out. Struggling against the tide, I remembered something else: Task Force 58 was pulling out of the area to rendezvous with Halsey's fleet after the raid on Chichi Jima. Don Melvin had probably radioed my position to friendly ships in the area; but realistically, if nothing showed up that day, my luck might have run out.

A half hour passed. An hour. An hour and a half. There was no sign of activity from the island, no Japanese headed my way. But nothing else was headed my way either. As it turned out, when my prayers were answered, it didn't come in the form of a large ship's outline on the horizon, but what appeared to be a small black dot, only one hundred yards away. The dot grew larger. First a periscope, then the conning tower, then the hull of a submarine emerged from the depths.

Was it an enemy sub or one of ours? It didn't take long to find out. A large bearded figure was standing on the bridge of the conning tower, holding a black metal object in his hand. As the sub drew closer, the object took form as a small motion-picture camera.

My rescue ship was the U.S.S. *Finback.* The camera buff turned out to be Ensign Bill Edwards. He stood there, filming away, while the sub continued to surface and half a dozen seamen came scurrying out to the forward deck. "Welcome aboard!" said one, who hauled me out of my bobbing craft. "Let's get below. The skipper wants to get the hell out of here." On shaky legs I climbed down the conning tower into the hold of the *Finback.* The hatches slammed shut, the horns sounded, and the sub's skipper gave the order to "Take her down."

In the sub's cramped wardroom, I was given a second welcome aboard by three other Navy airmen, rescued by the *Finback* a short while before. Silently I thanked God for having saved my life and said a silent prayer for the safety of my fellow crew members. Later I learned that neither Jack Delaney nor Ted White had survived. One went down with the plane; the other was seen jumping, but his parachute failed to open.

As a member of VT-51, I thrived on the feeling of freedom that came with flying an airplane. I was part of a team, yet on my own. But living with the officers and crew of the *Finback,* I learned about a different kind of teamwork, as well as danger.

Whatever the aviators on board might have thought originally, the *Finback* wasn't a rescue vessel but a combat ship on patrol. Much as we wanted to get back to our squadrons, we'd have to bide our time until the sub put in at Midway at the end of its war patrol.

Among other things, biding time on a submarine meant looking at the war inside out, being on the receiving rather than the delivery end of an air bombing. People talk about the risk of combat flying, but in a plane you can fire back and maneuver; on a sub you breathe stale air and sweat in the belly of a metal tube under fire.

The *Finback* sank enough enemy tonnage on that patrol to earn its skipper, Commander R. R. Williams, the Silver Star. He and his crew deserved it. Running on the surface, we were attacked by a Japanese Nell bomber. Below the surface, we were depth-charged: the sub would shudder, and the visiting airmen would give anxious looks at members of the crew. They'd reassure us, "Not even close."

It was close enough. The Navy awarded me a Distinguished Flying Cross for completing the mission on Chichi Jima, but what happened at the island was over in a hurry. Taking depth charges in a sub—even for ten minutes—could seem like an eternity.

But my month aboard the *Finback* had its better moments. There was the human element: I made friendships that have lasted a lifetime. I had a chance to reflect on the greater loss suffered at Chichi Jima. Six days after my rescue, I wrote a letter, later mailed to my parents, that described my feelings at the time:

"I try to think about it as little as possible," I said, "yet I cannot get the thought of those two out of my mind. Oh, I'm O.K.—I want to fly again and I won't be scared of it, but I know I won't be able to shake the memory of this incident and I don't believe I want to completely."

Then there were the better moments spent standing watch on the tower during the midnight to four A.M. shift, when the *Finback* ran on the surface to recharge its batteries. The sub moved like a porpoise, water lapping over its bow, the sea changing colors, first jet black, then sparkling white. It reminded me of home and our family vacations in Maine. The nights were clear and the stars so bright you felt you could touch them. It was hypnotic. There was peace, calm, beauty—God's therapy.

I still don't understand the "logic" of war—why some survive and others are lost in their prime. But that month on the *Finback* gave me time to reflect, to go deep inside myself and search for answers. As you grow older and try to retrace the steps that made you the person you are, the signposts to look for are those special times of insight, even awakening. I remember my days and nights aboard the U.S.S. *Finback* as one of those times—maybe the most important of them all.

I rejoined the *San Jacinto* and VT-51 exactly eight weeks after being shot down, in time to take part in strikes against enemy positions and shipping in the Philippines. In October 1944 American troops had landed at Leyte; in November our squadron was in action at Manila Bay and in the Luzon area. We also got news that over one hundred B-29s, taking off from Saipan, had bombed Tokyo. Three years after it had begun, the war in the Pacific was coming full circle, a noose tightening around the Japanese home islands.

In December VT-51 was replaced by a new squadron, and after flying fifty-eight combat missions I was ordered home. No reunion could have been scripted more perfectly.

I arrived Christmas Eve. There were tears, laughs, hugs, joy, the love and warmth of family in a holiday setting.

Barbara and I were married two weeks later, January 6, 1945, at the First Presbyterian Church in her hometown, Rye, New York, with a close friend from VT-51, Milt Moore, as a member of the wedding party.

A few months later I was reassigned to VT-153, a Navy torpedo bomber group being readied for the invasion of Japan. Everything I'd experienced in my year and a half of combat in the Pacific told me it was going to be the bloodiest, most prolonged battle of the war. Japan's war leaders were unfazed by massive raids on Tokyo. They seemed bent on national suicide, regardless of the cost in human life.

Now, years later, whenever I hear anyone criticize President Truman's decision to drop the atomic bomb on Hiroshima and Nagasaki, I wonder whether the critic remembers those days and has really considered the alternative: millions of fighting men killed on both sides, possibly tens of millions of Japanese civilians. Harry Truman's decision wasn't just courageous, it was far-sighted. He spared the world and the Japanese people an unimaginable holocaust.

I was stationed at Oceana Naval Air Station, Virginia, on the mid-August day when the President announced that the Japanese had sued for peace. Barbara and I were living in Virginia Beach. The announcement came at seven P.M. Within minutes our neighborhood streets were filled with sailors, aviators, their wives and families celebrating late into the night. We joined in the celebration, then, before going home, went to a nearby church filled with others giving thanks and remembering those lost in the war. After four years it was finally over.

We were still young, life lay ahead of us, and the world was at peace. It was the best of times.

YALE'S HITTING BIG FACTOR
IN TEAM'S DIAMOND SUCCESS
*The ability of the Yale Baseball team to back
up some mighty impressive pitching on the part of*

> *Frank Quinn and Walt Gratham with some solid*
> *base hits is one of the big reasons for the six game*
> *winning streak the Elis have put together this*
> *Spring.*
>
> *Leading the Yale hit parade is Bob James, a*
> *sophomore outfielder . . . who is currently*
> *powdering the ball at a .452 clip, while three other*
> *Eli regulars have averaged better than the coveted*
> *.300 level.*
>
> *After an impressive debut, George Bush, the*
> *Eli's classy first baseman, is hitting .167, but he has*
> *developed into a long ball hitter and has given en-*
> *emy outfielders a lot of running exercise. . . .*
>
> New Haven Evening Register
Spring 1946

What brought me to Texas . . .

The truth? I wish I could have answered, "A fat contract to play professional baseball"—the kind of contract
my teammate Frank Quinn got from the Red Sox after he
finished Yale ("fat" in those days being anything over fifty
thousand dollars; if Frank were in his prime today, he'd be
making a million dollars a season).

Frank was a phenomenal college player who helped
pitch our team to two straight Eastern regional intercolle-
giate championships, in 1947 and '48. I was team captain in
'48, happy to be called "a classy first baseman," but was
strictly in the lower half of the batting order when it came to
hitting. "Good field, no hit" was the way they described my
kind of ballplayer in those days—at least when I started my
playing years at Yale. But with practice I improved from
season to season. By my senior year a better description of
my style would have been "Good field, fair hit."

Once, after an especially strong day at bat in a game at
Raleigh, North Carolina—I think I was four for five, with a
couple of extra-base hits—some scouts approached me as I
left the field. But that was the first and last nibble I ever got
from the pros.

I did, however, get a lot of advice on how to improve

my hitting, not only from our Yale coach, Ethan Allen, but also from the head groundskeeper, Morris Greenberg. In my first season, Morris watched me in the batter's box a few times, then came to the apartment where Barbara and I were living on Chapel Street and slipped a note under the door. "Dear Sir," it began.

> After watching you play since the season started, I am convinced the reason you are not getting more hits is because you do not take a real cut at the ball. I am confident that if you would put more power behind your swing, you would improve your batting average 100%. I notice at the plate you are not going after any bad balls, and with the good eye which you have, I would suggest that the above be tried out.
>
> Your friend,
> Morris Greenberg

My first reaction on reading the letter was to call Morris and thank him for sending it; my second was that he might be onto something. I'd been so wound up in batting techniques—how to meet, pull, hit the ball to the opposite field—that I was swinging defensively. Not striking out much, but strike out or ground out, the bottom line's the same: no risk, no gain. So I decided to take Morris's advice and put more practice time into attacking the ball. It didn't get me a pro contract, but it did bring my batting average up to a respectable .280 by the time I played my last game.

That was in the finals of the College World Series at Kalamazoo, Michigan, in June 1948, two and a half years after I was discharged from the Navy and entered Yale. Like other married veterans in the late 1940s, I was on a fast track to get my degree and make up for lost time. It was college with a difference—not the Frank Merriwell version of campus life that existed before the war.

For one thing, Barbara, young George—he was born in July 1946—and I lived off campus, in a sprawling old house that had been divided into small apartments. To be exact, thirteen small apartments. Not to make too much of the postwar housing shortage, but there were a dozen other veterans' families sharing the house with us—each with one child, except for Bill and Sally Reeder, who had twins. That made forty in all.

But what the residence at 37 Hillhouse Avenue lacked in space it made up in other ways. When you lived forty to a house, twenty-four hours a day, you either get to like each other or you move on. We made some close and lasting friendships at 37 Hillhouse, and the New Haven address was unbeatable—next door to Charles Seymour, the president of Yale.

There was just a trace of political activism on campus; two years behind me, Bill Buckley was getting ready to stir the pot with his first book, *God and Man at Yale.* But aside from following the front-page news—the beginnings of the Cold War, from the Russian takeover of Eastern Europe to the Berlin Blockade—I wasn't politically involved. Most of the other veterans on campus felt the same. We were members of what one magazine writer, comparing us to the young political activists of the 1930s, called "the Silent Generation." But it wasn't that we were really silent or didn't care what was going on in the world, only that after four years of war we had a lot of catching up to do. I came back to civilian life feeling that I needed to get my degree and go into the business world as soon as possible. I had a family to support.

I was majoring in "the dismal science," economics, but didn't find it dismal at all. I enjoyed the work, studied hard, did well enough in class to earn Phi Beta Kappa and other honors. Technically my minor was sociology, but only technically. My real minors, as far as my attention span went, were soccer and baseball. Especially baseball.

The player I looked up to most as a kid was Lou Gehrig, the Yankees' first baseman. Gehrig had played college ball at Columbia and set a standard of quiet excellence, on and off the field. Nothing flashy, no hotdogging, the ideal sportsman. He could field, hit, hit-with-power, and come through in a clutch. A great athlete and team leader.

I never got to meet Gehrig, but one of the biggest moments of my senior year came when his teammate, "Babe" Ruth, visited Yale to give the school library the original manuscript of his autobiography. It was the afternoon of our home game against Princeton, and as team captain, I took part in the pregame presentation ceremony. When Ruth turned the manuscript over to me, his hand trembled and his voice could barely be heard. It was obvious that he was dying of cancer; but some of the young, free-spirited "Babe" was still there, very much alive. "You know," he said, winking, "when you write a book like this, you can't put *everything* in it." The ceremony was one of his last public appearances.

A few weeks later, I put on my baseball uniform for the last time. Yale was playing in the 1948 NCAA College World Series, at Hyames Field in Kalamazoo, Michigan. We were competing for the national championship the second year in a row. As Eastern Region champions, we'd played in the first-ever College World Series in 1947, losing to California. A turning point in that series came when we gave up an intentional walk to fill the bases, with two out. We were playing percentages: Cal's pitcher was coming to bat, and we figured that he'd either strike out or pop up. But scouting in those days wasn't what it is today. Cal's pitcher was Jackie Jensen, who later became one of the Boston Red Sox's best right-handed power hitters. The last time I saw the ball it was headed for downtown Detroit.

We had no better luck in 1948, this time losing to Southern Cal in a best-of-three series, two games to one. Sparky Anderson, who went on to manage the Cincinnati Reds and Detroit Tigers to world championships, was then batboy for the Trojans. They kept him hopping with a three-run rally in the ninth inning of the first game. But bottom of the ninth, we came back. Bases loaded, nobody out—then, just like that, Southern Cal pulled off a triple play to end the game. With Frank Quinn pitching, we won the following day, but the Trojans took the third game and the title.

Losing the national championship the second year running was a letdown, but just taking part in a title game was something our team felt proud of. We'd beaten the best teams in the East to get to the College World Series—North

Carolina, N.Y.U., and Illinois—and it never occurred to us that losing our final game could ruin an otherwise good season.

We could thank our coach, Ethan Allen, for that. He always kept things in perspective. In addition, most of us had served in the war. We knew there were worse things that can happen to you in life than losing a ballgame. In any case, when we left Kalamazoo in 1948 we were only disappointed, not devastated.

I headed straight home from Kalamazoo to gas up my '47 Studebaker, say good-bye to Barbara and little George, and start the long drive to Texas. Graduation ceremonies had been held before the series and my job with Ideco was waiting. Heading south, I stopped over to see a ball game in Birmingham, Alabama. Frank Quinn was already there, earning his bonus for the Red Sox's Southern Association team. The luck o' the Irish.

I was headed to Odessa after considering and rejecting several options, though in some cases the options rejected me.

One option was applying for a Rhodes scholarship. Graduating with honors and being a two-letter man in sports, in addition to other college activities, gave me a good shot at a Rhodes, according to my faculty counselor. But attractive as that possibility was, it would have meant putting off my entry into the business world. Even if I were accepted, there was no way that Barbara, little George, and I could spend a year in England without outside financial help. The same was true of graduate school in general.

And again, I'd lost four years in the war. I wanted and needed to get into the real world, to get a job. So like other seniors, I began my job search. Procter and Gamble, for one, had a training program going. I interviewed, but nothing came of it.

Then Neil Mallon entered the picture to lend a helping hand, and not for the first time. A close family friend, he was surrogate uncle and father-confessor to all the Bush children while we were growing up. Recalling my wartime experience in Corpus Christi, Neil had a suggestion—and a job offer to back it up. "What you need to do is head out to Texas and those oil fields," he said. "That's the place for ambitious young people these days."

Neil was the head of Dresser Industries, parent company of Ideco (short for the International Derrick and Equipment Company). They had an opening for a trainee in West Texas. I went to Dresser's main office—then in Cleveland, Ohio—where Neil outlined the job. "You'll be an equipment clerk," he explained. "There's not much salary, but if you want to learn the oil business, it's a start." He might have added that if I really wanted to find something different in life than what I'd known, the place to find it was West Texas.

Heading into Texas in my Studebaker, all I knew about the state's landscape was what I'd seen from the cockpit of a Vultee Vibrator during my training days in the Navy. There was ranchland, some of it rolling, other parts flat. The countryside had looked sparsely covered, but nothing like what could be seen traveling down Highway 80 toward Midland-Odessa. Once past Abilene, it was all dry topsoil, tumbleweeds, and a few trees. I'd had the impression (probably from watching Randolph Scott movies) that Abilene was cattle-grazing land, but it was hard to imagine how the barren area around me could support cattle, or that underneath this arid soil might be a fortune, even several fortunes, in minerals.

Just outside Abilene I pulled over to a wooden-frame restaurant for my first West Texas–style lunch. There were the signs advertising beer outside the roadstop. They added up to more evidence that Texas was in a different world:

LONE STAR . . . JAX . . . PEARL . . . DIXIE

Inside I passed over the national brands and asked for either a Lone Star or a Pearl, to mark my arrival in Texas (but not as a Texan; that didn't come as easily). My eyes ran down the menu, falling finally on "Chicken-Fried Steak." Nothing like that had ever been served at the Corpus Christi Naval Base mess hall, but after calling for a local beer there was nothing to do but go the full West Texas route.

"Chicken-fried steak," I said, as if knowing what I'd

ordered. Would it turn out to be a steak fried like a chicken, or a chicken fried like a steak? The waitress nodded, picked up the menu, and headed toward the kitchen. About ten minutes later she reappeared with the answer: It was a medium-grade steak smothered in thick chicken-type gravy. At the time I weighed about 180 pounds, thin for my height. Calories meant nothing, and at age twenty-four I couldn't have cared less about cholesterol, even if I'd known what cholesterol was in 1948. But even now, at 195 pounds, and nearly forty years older, I count chicken-fried steak as one of my favorite Texas delicacies. The only difference is, I don't eat it at midday, not when I have an afternoon workload.

A little later I drove into Odessa for the first time. It was another eye-opener because of the difference between the landscapes I knew and West Texas landscapes. I knew what industrial towns looked like back East, but I'd never seen a whole townful of equipment yards. As I headed toward the Ideco store—just a small, rectangular tin-roofed building, with a loading dock—I passed drilling masts, derricks, and draw works; rack on rack of casing, drill pipe, and tubing; and row on row of sucker rods. At the time, of course, I didn't know that's what they were called. But I learned, in a matter of days.

My coworker, Hugh Evans, saw to that.

Barbara and young George came to Odessa after I'd located a place for us to live: a shotgun house on East Seventh street, with a makeshift partition down the middle that divided it into two apartments. We had one bedroom, a small kitchen, and a shared bathroom. An old water-drip window unit that cranked up like a West Texas dust storm drew cool air into the bedroom on hot summer nights.

The unit wheezed but wasn't noisy enough to drown out the socializing on the other side of the partition. Our neighbors, a mother and daughter, entertained a long line of male guests every night. We shared one of the few indoor toilets on East Seventh, and the guests kept it occupied from dusk to dawn.

One house over lived an Oklahoma couple, Jack and Valta Ree Casselman, and across the unpaved street was Otis Miller, a native Texan who listened patiently for a month while his new neighbors from the East mispronounced his name, calling him *"O*-tis" when it was really *"Ah*-tis." It was our first lesson in Texas phonetics, but there would be others, as I visited nearby oil fields, traveling through towns called Muleshoe, Wink, and Notrees.

The summer months passed, and the daily temperatures fell, bringing on "the Season"—not just autumn, but the one thing in Texas that ranked equal to, if not greater than, oil prices as the subject of morning coffee conversation at Nell's diner.

Barbara and I were sports fans, but we'd never seen anything like the football fever that overtook West Texas from September through November. When the Odessa Broncos played Abilene, San Angelo, or Midland—especially Midland—there wasn't any point trying to talk about anything else, either twenty-four hours before or after a game.

It was during the peak of the season of '48, my first autumn as an Ideco trainee, that Bill Nelson gave me my first real sales assignment. A tough one: the prospect neither understood nor spoke English.

"Dallas is sending over a customer," Bill said glumly after hanging up the phone one morning, "a foreigner."

"Where from?" asked a field salesman, Leo Thomas.

"Yugoslavia," said Bill. "Not just a foreigner, but a damn Communist."

This was the early postwar period when the United States had just begun giving foreign aid to Yugoslavia to encourage Marshal Tito's split with Moscow. But Bill had his own foreign policy, and he wasn't too happy about babysitting a Marxist engineer, sales or no sales. He looked at Leo Thomas. Leo looked at Hugh. They all looked at me. The message was clear: As the closest thing to a foreigner in Odessa, Texas, I'd just been nominated to show our Yugoslav guest around.

I felt sorry for the guy from the moment he stepped off the train, a bewildered expression on his face and a Yugoslav–English dictionary in his hand. His Ideco guide had barely mastered the language of the oil fields, but somehow we managed to communicate and I was able to answer most of his questions about the company's drilling-rig inventory. Then, after dinner on his last evening in town, Barbara and I decided to give him a real taste of Americana.

It was the most feverish Friday night of the season: Odessa against Midland, the grudge game to settle bragging rights between the two towns for the next twelve months. There was an overflow crowd of twelve thousand-plus fans in the stadium, rattling the stands from the opening kickoff. Our guest put his hands to his ears, then shook his head. This wasn't the sport called football that he'd grown up with back in Belgrade.

Barbara and I could empathize. Even without a language barrier, it would take us several seasons, living in both Odessa and Midland, before we understood the game, not as we knew it back East but West Texas–style, as a quasi-religious experience.

It was the end of my first year on the job.

The Ideco supply store in Odessa had a traditional holiday party the afternoon before Christmas every year.

Right there in the store. Nothing fancy. Customers came in from the field; business friends and neighbors dropped by. Cold cuts, potato chips, pretzels, drinks on the house. Lots of drinks on the house.

I was never much of a drinker, either in the Navy or in college. One or two drinks at the most. If anyone had asked me what my limit was, I could honestly have answered that I didn't know; I'd never pushed it.

Until that Christmas Eve in Odessa, 1948.

The customers started dropping by the store in midafternoon. I was helping mix the drinks. Actually, I was pouring them, since Odessa in those days wasn't much of a mixed-drink town. Just whiskey straight; for some, maybe a little branch water to stretch it out.

Naturally, as one of the hosts, I wanted to hold up my end of the party. Midafternoon ran into early evening. I was still holding up pretty well when the first group of guests started leaving. Then a second group started drifting in.

I hadn't counted on that. Nobody had told me that these Odessa Christmas parties ran in shifts.

Barbara was waiting at home. We had the tree to decorate. Still, I had a job to do. I was an Ideco trainee, and this was part of my training. If this was how they celebrated Christmas Eve in the oilfield supply business, it would be one more learning experience.

Early evening ran into late evening. Finally the last guest on the last shift left, though I'm not sure exactly when. Leo Thomas filled me in the day after Christmas, when we got back to work. It was Leo who told our boss, Bill Nelson, not to worry, that he'd get me back home.

He did—in the back of the company pickup. Then he stretched me out, gently, on the lawn in front of our house. Leo was very apologetic, saying he should have kept a closer eye on me, this being my first company Christmas party and all.

That, at least, was the way Barbara told the story of our first Christmas Eve in Texas, back in 1948. And when reminded, she continues to tell it. Forty years later I still have to take her word for it.

Three

EITHER
AN A OR A Z

> *I don't remember when we first met but early
> on many friendships just developed naturally, with-
> out any special effort. We lived in the same small
> town, knew the same group of people, had children
> about the same ages, and were associated by our
> mutual interest in the oil industry. Somebody had a
> rig, someone knew of a deal, and we were all look-
> ing for funds. Oil was the thing in Midland.*
>
> *Excerpt of letter from C. Fred Chambers, 1986*

We were home again. Not Connecticut, but back home
in Texas. After a little less than a year in Odessa, Dresser
Industries had transferred me to California, where I first
worked in Huntington Park, then Bakersfield.

At Huntington Park, I was an assemblyman at another
Dresser subsidiary, Pacific Pumps. Paying my dues, liter-
ally, and attending meetings as a member of the United
Steelworkers Union. In Bakersfield, I became a full-fledged
Ideco salesman, selling drilling bits.

It was the salesman's life: on the road through the hot
summer months, working out of a suitcase. I'd load my car
up with bits and head one hundred miles up to Carrizo
Plains or the Cuyama Valley, going from rig to rig, finding
out what size bit the customer would need and what type of
rock formation he'd be drilling into. I drove at least a thousand miles every week.

We lived for a time in Whittier, then Ventura, then
Compton. Robin, our first daughter, was born in Compton
in 1949. Beautiful hazel eyes, soft blond hair. Now it would
be four for Texas when Dresser headquarters sent word
transferring me to Midland.

Barbara and young George couldn't wait to get back. Neither could I. California was fine, but the oil boom was on in Texas. And Midland, the heart of the Permian Basin, had come into its own as the biggest boomtown of them all.*

Old-timers around Midland in the early 1950s could tell you that this wasn't the city's first boom. Half a century before, it was known by local citizens as "the Queen City of the Prairies," a farming, cattle, and sheep-ranching center connected to the outside world by the Texas & Pacific Railway company.

In his book, *Legacy,* Texas historian Gus Clemens notes that the quality of Midland soil in those days was measured not by oil rigs but by Texas-size "peaches . . . more than 10 inches in diameter." One lure for settlers in the area was Midland's convenience to larger urban centers. According to a promotional flyer, it was possible to leave town on a night train "and arrive in Dallas for breakfast."

There had been exploration in the area since the 1890s, but the first true oil strike came in Reagan County† in 1922. Known as "the Miracle of St. Rita," it was developed by the Texon Oil and Land Company. After over a year of drilling, Texon had gone to three thousand feet with no sign of oil. The company considered abandoning the operation. Then, as Clemens tells the story, on May 28:

> [T]here was a great hissing sound, followed by a deafening roar and the crash of debris on the roofs. Running outside, the drillers watched in awe as a tremendous head of oil spewed above the weather-beaten derrick and drifted across the prairie, coating everything in greenish-black. . . . The well gushed three times on the 28th, twice on

---

* Though California was the place to be for my great-great grandfather, James Smith Bush, who, exactly one hundred years earlier, had left a country store in Rochester, New York, to become one of the original forty-niners. "He liked the country so well that he started east in 1851 to get his family, intending to take up permanent abode in the far West," according to a family history. "He never reached home but, dying on the voyage, was buried at sea."

† Named after a political figure, but not from California. John Henninger Reagan had been a U.S. Congressman, then Secretary of the Treasury of the Confederacy during the Civil War.

the 29th, and settled down to one gusher a day by the 30th. . . . On June 10th, the Orient Railroad ran a special train to the site carrying more than 1,000 people. When the gusher came in at 4:40 P.M., the crowd stood spellbound as petroleum spewed above the derrick with a roar so loud that people had to shout in each other's ears. W. H. Worley, an oil expert from Arkansas, reported: "There is no question but that this is an oil well. All speculation as to that is now wiped out." . . .

Other outside speculators, not as reserved as Mr. Worley, converged on the area, and by the end of the decade of the 1920s, Midland was calling itself the oil capital of West Texas. But as people in the oil industry know, for every boom there's a bust.

The oil was still in the Permian Basin in the 1930s, but the Depression and new finds in East Texas produced a glut that brought prices down. "By the end of 1931," writes Gus Clemens, "West Texas oil sold for as little as 10 cents a barrel, and oil men ruefully commented that a barrel of water . . . was worth more than a barrel of oil."

Boom years returned in 1934–35. This time the major oil companies moved in. World War Two kept the wells pumping, and by 1945 Midland's population had grown to 14,000. With the end of the war, the area braced for another economic downturn, but new discoveries would attract worldwide attention, leading Midland into its greatest growth period. In 1945, when I was being discharged from the Navy, the town had only three office buildings. But by the late 1950s, after the Coke, Scurry, and Spraberry finds, it had a skyline that qualified it as "the Tall City of the Plains."

There would be other boom-and-bust cycles, but Midland's future course was set. As Bill Collyns, then editor of the Midland *Reporter Telegram*, saw it, "Everything really took off after the war."

"The major oil companies built first, then the independents came in," recalled Collyns. "Pretty soon Midland was the headquarters of the independent oil man in Texas. During the 1950s almost every square foot of space was rented, so we built more offices. People said we were overbuilding, but that wasn't the case. Almost every building made money for the investors. It was hard to go wrong in Midland."

That was the Midland the four Bushes moved to in 1950, a magnet for other young people, not only from surrounding states but the East. We settled into a house on East Maple Street in a neighborhood that became known as "Easter Egg Row."

If the term had been around at that time, "Easter Egg Row" would probably have been called "Yuppieland West." It was the first mass housing project in Midland, built by an Arizona contractor named Cunningham. The houses all had the same floor plan—847 square feet—and sold for $7,500. But Cunningham knew all Texans were individualists, so he hit on a way to give each home its own identity. The rectangular houses were placed in different positions on each lot, with each painted a different luminous color. The Bush family's Easter egg came in light blue.

The time, the place, and the prospects for the future were all bright for families moving to Midland in the early 1950s. We were all, as Pittsburgh transplant Earle Craig understates it, "young people with a considerable amount of ambition." There wasn't anything subtle or complicated about it. We all just wanted to make a lot of money quick.

Quick, but not easy. We were young in the business, but still had enough experience to know that much. It would take energy, perseverance, single-minded dedication—and, of course, a little bit of luck.

Exciting as the oil business was, life in a town with a single-track mind had its drawbacks.

If you were married, with a young family, you also needed an understanding wife. Most of the wives on Easter Egg Row had come to the West Texas plains from large cities. Later there would be a local symphony orchestra and community theater; Barbara and I, with our friends from the Row, pitched in to support these and other community projects. But in the early days, social life was limited.

The big event of the week along Easter Egg Row was the after-church Sunday hamburger cookout. The scene was

straight out of Norman Rockwell: kids playing, dogs bark-
ing, and, depending on the season and the personnel available, either a touch-football or a softball game to round out
the festivities.

There was a unique warmth and camaraderie to the
friendships Barbara and I made in those years, a lot like the
attachment I felt to my shipmates and the members of my
squadron during the war—except that now it extended to
families. It also extended beyond Easter Egg Row and Midland to neighboring towns where other young oil families
had settled. We would get together with the Lubbock crowd
every once in a while in a kind of two-city neighborhood
barbecue.

One of those get-togethers gave me a chance to tell my
future grandchildren that I'd once played in a touch-football
game against not one but two All-American greats—Bobby
Layne of Texas and the Detroit Lions and Pittsburgh
Steelers, and Glenn Davis, Army's "Mr. Outside" during
the war years. Davis had brought with him Terry Moore, a
glamorous young actress, and it created quite a stir in Midland, having a real movie star come to town. Wives and kids
of the players flocked to the junior high football field for a
glimpse of our glamorous celebrity, only to find Terry with
her hair in curlers and her figure concealed by a sweat shirt
and blue jeans.

The game took place April 29, 1951. Billed as the First
Annual Martini Bowl, it was between the Midland Misfits
and the Lubbock Leftovers. Layne, who played quarterback
for Lubbock, wanted to beat hell out of us. Davis, who
played halfback, opted for mercy. The game ended in a tie.

The mimeographed program for that classic featured
advertisements by "Liedtke & Liedtke, Attorneys at Law,"
and the "Bush-Overbey Oil Development Co., Inc. (Petroleum Bldg., Phone 1678)."

Bill and Hugh Liedtke were Oklahoma transplants to
Midland. Bill had set up a law practice after getting his
degree from the University of Texas. His brother Hugh, also
a lawyer, joined him following a year of study at Harvard
Business School. When Hugh demonstrated a flair for work-

ing out innovative financing plans, the Liedtkes soon got into the business of buying and selling oil leases.

Bush-Overbey was in its first year as an independent oil company. It was formed, as my partner John Overbey recalls, in late 1950, when I "caught the fever and decided there must be a better way to participate in the excitement than selling hardware for Ideco."

The Overbeys lived across the street from us on Easter Egg Row. John was an independent operator, trading in oil leases and royalties. As neighbors—and after a while good friends—we spent hours on end talking about oil deals. When the temptation to strike out on my own got too great to resist, John seemed the ideal person to link up with. Still, I had an obligation to Dresser, especially to Neil Mallon, who had brought me to Texas.

The decision came hard because staying with Dresser could mean moving up the executive ladder in a major corporation closely tied to the oil industry. But I'd "caught the fever."

The hard part came when I traveled to Dresser headquarters in Dallas to break the news to Neil.

At age twenty-six, I didn't just respect Neil, I was awed by him. Barbara tells the story of my buying a small tape recorder to put by our bedside in Midland. When inspiration struck in the middle of the night—say, a brainstorm on financing some leasing deal—I'd get up, turn on the light, and tape my thoughts. It was only an experiment, I told her; Neil had some of his best ideas at night, and that was his way of making sure they didn't slip his mind. Barbara wasn't impressed. Neil Mallon wasn't married, she pointed out; he didn't have a wife who needed her sleep. (The experiment ended with no great loss to Bush-Overbey: unlike Neil's, my late-night brainstorms were gibberish in the light of dawn.)

Now, two and a half years after Dresser had hired me as a trainee, I was leaving the company. How would Neil react? It would be hard to tell from his demeanor. On his most hectic days he stayed under control, never showing anger or raising his voice.

He heard what I'd come to say, then took off his glasses

to clean them, collecting his thoughts. Then he got up and went into the next office, returning with a legal-size yellow pad. He began writing, talking quietly as he wrote. "I really hate to see you go, George," he said, working his way down the pad, "but if I were your age, I'd be doing the same thing —and here's how I'd go about it."

In the next half hour I got a crash course not only in how to structure but how to finance an independent oil company.

Neil Mallon was a friend and a mentor second only to my father. Watching him operate, I learned that an executive doesn't have to bully or browbeat the people under him in order to run an organization efficiently. What he taught me that day—a lesson that's stayed with me ever since—is that whenever anyone working for you wants to move on, don't stand in the way. Lend a hand.

I left Neil's office with a tremendous weight off my shoulders. Of course, the real weight had just been added. In a few weeks, the only paycheck coming in would be from *Bush-Overbey Oil Development Co., Inc.* And along with John Overbey, I'd be responsible for making sure there were funds in the bank to cover it.

For an independent West Texas oilman in the boom years of the early 1950s, the office was the place you were least likely to be found on any given day. As my own boss, I was on the road more than I'd been as a salesman for Dresser. The travel was far, wide, and varied. But never routine. That was the lure of the independent oil business— one day you were on a dusty road on some distant ranch, searching for landowners; the next day you were in a yellow cab in a big city, searching for funds.

In March of 1951, while the company was still finding its legs, the talk around West Texas was about a major oil strike in, of all places, North Dakota. The strike was known as Amerada Iverson No. 1. It was in a region with no oil-producing history—in other words, just the kind of "what the hell do we have to lose?" proposition Bush-Overbey thrived on.

Small operators often worked on projects together, and Gary Laughlin, another East Maple Street neighbor, was an independent who owned a Beechcraft Bonanza B-35. (Gary was another ex-Navy aviator, a Marine who'd flown Corsairs during the war.) Not long after we heard of the North Dakota strike, the two of us were headed north to Minot, the largest airfield in the area.

Once in Minot we rented a jeep with a top and side curtains—it was spring in Midland but still winter in the Dakotas—and headed for the county seats where land records were kept. Knowing how to read land records in a strike area is the less glamorous, but necessary part of the oil business you never see on "Dallas."

Gary and I were looking for farmers to sell us royalty, or mineral, rights. Most landowners own not only their land but the rights to what's beneath the surface. An oil company —call it Company A—comes along and buys a lease, at a fixed price per acre, which gives the company the right to explore for minerals, for a certain length of time. But the landowner normally retains what are called royalty rights; he gets to keep one out of every eight barrels—the percentage may vary—that the company produces.

But there's always the chance, of course, that Company A will drill and end up with a dry hole. That leaves the landowner with his rental money, but one eighth of nothing in royalties. This is where risk takers like Bush-Overbey and Gary Laughlin enter the picture. We were "independent" oil companies trying to get in on the action. Our proposition to the farmer-landowners was this: "We'd like to buy a percentage of your royalty rights. True, if the well comes in, you'll get less royalty money. But if it doesn't—well, a bird in the hand . . ."

That's one way an independent oil company operates, by investing—"speculating" is another word for it—in royalty percentages. Another way is by investing in what are known as "farm outs" of mineral rights.

For example, an independent goes to a major oil producer—say, Standard of Texas or Gulf—and says, in effect, "You have four sections of land leased in Oz County. Okay, you can hedge your risk. Sell me two of the sections; I'll drill and see if there's oil. If I hit, you've found out there's oil in the area without having to put your money into an exploratory operation; if I don't hit, it's my hard luck: you've learned the area is dry, without having to spend any of your own drilling money."

Still another way an independent operator can hit it big is by actually competing with the major companies in buying leases from mineral owners. How could Bush-Overbey ever hope to compete with Standard or Gulf? Because we were smaller, had no bureaucracy and more flexibility in making a decision on whether to go with an investment. We could move faster—provided, of course, that we could come up with the money.

To get the money, we'd have to attract investors outside the business, people willing to take a risk on an oil venture. If we struck oil, our investors would get a percentage of the income, depending on the amount of their investment; if the well proved dry, they could write off their losses.

There are still other ventures—getting a farm out, then bringing in a major company as a single-project partner—but whatever the arrangement, an independent's stock-in-trade is always risk taking.

In North Dakota, as things developed, the biggest risk Gary Laughlin and I took was just flying there. At times we didn't know where we were. And when we did know where we were, the people we tried to do business with had a hard time understanding what we were doing there.

In McKenzie County, bordering Montana, we offered landowners $1.25 an acre for mineral rights. Can't make the deal, they said. Rights have already been bought by something they called "the Mongolia Oil Company." (It turned out to be "Magnolia," now Mobil.) We explained to them that Mongolia had the drilling rights; what we were talking about were royalties on the mineral rights. Our offer stood at $1.25.

They were baffled by these odd Texans, who were willing to pay hard cash for an outside option on minerals that might not exist; but they took our money, we got our rights, and after a few days we headed back to Minot to fly home.

That's where the real risk taking began.

We fueled up Gary's Beechcraft and checked the weather. Wind and weather permitting, we figured to make Midland nonstop. The forecast was for generally low ceilings, with a few scattered thunderstorms along the way. No big problem there, so we took off and headed south. It wasn't long, however, before we realized the forecast had been wildly optimistic.

The weather was rough, so we tried to climb over it; but climbing, we ran into clouds, colder temperatures, and ice. We tried to duck below again, looking for light areas. Gary was a good pilot; but without deicing equipment—and with zero visibility—the situation looked as bad as anything either of us had seen during the war, until, weaving our way around Montana, we managed to find a slight opening in the clouds above Miles City. We came down, one of the happiest landings in both of our flying careers. The people at the Miles City airport looked at us as if we were crazy.

They were right. For all our jeep-jockeying around North Dakota, the most that came of it was something to talk about when we got back to Midland. Oil was later discovered near the minerals we'd bought, but after expenses we came out losers.

Looking for oil plays, anytime, anywhere, was one end of the Bush-Overbey independent oil operation. Looking for investment money was the other. Most big investors were in the East, so we spent as much time scouring the big cities for funds as we did the farmlands for oil rights.

My uncle, Herbie Walker, had helped us with funds and his expertise as an investment banker when we started the company. But in business as in politics, you can only go so far relying on the backing of relatives and friends. Along with other independents, we stayed busy working up leads and contacts—possible investors interested in getting into the oil action in Texas or, at worst, looking for tax write-offs.

One such contact—probably the best I ever made during those early days at Bush-Overbey—was Eugene Meyer, the owner of the Washington *Post,* and father of the present

owner, Katharine Graham. Fred Chambers and I were looking for funds for a surefire producer in West Texas. The
question wasn't whether the well would produce, only how
much. Since I'd met Meyer before—Brown Brothers, Harriman and Company managed a lot of his accounts—I gave
him a call. He said yes, he did put money into oil deals from
time to time, but only after a specialist looked the deal over.

The specialist was less than effusive. On the other hand,
he didn't pour cold water on the deal. It was just that he'd
seen a load of bright-eyed young entrepreneurs come by, all
wanting Eugene Meyer's capital to finance surefire deals.

Mr. Meyer agreed to see us anyway. We were invited to
breakfast at his home. Over bacon, eggs, and coffee, we re-
viewed the proposal again. He listened patiently, made some
small talk, then said he had an appointment but would drop
us off to catch our train at Union Station. Fred Chambers
still remembers that chauffeur-driven ride and the fur lap
robe our host used to keep our legs warm on a brisk Washington day.

What I remember about the ride is the sinking feeling I
had as we neared the station. Our host just didn't seem
interested in the details of our proposition. I was afraid to
press him, even as we entered the road to our drop-off point.
At age twenty-seven, you don't turn to a Eugene Meyer and
say, "Well, which is it, in or out?" So I simply resigned
myself to the fact that we had had a fine breakfast and could
tell our neighbors on the Row about the inside of Eugene
Meyer's limousine.

The limo pulled up to the curb. We were about to say
our good-byes when, at long last, our host spoke. "Okay,"
he said quietly, "put me down for $50,000." Just like that. I
was braced for a polite, "Thanks, I'll let you know," but he
made his decision on the spot, betting, I believe, not so
much on the project as on us.

Then, before his car pulled away, Mr. Meyer rolled
down the window. "You say," he asked, "this is a good tax
proposition?" We nodded, enthusiastically. "Okay," he said,
"then put my son-in-law down for . . ."

Our surefire proposition didn't do as well as we'd
hoped, though from a tax standpoint the investors came out

ahead. But Eugene Meyer never looked back. We had other oil-business dealings over the years, most of them profitable, all enjoyable.

> *Excerpt, letter from John Overbey, 1986*
>
> *Bush-Overbey rocked along and made a few good deals and a few bad ones, but somehow managed to stay in the black the entire three years of its existence. The Scurry County boom began to fade in 1951–52, but was replaced by the Spraberry boom. We were active in the Spraberry boom, and I remember one trade in particular you made for a piece of property there.*
>
> *You telephoned an absentee owner who lived in East Texas, and after much haggling settled on buying part of his Reagan County royalty for $150 an acre. After you both agreed, you suggested an exchange of telegrams to verify the deal in writing. The East Texas seller demurred, saying a deal was a deal and "My word is my bond."*
>
> *You, having been indoctrinated in the oil patch myth that a handshake was all the contract you needed, agreed to forego the exchange of telegrams and sent him a deed and a draft in the mail. Ten days passed and you didn't hear from the guy, so you called him again. Yes, he said, he'd received your deed and draft but sold the property to Nash Dowdle instead, for $151.50 an acre. Apparently his "bond" was worth $1.50 an acre.*
>
> *According to the recent news, our friend Hugh Liedtke is still making oil deals on a handshake; but he seems to make them a bit more profitable.*

Bill and Hugh Liedtke still had their licenses to practice law, but their law books, except for the ones on leases and mineral rights, were gathering dust. The Liedtkes had long since abandoned the courthouse for the oil fields, as independent oil operators with offices next door to Bush-Overbey. Then, in 1953, Bill and Hugh suggested we join forces: they'd raise $500,000, Bush-Overbey would raise $500,000, and the two companies would be rolled into one entity. We'd buy producing properties on the oil-payment plan, with the $1 million for equity.

Agreed. Now, what would we call our new company? Late one night, Hugh and I were going over possible names. We wanted something that would attract attention, a company name that would "stand out," as Hugh said, "when somebody opens the phone book."

Deep-voiced, with a pronounced Oklahoma drawl, Hugh was impressive even in his younger days, before he became "Mr. Pennzoil," a legend in the U.S. domestic oil industry.

"It ought to start with either an *A* or a *Z,*" he said, "so it comes either first or last in the pages under 'Independent Oil Operators.'" Nothing in between that could be lost in the shuffle—that was Hugh's m.o. right from the start.

The movie *Viva Zapata!,* starring Marlon Brando, was playing in downtown Midland. It was the story of Emiliano Zapata, the Mexican rebel leader who led a revolt for land reform in the early 1900s under the slogan "Tierra y Libertad"—"Land and Liberty." We couldn't afford a public-relations counsel, but if we had one he would have told us that was exactly the corporate image we were looking for.

And that's the way Zapata Petroleum was born. The following year it would spin off Zapata Off-Shore, and in time, under Hugh Liedtke's imaginative management, merge into Pennzoil.

Zapata: There was a winning chemistry about the company. We could sense it.

I was at the Ector County courthouse, twenty miles from Midland, checking land records, when Barbara called. She said Dr. Wyvell wanted to see us, right away. Dorothy Wyvell was the children's doctor. In a town the size of Midland, more than a doctor, she was a warm, personal friend.

When we went into the doctor's office and sat down, all I knew was that Robin had been in for a checkup because she'd been acting listless. But I knew something was seriously wrong before Dr. Wyvell said a word. She was normally a person of great composure, a reassuring presence whenever one of the kids got sick. But that day her eyes were misting, and she was having a hard time putting her thoughts into words.

Some tests had been run to see what was the matter with Robin, the doctor finally said. The results were back. Robin was a very sick child. She had leukemia.

Barbara seemed to understand the full meaning of what the doctor had said, but I didn't at first. When I asked what could be done, the answer stunned me. Nothing, said Dr. Wyvell. The disease was rampant. Robin's case was advanced, and she had only a short time to live. It might be a few weeks; it might be only days. Her deeply felt counsel to us was that we take Robin home, keep her as comfortable as possible, and let nature take its course.

Dr. Wyvell loved Robin. She just didn't want to see any of us hurt any more than necessary.

After we came home from the doctor's office, I called my uncle, Dr. John Walker, in New York City. He was president of Memorial Hospital there and a former cancer specialist. When I told him the news about Robin, he urged us to bring her to New York, where early research into leukemia was being conducted at Memorial Hospital by the Sloan-Kettering Foundation. Maybe nothing could be done, he told us, but we would never forgive ourselves if we didn't try. Even if the odds were a hundred million to one, said John, "You've got to give life a chance."

We flew to New York, checked Robin in at Memorial Hospital, and prepared for a long vigil. The treatments began. In the next six months there were periods of remission, when Robin almost seemed to be the healthy little girl we'd always known. I remember once walking with her when she was holding my hand and laughing. Because of her blood transfusions, she was especially beautiful and full of life that day. I ran into an acquaintance, we talked briefly, and as we got ready to move on, he asked, "George, how is your other kid doing—the one sick with leukemia?" He had no idea he was talking about the vivacious little girl beside me.

But despite these periods of remission, the doctors kept

telling us not to get our hopes up. Their prognosis was the same as Dorothy Wyvell's. Robin had the highest white blood cell count they'd ever seen in a patient. They'd do their best, but there was nothing known to medical science that could help.

Spring passed into summer, summer into fall. Barbara stayed at the bedside; I shuttled between Midland and New York City.

Prayer had always been an important part of our lives, but never more so than during those six months. Barbara and I sustained each other; but in the end, it was our faith that truly sustained us, as gradually but surely, Robin slipped away. She was three years and ten months old when she died. To this day, like every parent who has ever lost a child, we wonder why; yet we know that, whatever the reason, she is in God's loving arms.

> *In August 1959, Zapata Petroleum, which previously had reduced its ownership of Zapata Off-Shore to 40%, sold the remaining stock to its subsidiary. ZOS became an independent company, and its securities were listed on the American Stock Exchange. . . . The headquarters offices moved to the Houston Club Building, and the company marked its fifth anniversary with a fleet of four rigs, 195 employees, and 2,200 stockholders.*
>
> *Excerpted from* VIVA, *bimonthly publication of employees of Zapata Corporation worldwide, twenty-fifth-anniversary issue*

The Bushes moved to Houston after Zapata split into separate entities, Hugh and Bill Liedtke concentrating on drilling-and-production, my interest being the offshore drilling-and-contracting end of the business. A psychologist might trace it to my younger days and conclude that it had something to do with my first love, the sea. Running an offshore drilling company would mean days spent on or over water; not only the Gulf of Mexico but oceans and seas the world over, wherever there was oil or the prospect of oil.

Dividing the business was all very amicable, done over a lunch. As Midland friend Jim Ritchie recalls the occasion, the Liedtkes would say, "Okay, you take this, we'll take that," and I'd say, "Fine, you get this, we get that." We started as friends and parted as friends, richer in more ways than one.

The start came with our buying 8,100 acres in the West Jamieson Field in Coke County. By the end of 1954 we had 71 wells producing an average of 1,250 barrels a day.

Hugh Liedtke recalls that before that play ran out it totaled 127 productive wells drilled, without a dry hole. People outside the business might view that as an incredible run of luck, like shooting sevens at a dice table. Actually, it was less luck than basic geology.

Our 127 wells were drilled under blanket-sand conditions. We knew there was oil in the area before going into the deal. It was a farm out, in partnership with the Perkins-Prothro Company, a major outfit in Wichita Falls. There was a risk, but not a wildcatter's all-or-nothing risk. Once the geologists and engineers decided where we should drill, the only question was how good the well would be.

The Jamieson Field wells weren't the most prolific wells in the world, by a long shot. But they were good wells, and as we continued drilling, our income piled up. We now had enough to invest in other productive West Texas oil properties, as well as turn our eyes seaward, to what I felt was the future of domestic oil production, offshore drilling.

THREE-LEGGED MONSTER
NEW DRILLING BARGE
LAUNCHING TUESDAY

Zapata Off-Shore Co.'s new three-legged drilling barge will be commissioned in Galveston Tuesday.

Named the Scorpion, *the barge will have a number of new wrinkles embodied in its mobile unit.*

For one thing, its three legs are a radical departure from the usual multiples of two. Also, its

> *equipment and arrangement are the newest and latest ideas.*
>
> *It was built for Zapata by R. G. LeTourneau, Inc., at Vicksburg, Miss., and towed to Galveston for outfitting. It weighs 9 million pounds and cost $3,000,000. . . .*
>
> *The over-all dimensions of the platform are 180 by 150 feet. The three legs or spuds, each 140 feet long, are driven into the Gulf floor and the body pushed above the reach of waves by electric motors.*
>
> *At Galveston for the ceremonies will be George Bush, Zapata president, of Midland, and a number of visiting oilmen.*
>
> *From the Houston* Chronicle, *March 18, 1956*

No one doubted that offshore drilling represented the future of the business, but what LeTourneau proposed was a giant leap into the future. He'd gone to major offshore companies like Kerr-McGee, and while they were interested in his revolutionary ideas, they were hesitant to back up their interest with money. Not only was LeTourneau's equipment different, but the man himself was unorthodox.

But we hadn't named our company Zapata in order to be gun-shy about going into revolutionary, high-risk ventures. We listened to R. G. LeTourneau, looked at what he had to offer, and decided to stake our offshore future on his three-legged monster.

That brought us a lot of publicity and some pats on the back for making a bold business move. The only problem was, the darn thing didn't work—at least, not at first. Put out to sea on its first assignment, the *Scorpion's* jacking system failed and the Gulf saltwater got into its gear boxes.

For LeTourneau, it was back to the drawing board. For Zapata, a major decision had to be made—whether to go ahead with another LeTourneau-designed three-legged rig, the *Vinegarroon,* to the tune of $3.5 million.

We took the gamble. Like Eugene Meyer betting on Fred Chambers and me years before, Zapata's management based its decision on our hunch about LeTourneau the man. And in time, LeTourneau's three-legged monsters—first the *Scorpion,* then the *Vinegarroon,* then the $6 million *Maverick*—became the state of the art in offshore drilling rigs.

LeTourneau was gruff, eccentric, a kind of George Patton of engineering. He was the man of action with a mystic touch, a dynamo, a creative genius. He'd come to us with a proposition: he'd build the *Scorpion* at his own expense. We'd advance him $400,000—refundable if the completed rig didn't work; if it did, he'd get an added $550,000 and 38,000 shares of Zapata Off-Shore common stock. Our feeling was that anybody who had that much confidence in himself was worth the gamble.

Despite the disappointment at Galveston, the gamble paid off. LeTourneau didn't go back to the drawing board, he came over the deck itself. We watched incredulously as he looked at his monster's legs, then at the rack-and-pinion gears. Then right there on the steel deck, he pulled out some chalk and sketched the changes that had to be made.

No engineer's drawings, not even a slide rule. But it worked. Redesigned, the *Scorpion* was back in the water, drilling for oil, within a month after its original failure. We signed on for the *Vinegarroon,* LeTourneau's second monster, in March 1957. It had an improved design, one strong enough to stand up to Hurricane Audrey, with hundred-mile-an-hour winds, its first time out. The paint was stripped off, but the rig kept pumping.

So you wanted some of the romance of Emiliano Zapata to rub off on you?

HUGH LIEDTKE: *It rubbed both ways. The shareholders that got in early and had a profitable investment, well, they thought Zapata was a patriot. But those that got in at one of the top swings in the market, and then the market fell, they thought Zapata was a bandit. We were lucky that the overall investment in Zapata turned out well.*

Did your experience in Zapata help you in your public life?

GEORGE BUSH: *The experience of dealing with people helped me enormously. I learned a great deal about leadership, and I learned about the economic system. I had studied in college about supply and demand, risk and reward, profit and loss, the importance of labor and morale. But I didn't realize how all those things work together until I was making decisions that involved life and death, and survival of the business. . . .*

But I think I learned the most about people. The oil field doesn't get credit for the fiber of its people. In those days, most of the oil-field workers didn't have much education. They came from an entirely different background than I did. But the way they devoted their lives to their work, their fierce loyalty, competitiveness, and spirit, were an inspiration. It made a lasting impression on me.

> *From* VIVA, *twenty-fifth-anniversary issue, excerpt of interview with Hugh Liedtke and George Bush (1979)*

Four

THE DIFFERENCE BETWEEN CHICKEN SALAD . . .

1. My Grumman Avenger torpedo bomber was nicknamed the "Barbara." I'm shown here filling out my flight log, aboard the carrier U.S.S. *San Jacinto*, 1944.

2. With the officers and crew of the submarine U.S.S. *Finback*, September 1944. I was rescued by the sub near the Japanese-held island of Chichi Jima after my TBM Avenger was shot down during a bombing raid. I'm kneeling, second from the left, and obviously happy to be there.

3. After a "secret" engagement, Barbara and I were married at her family church in Rye, New York, on January 6, 1945. I had just returned home after duty as a TBM Avenger aviator in the Pacific.

4. Meeting the "Babe" was one of the highlights of my 1948 season as captain and first baseman of the Yale baseball team. He'd come to New Haven to give the university library the manuscript of his autobiography. Another highlight that season was our winning the NCAA Eastern regional championship for the second year in a row.

5. The Vinegarroon —one of engineer-designer R. G. Le Tourneau's "three-legged monster" drilling rigs that Zapata Off-Shore pioneered in the Gulf of Mexico in the 1950s. Cost: $3.6 million. Barbara and I left Midland and moved to Houston when I became president and C.E.O. of the company.

6. Viva Zapata! Hugh Liedtke and me at Zapata Petroleum in Midland, Texas, in 1954. Hugh, his brother Bill, and John Overbey were my partners in the independent oil company that took its name from the Marlon Brando film that was featured at a Midland theater. I was thirty years old at the time.

7. In 1964 I ran for the United States Senate in my first campaign for public office. At the Republican National Convention in San Francisco, I was a Goldwater for President supporter, and Barry later campaigned in Texas on my behalf.

8. Next stop, Washington. Barbara and I couldn't have been happier than when the results were announced and we learned that I'd been elected to Congress in November 1966.

9. At the Capitol, 1967. Barbara and me with our growing family after I was elected to Congress. Left to right: Dorothy, Marvin, Neil, Jeb, George, Barbara, and the representative from Houston's Seventh District.

10. Speaking to the U.N. General Assembly in October 1971.
As U.S. Ambassador to the U.N., 1971–73, I met and got to
know leaders and diplomats from all parts of the world.

11. Bicycles were the most popular way to travel when Barbara and I were in Beijing during my time there as American envoy to China, 1974–75. I recall two memorable meetings, one with Chairman Mao, the other with then Vice Premier Deng.

12. Walking the grounds at CIA headquarters in Langley, Virginia, with President Ford. I returned from China to become director of Central Intelligence and served in that office through 1976.

13. Getting in shape for my run for the White House in 1980. I
started jogging during my days as CIA director. Here our
family cocker spaniel, C. Fred Bush, joins me for part of the
way in one of my three-mile jogs in Maine, the summer of '79.

> HOUSTON, November 1 (AP)—U.S. Sen. Ralph
> Yarborough, D.-Tex., told Harris County support-
> ers Saturday that his opponent, George Bush, is
> "the darling of the John Birch Society in this Sen-
> ate campaign."
>
> —News report, November 1, 1964

Sometimes you don't laugh at it until years later, but
other times it's funny enough to laugh at when it happens.
"I really hate to show you this, George," said a campaign
staffer, handing me the Yarborough story, "but I think you
ought to know. . . ."

It was the Sunday before the vote. I was tired and must
have looked it. Everybody seemed extra solicitous about my
feelings, as if I were a floating rally balloon that might pop
when touched. But I'd never felt better, not since the campaign began. It was the runner's high that hits a candidate
when finally, after months of pursuit, he sees the goal in
sight.

The goal wasn't just the end of the race but winning it.
And we were going to win, no doubt about it. The polls
showed a Lyndon Johnson landslide over Barry Goldwater
in Texas, but the U.S. Senate race was neck and neck. Something was in the air.

That was a side effect of my campaign runner's high:
absolute confidence that all the work put in, not only by me
but my family, staff, and volunteer workers, would be re-
warded on election day. No newspaper story or last-minute
campaign charge was going to change that.

How could it? Everything that could possibly be said or
printed about me had already been said or printed—includ-

ing the charge, in a full-page newspaper ad, that a vote for
me, like a vote for Goldwater, could lead to nuclear war.

A campaign is a learning experience. In the year and a
half since I'd entered the race for U.S. Senate against Ralph
Yarborough, I'd learned a great deal. Barbara and I had
traveled Texas, from the Panhandle to the Rio Grande,
Wichita Falls to Beeville. There's no better way to learn
about the state, its people, its diversity. And I'd learned a lot
about myself, too. Actually, about *ourselves.*

For example, I'd learned something about Barbara's father, Marvin Pierce. It showed up in a John Birch pamphlet
early in the race. Mr. Pierce, the pamphlet said, was president of the McCall Corporation.

That much I knew.

McCall's published *Redbook Magazine.*

I knew that, too.

Redbook was, as the name suggested, an official publi-
cation of the Communist Party.

That I hadn't known.

Then there was the heavy-set guy who taught me something about one of my contributors that I hadn't known.
Roy Goodearle, one of my campaign advisers, and I were
working the crowd at a political barbecue in the Panhandle
district. We were handing out campaign cards: HELP BUILD
A GREATER TEXAS. HELP BUILD A GREATER NATION. SEND
GEORGE BUSH TO THE UNITED STATES SENATE.

"Bush. Yeah, I've heard of you," the guy said after I
handed him a card. "But I can't support you."

"Sorry to hear that," I said, thinking he meant he could
never support a Republican candidate. That's what people
usually meant when they reacted that way. *I like you personally, Bush, but you belong to the wrong party.*

Remember, this was 1964. We were building the Republican Party in Texas, but the going was slow, especially
in the rural areas. But my being a Republican wasn't the
thing bothering the guy. It was something worse than that.

"You've got Eastern money in your oil business, right?"

"Some," I said. Roy Goodearle was tugging at my
sleeve. "Why? What's your point? Everybody that's drilling

either goes to the West Coast or East for investors. It's the nature of the business."

My questioner shook his head, not even listening to my answer. "What about some of your campaign contributors?" He mentioned a prominent Houston attorney whose contribution had been either one hundred or five hundred dollars.

"What about him?" I asked. Roy was tugging harder.

"What about him? See, Bush, that's what I mean. You either don't know or don't care."

"Don't know or care about *what?*" I asked. By this time Roy had stopped tugging and had taken me by the arm, urging, "Come on, George, we've got to move along."

"Know," said the man, slowly tearing up my campaign card and depositing it at my feet, "that the sonofabitch is a member of the Council on Foreign Relations."

The lesson was that in the minds of some voters the Council on Foreign Relations was nothing more than a One World tool of the Communist-Wall Street internationalist conspiracy,* and to make matters worse, the Houston lawyer had also worked for President Eisenhower—a known tool of the Communists, in the eyes of some John Birch members.

I pictured that shredded campaign card lying at my feet as I read Ralph Yarborough's description of me as the "darling of the Birch Society." Ralph, I concluded, must be getting desperate when he comes into my home county and says something like that. It was well known in Houston that I was on the Birch Society's political hit list.

Yarborough's strategy was obvious—to tie his campaign to Johnson's and to label me an "extremist." Johnson was running two to one ahead of Goldwater in the Texas polls, campaigning on a one-note theme that if Barry were elected President he'd either blow up the world or do something reckless like get American troops involved in a land war in Vietnam.

---

* A decade and a half later, running for President, I ran into some of the same political types on the campaign trail. By then, however, they'd uncovered an international conspiracy even more sinister than the Council on Foreign Relations—the Trilateral Commission, a group that President Reagan received at the White House in 1981.

Learning that I was a John Birch favorite came as a surprise, but the hardest campaign lesson of all was finding out I wasn't a Texan—at least not by my opponent's definition. According to Yarborough, I was a "carpetbagger" who'd come down from Connecticut. Even Lyndon Johnson, on a campaign swing around the state, raised the point, though I calculated that after sixteen years of living, working, and bringing up a family in Odessa, Midland, and Houston, my credentials as a Texan were pretty strong.

I could handle that charge, even when it came from a President. (After all, I'd spent more time in Texas since 1948 than LBJ.) But the charge that couldn't be handled—because it was true—had to do with my party affiliation. Despite the fact that Eisenhower had carried the state twice in the 1950s—I'd done grass-roots work in Midland for both campaigns—Texas was still a straight-lever, Democratic state. When Texans held an election, they practically put up a notice: PUBLIC OFFICE AVAILABLE—NO REPUBLICAN NEED APPLY.

True, John Tower, a conservative college professor, had run as a Republican and won Lyndon Johnson's Senate seat in 1961, after LBJ became Vice President. But Tower was an exception—the only Republican to win a statewide election since the mid-1800s. Over most of the state in the early 1960s, the Texas Republican Party was a Ma Bell operation—call a meeting of local Republicans, and you wouldn't need much more space than a phone booth.

The idea that I might have a role in changing that—in helping build a two-party system in Texas—didn't occur to me in the early and mid-1950s. My first priority in those years was to build a business and make enough money to take care of my family and our kids' educations.

Privately my own political philosophy had long been settled. I supported much of Harry Truman's foreign policy in the late 1940s. But I didn't like what he and the Democratic Party stood for in the way of big, centralized government—the attitude that "Washington knows best" and the policies and programs it produced. I considered myself a conservative Republican, but I didn't have much chance to get into any deep ideological discussions during my early years in Texas when I was painting oil rigs in Odessa.

Politics entered into my thinking in other ways in the years that followed, especially after Dad went to the Senate in 1953. But they were ways that rankled and still do, thirty years later. They involve the political activities of a certain kind of entrepreneur who believes that everything is for sale and what can't be bought can be bullied. I learned that the oil business in those days had its share of this breed—of what President Eisenhower, in a moment of pique, called "an irresponsible and small segment of the industry."

What Ike was referring to was the way some oil lobbyists stepped over the line, working to pass the gas deregulation bill in 1956. It was a good bill, in my opinion, because deregulation would encourage more independent producers to explore for natural gas, which would increase the supply and ultimately lower prices. But my opinion was that of a Texan in the oil business, and it differed from my father's, a Senator representing a gas-consuming state. He and his Connecticut constituents were opposed to the bill. I thought they were wrong in believing deregulation would mean higher-priced natural gas; but that was Dad's and his region's view thirty years ago.

With a major lobbying effort behind it, the bill passed the House in 1955. When it went to the Senate in 1956, the pressure became intense. Charges surfaced that the oil-and-gas industry was trying to buy votes and strong-arm opposition senators.

Along about this time, calls started coming into my office from big names in the business. The subtler ones asked whether I could get my father turned around on the bill; the ham-handed types said that I'd damn well better get my father turned around. I tried to keep my emotions under control—even when some of the callers got abrasive. My answer was always the same: I disagreed with my father's position but respected it. Yes, I'd told him how I felt on this and other issues, but never on the basis of self-interest. He'd heard me out but remained opposed to the bill.

Calls were then made to my former boss, Neil Mallon, at the Dresser Company. The head of Phillips Petroleum,

K. S. (Boots) Adams, told Neil that "if Prescott Bush doesn't vote for this bill, you can forget selling any more Dresser equipment to Phillips, and you can tell George Bush to forget his offshore drilling business."

Then one morning, at two A.M., I got a call at home from one of the more aggressive lobbyists in the business, who worked for Sid Richardson. Richardson was the Texas oilman said at the time to be the richest man in the world. He was a prime mover of the bill. His lobbyist was calling from Corpus Christi, dead drunk, and, as he put it, tired of pussyfooting around. It was like this, and I damn well better understand it: Unless my father "got right" on deregulation, "That's all she wrote for you, Bush, because we're gonna run your ass out of the offshore drilling business."

It was heavyweight talk, because if anybody in America could run somebody out of the drilling business, it was Sid Richardson. The next morning—earlier than usual, because I hadn't slept much after the call—I went by Tom Fowler's house on the way to work to tell him about it. Tom was an experienced hand in the oil business whose judgment I valued then and still do. He was one of the first friends Barbara and I made after moving to Midland. Tom knew Sid Richardson. Even before I'd finished my story, he assured me that "this isn't Sid, it's his fool lobbyist. You just go to your office, G., and let me put in a call of my own. We'll have that idiot eating crow—feathers, beak, and all."

Just before lunch I got another call from Richardson's man. He sounded hoarse, as if he were recovering from a hangover or, in Tom Fowler's words, had just swallowed the crow's beak. "Sorry about last night, George," he said. "I got too involved. Forget what I said, it was all a mistake."

It damn sure was. One of many mistakes, it turned out. Every organization, whether in the public or private sector, has to guard against overzealous operators who get "too involved" carrying out their jobs. Not only can they get the people they work for in trouble, but they manage to foul up the very thing they're trying to achieve. Because of the heavy-handed lobbying that went into passage of the gas deregulation bill, President Eisenhower vetoed it, blasting the "incredible stupidity of the industry" and later describing the affair in his diary as the sort of thing that can make "American politics a dreary and frustrating experience for anyone who has any regard for moral and ethical standards."

But the incident didn't dampen my growing interest in going into politics. I'd achieved everything I'd hoped for when we moved to Texas. I'd helped build a company from the ground up. Most of my investments, despite the ups and downs of the oil business, had been profitable. Zapata Off-Shore was thriving. We had financial security, warm, close friends, and a comfortable home. I was still young, only in my thirties—young enough to look for new challenges.

Politics is always in the Texas air, and beginning in the late 1950s, I began to talk to close friends about my growing interest in public service. The advice they gave me was that if I was serious about running for office, the sensible thing to do was switch parties.

These were Democrats talking, but some were influential figures in Texas politics, like Lyndon Johnson's friend George Brown, of Brown & Root Construction Company. They mentioned several possibilities, including a chance at a U.S. Senate seat, if I crossed over and became a Democrat. The transition, they said, would be painless: In Texas there are really two Democratic parties—conservative Democrats on one side, liberal Democrats on the other. I'd just take my place on the conservative end of the Democratic spectrum.

The argument made pragmatic sense, but I just couldn't see it. Philosophically I was a Republican, and the idea of a party switch didn't sit well with me. Besides, fresh winds were blowing in Texas politics. Well-known Texans, like Peter O'Donnell, the Republican state chairman, and Thad Hutcheson, a prominent party leader, were trying to build a statewide Republican organization.

The case against Republicans, as far as Texans were concerned, went back a century, to the Civil War and the Reconstruction era. The state was solidly Democratic, and the allegiance of Texans to "the party of our fathers" became even stronger during the lean years of the Depression.

The Democratic campaign line in the 1930s was that the "Hoover Republicans" were responsible for unemployment and farm foreclosures; Franklin D. Roosevelt and the Democratic Party were said to be the only friends the people had.

Beginning in the 1950s, however, cracks began to show in the post-Roosevelt Democratic Party in Texas. The split between Democratic liberals like Ralph Yarborough and conservatives like Governor Allan Shivers grew wider. Dwight Eisenhower twice carried the state, by landslide numbers, in national elections. John F. Kennedy, despite the presence of native son Lyndon Johnson on his ticket, almost lost Texas to Republican Richard Nixon in 1960.

Something was stirring at the political grass roots in Texas, especially in Houston and Harris County. Nixon carried Houston over Kennedy—the largest metropolitan area in the country to go Republican in 1960.

Texas Democrats had grown fat and complacent. I felt they'd lost touch with the people. A new generation of Texans had come up, young people more interested in the future than in horror stories about Reconstruction and Herbert Hoover. These were the voters who could turn Texas into a genuine two-party state.

On a sunny Saturday morning in the spring of 1962, Roy Goodearle, Tom and Nancy Thawley, Jack Steel, and other local Republican leaders met with me at our house on Briar Drive to talk about their plans to build the Republican Party in Harris County.

Goodearle was a young independent oil man. He'd been active in Texas Republican politics for several years and was just beginning to acquire the gray strands and reputation for political savvy that would later earn him a Washington reputation as "the Silver Fox." He began by saying that the Harris County Republican organization was suffering growing pains. Along with increased interest in the party had come factions. One particular faction, composed of members of the John Birch Society, was threatening a takeover.

The John Birchers had a fixed idea of what was good

for the country and were intolerant of any view but their own. As far as they were concerned, America was divided into three kinds of people: (1.) those who agreed with the Birch line; (2.) Communists; and (3.) those who disagreed with the Birch line and were tools of the Communists, wittingly or unwittingly.

It was clear that a John Birch Society takeover of the Harris County party would mean that all the gains Republicans had made in recent years would be jeopardized.

As we settled down to lunch, Goodearle explained that a Birch candidate for county chairman had been narrowly defeated in a recent vote; but now the elected chairman was leaving, and it was up to the party's executive committee to choose his successor. Unless another strong candidate entered the race, a Bircher would become county chairman. The campaign would be tough because the Birchites were well-organized and zealous. Whoever ran for county chairman against their candidate would have to work overtime, touring the county, visiting every precinct, making speeches every night for several weeks.

Goodearle and the group wanted to know whether I'd be interested in entering the race. I didn't really need time to think it over. This was the challenge I'd been waiting for— an opening into politics at the ground level, where it all starts.

In the next few weeks Barbara and I got our first taste of what would become a way of life in later years. We were on the road every night, campaigning from precinct to precinct. Sometimes I drew as many as fifty people to precinct meetings, sometimes as few as two. I was an optimist even then. There was an upside to having small audiences; if my speech bombed, word wouldn't get out as fast.

It was another apprenticeship, like my days in Odessa. We made all the meetings, with me working on audience eye contact (easy when there were only four eyes in the audience) while Barbara—sitting on the platform behind me— took up needlepoint. It was a way, she explained, of staying awake at ten P.M. while listening to a speech she'd heard 150 times before.

The speech itself was about building a two-party system in Texas and what Republicans had to offer the people of Houston as a political alternative to the old-line Democratic establishment. It was a campaign style I was comfortable with. Just as people listening to a candidate running his first race learn something about the candidate, the candidate learns something about himself. I found out that jugular politics—going for the opposition's throat—wasn't my style. It was a lesson carried over from my experience in business. When competition gets cutthroat, everybody loses. Sometimes confrontation is the only way to resolve problems— but only as a last resort, after all other avenues have been explored.

That was the approach I took in my first campaign, and it was the approach I stayed with in chairing the Harris County Republican Party the next two years. There was no point trying to resolve the deep ideological differences in the membership, so I shifted the emphasis to the nuts-and-bolts of building the party organization. My theme was that we all shared basic conservative views, but to be effective we had to concentrate on tackling the Democrats, not each other. By the end of 1963 our membership had grown and we'd raised enough money to move the headquarters to a better location.

The Birchites were still grumbling, but that was another lesson I carried over from my experience in business: You can't keep everybody happy.

YARBOROUGH IS OUT OF STEP
WITH TEXAS VOTERS, BUSH STATES

George Bush, who swept to a landslide victory over Jack Cox in Saturday's runoff election for the Republican Senatorial nomination, has pledged himself to a successful campaign against Democrat incumbent Ralph Yarborough. Texas Election Bureau returns from 249 counties, 226 complete, show Bush 49,548, Cox 30,122.

—*Corpus Christi* Beacon Press, *June 18, 1964*

The irony was that Ralph Yarborough would be re-elected riding Lyndon Johnson's coattails when only a year before, Yarborough had called LBJ "a power-mad politician." The feeling between the two men was so bitter that when President Kennedy came to Dallas on November 22, 1963, it took all his powers of persuasion just to get his Vice President and the Democratic senator from Texas to shake hands.

But now Johnson was President, and as *Time* magazine reported, "it would be a blow to LBJ's personal vanity if his own home state were to elect Bush to join Republican John Tower in an all-GOP Texas Senate team."

"If Lyndon would stay out of it," *Time* concluded, "Republican Bush would have a chance. But Johnson is not about to stay out of it, which makes Bush the underdog."

It had been a long, hard underdog's campaign since the day party chairman Peter O'Donnell persuaded me to challenge Yarborough. My experience in Harris County had helped, but the party primary and runoff campaigns taught me new respect for how much territory Texas covers. The polls showed that my greatest handicap as a statewide candidate was that I was known in Houston, Midland, and Odessa, but over much of the state I was just a name and smile on a campaign billboard.

By early October, however, I was closing the "George Who" gap with the help of a shirtsleeve campaign, using the Black Mountain Boys and Bluebonnet Belles to bring in and warm up the crowds.

OLD-FASHIONED
POLITICAL RALLY
FOR
GEORGE BUSH

FREE!	*FREE!*
Soda Pop!	*Live Music*
Ice Cream!	*On the Stage*

Balloons for the kids!
Don't Dress Up—Just Come as You Are
Saturday, October 17, 7:00 p.m......
in Our Fine Memorial Auditorium

It was the kind of campaign not generally identified with Republican candidates, a leaf taken from the old Texas populist book. And after visits by Barry Goldwater, Richard Nixon, and other nationally known figures, the race got tight enough for my opponent to help my name identification with personal attacks. Being called a "carpetbagger" stung, but it meant we had Yarborough running scared. Things were looking up. . . .

If only Lyndon had stayed out of it.

IT'S LBJ BY A RUNAWAY
Ralph Wins in Texas Sweep

. . . Senator Yarborough claimed victory early Tuesday night, and Bush conceded at 11:30 p.m.

"The figures indicate that we have lost," Bush said. "I have been trying to think whom we could blame for this and regretfully conclude that the only one I can blame is myself. I extend to Sen. Ralph Yarborough, who I believe beat me fair and square, my best wishes."

The Houston Post, *November 4, 1964*

In Midland I was bitten by the bug that led me into the oil business. Now I'd been bitten by another bug. In February 1966, fifteen months after my unsuccessful race for the U.S. Senate, I resigned as chairman and CEO of Zapata to devote full time to running for Congress. It would have been unfair to the company's stockholders and employees to do otherwise. The 1964 Senate race taught me that it takes a total commitment to be a candidate. Zapata, like any successful business, needed hands-on leadership from its front office.

The truism is don't burn any bridges behind you. Under certain circumstances, however, bridge burning has something to be said for it. Resigning as operational head of Zapata left me with only one direction to go. That was forward—to win the Congressional seat in the newly formed Seventh District of Houston, then head for Washington.

Buster Whittington, one of my Zapata colleagues, couldn't understand what had gotten into me. Buster later told a reporter that when he asked "why the hell he was giving up all this to take some $18,000-a-year job" my answer was, "I can't explain it to my wife, so how the hell am I supposed to explain it to you?"

Actually, I didn't have to explain it to Barbara. She shared my concern for the way things were going in the country and my feeling that we had an obligation to put something back into a society that had given us so much.

Aleene Smith was one of the first people outside the immediate family to sense that the 1964 Senate race had a profound impact on my outlook on life. Aleene was my secretary and later joined our Washington staff. She told the same reporter who interviewed Buster that when I came back to the office after the Yarborough race, "he just didn't have his heart in making money anymore."

It was a fair observation, though with a family of seven, you don't really get cavalier about the importance of earning money. Barbara and I now had a full household—George, Jeb, Neil, Marvin, and our youngest, Dorothy.

At the same time, we'd put enough away to take care of the kids' schooling and to live on a congressman's income. We weren't rich by big-league Texas-oil standards, but money was no longer the ultimate measure of achievement I saw it as in my younger days. Having passed the age of forty, I'd concluded there were other important ways to contribute to our children's future. Going to Washington as a member of Congress was a step in that direction.

To get there I'd have to defeat Frank Briscoe, a conservative Democrat. As district attorney, Briscoe had won re-election by a three to one margin two years before. At the same time, I carried the precinct boxes in the new Seventh District by an eight to five margin against Yarborough. It figured to be a close race.

Jim Allison, a close friend from Midland and one of the hardest-working people I've ever known, came down to manage my campaign. Harry Treleaven took a leave of absence from his national P.R.-advertising agency to develop a media program. The big issues at the time were the Vietnam war and federal spending programs under LBJ's Great Society. Another issue was the state's right-to-work law.

My opponent and I both supported the Administration's Vietnam policy, were pledged to cut federal spending, and favored the right-to-work law.

In a political contest without clear-cut ideological distinctions between the candidates, the decision for the voters comes down to which candidate would be a stronger voice for the district on Capitol Hill. Treleaven, an experienced political P.R. pro, recommended that we key our campaign to the idea of "action"—ELECT GEORGE BUSH TO CONGRESS AND WATCH THE ACTION—with a picture of the candidate in shirtsleeves, coat slung over his shoulder. That became our campaign theme. But themes alone don't win elections, unless there's follow-through at the organizational level. We worked the idea of "action" into everything we did, saturating neighborhoods with volunteer door knockers and bell ringers at the end of each working day.

It was a critical off-year election for the Republican Party nationally. Richard Nixon, building a base for his 1968 presidential campaign, toured the country on behalf of Senate and congressional candidates. He traveled to Houston for our kickoff. House Republican leader Jerry Ford came down for a fund-raiser in mid-October. The campaign attracted national attention as a test of whether the GOP could come back after the Democrats' landslide victory in 1964.

We could and did.

GEORGE BUSH EASILY
DEFEATS BRISCOE

GOP Gains 40
Seats in House

—The Houston *Post,* November 9, 1966

If there was a disappointing aspect in the vote, it was my being swamped in the black precincts, despite our making an all-out effort to attract black voters. It was both puzzling and frustrating. As district attorney, my opponent had been criticized by black leaders in the community, and his campaign went so far as to make an issue out of my sponsoring a black girls' softball team.

My hope had been that a Republican candidate might be able to break the Democratic Party's grip on black voters in the area. As GOP county chairman, I'd placed our party funds in a black-owned bank and opened a party office with a full-time staff near Texas Southern, one of the state's major black colleges. Running for Congress, I talked about the possibility of a breakthrough of this kind not only with local black leaders but with a longtime friend, Bill Trent, a national leader who chaired the United Negro College Fund when I headed the UNCF drive on the Yale campus in 1948.

It seemed important in 1966—and it still does, in the 1980s—that the party of Lincoln both deserve and attract increased black support and participation. As straight-ballot voters, blacks are taken for granted by the Democratic Party, a condition not in their best interest or the best interest of our political system.

The civil rights open housing bill came before the House of Representatives in April 1968, while the country was still going through the trauma of Martin Luther King Jr.'s assassination. It was the most controversial bill I would vote on during my four years in Congress. Rose Zamaria, my administrative assistant, reported on the mail count each day. Letters from the district were overwhelmingly against the bill. After I voted for it, the mail got heavier. And uglier. Threats were directed not only against me but against members of my staff.

Written responses alone wouldn't satisfy the people in my district opposed to open housing. It was an emotional issue that would have to be talked out, face to face.

A week after the vote, I flew home to a rally held in the Memorial-West section of the district. The place was jammed. Judging from the boos and catcalls when I was introduced, it was also seething. The tone was set by another speaker on the program, who predicted that the open housing bill "will lead to government control of private property, the Communists' number one goal."

The theme of my opening remarks, once the audience had settled down, was Edmund Burke's definition of a legislator's function in a free society. "Your representative owes you not only his industry, but his judgment," wrote Burke, "and he betrays instead of serving you, if he sacrifices it to your opinion."

That explained the way I saw my job as their congressman; but there was something else that needed saying, whether or not my all-white audience agreed with it. It had to do with the reason the open housing bill deserved their support as well as mine.

I reminded them that even as we met, black Americans were fighting in Vietnam to protect our freedom and way of life. How did they feel about a black American veteran of Vietnam returning home, only to be denied the freedom that we, as white Americans, enjoyed?

"Somehow it seems fundamental," I said, "that a man should not have a door slammed in his face because he is a Negro or speaks with a Latin American accent." Open housing, I summed up, offered a ray of hope for blacks and other minorities "locked out by habit and discrimination."

As I talked, the catcalls that had greeted my introduction stopped and the audience seemed to settle down. In most cases I can pick up some hint as to how a speech is being received, but that night I didn't get a reading until the very end.

I finished, looked out at row after row of silent faces and turned to thank the program moderator. It was then that the applause began, growing louder until there was a standing ovation. All the ugliness that had gone before seemed to wash away, and I sensed that something special had happened: There had been a change of mind and heart on the part of some—not all, but some—of the people who were there.

More than twenty years later I can truthfully say that nothing I've experienced in public life, before or since, has measured up to the feeling I had when I went home that night.

• • •

The congressional class of 1966—House members first elected that year—came to Washington at a time when the country was sinking into quicksand in Southeast Asia and our inner cities were being torn apart by racial conflict. Two years before, Lyndon Johnson had been at the peak of his power. Now LBJ's influence was slowly ebbing.

It wasn't just the off-year election comeback Republicans had made in Congress. The President was also losing control over members of his own party. An odd turn of political events was taking place. Democrats on Capitol Hill and elsewhere were becoming harsh critics of their President's Vietnam policy, while most Republicans, led by Everett Dirksen in the Senate and Jerry Ford in the House, remained its staunch defenders.

LBJ had a phrase for Democrats who were abandoning him. He said they'd "painted their asses white and ran with the antelopes."

One Democrat who supported LBJ on Vietnam—though he didn't go along with his Great Society program—was G. V. (Sonny) Montgomery of Mississippi. Though on opposite sides of the political aisle, Sonny and I became close friends during our first year together in the House.

Most first-term Congressmen arrive in Washington with big ideas, ready to introduce new laws and implement bold plans to save the country. But as a freshman member of the House, you're only one of 435 lawmakers—535 counting the Senate—and at the absolute bottom of the totem pole. Your constituents are less interested in the one-minute foreign-policy speech you inserted into the *Congressional Record* than they are in how well you unsnarl the bureaucratic red tape that's holding up their pension checks or Small Business Administration loans—which is just as well because, as a freshman, there's not much you can do to shape foreign policy.

In short, you've got a lot to learn about the way Congress works. And for that, in a legislative body as large as the House of Representatives, you look to the people who've been around longest—the House leadership—for guidance.

In Sonny's case, the Democratic leadership at that time was headed by Speaker John McCormack and Majority Leader Carl Albert. In my case—and that of my close Republican friends, Bill Steiger of Wisconsin, Tom Kleppe of North Dakota, and John Paul Hammerschmidt of Arkansas —we looked to Minority Leader Jerry Ford and Minority Whip Mel Laird.

Each of these House leaders—McCormack, Albert, Ford, and Laird—understood the four rules of leadership in a free legislative body:

First, no matter how hard-fought the issue, never get personal. Don't say or do anything that may come back to haunt you on another issue, another day.

Second, do your homework. You can't lead without knowing what you're talking about. In later years, whenever I'd hear anyone make a slighting comment about President Ford's grasp of issues, I'd point out that in four years in Congress I'd never run into anyone who had a better grasp of the details of pending legislation than Jerry Ford when he was House Republican leader.

Third, the American legislative process is one of give and take. Use your power as a leader to persuade, not intimidate. It's significant that legislative leaders from both parties over the years have been those members who aren't inclined toward bluster and bombast.

Fourth, be considerate of the needs of your colleagues, even if they're at the bottom of the totem pole.

One House leader I'll always remember in that connection is Wilbur Mills. As chairman of the Ways and Means Committee, Wilbur was one of the most powerful members of the House during my two terms there. Though a freshman, I was named to fill the open Republican slot on Ways and Means, and came to respect the Democratic chairman as a model of what a good congressional leader should be.

Wilbur was a worker and he kept the committee working. No overseas travel—they were all "junkets" as far as he was concerned. He figured we had a job to do right where we were, in Washington. He was the acknowledged master of his field—tax legislation—and when he talked, his colleagues listened and learned. Best of all, however, Wilbur was unfailingly courteous, a leader who got his way not through bullying but by patiently working out a consensus.

Whenever hearings were held, my Republican colleague from upstate New York, Barber Conable, and I would show up and take our seats at the far end of the committee table. I don't remember how many hearings we attended. Over the years the bills and issues blur together. But one thing that still stands out is that no matter how late the hour, the chairman would keep the committee in session until the youngest, most junior members had a chance to ask the witness questions.

Most hearings before Ways and Means were technical and didn't draw much media attention. This didn't make the job of my press secretary, Pete Roussel, any easier. On one occasion, however, we held hearings on a bill that drew a star witness, Walter Reuther, head of the United Automobile Workers.

The hearing dragged on, late into the afternoon. Most of the other members of the committee had asked their questions and left. Reuther had pretty much said what he had to say. He had a plane to catch, but there were still reporters in the room, and Chairman Mills, seeing me at the end of the committee table, said that while he understood the witness's time constraints, "I believe Mr. Bush has some questions he wants to put to you."

Wilbur hadn't forgotten what it was like being a freshman Congressman and how important it was that I let my constituents back in Houston know I was on the job. At the same time, he knew I wouldn't forget that he'd seen to it that I had a chance to question a news-making witness.

That's how I remember Wilbur in his peak years. Later he went through a terrible personal ordeal, was laughed at and ridiculed as an alcoholic. But to his credit, he showed the same strength and character in recovering from that illness that he showed when he was operating from the center of power on Capitol Hill.

I had great respect for Wilbur Mills during my years in Congress. Twenty years later, I still do.

· · ·

I'm a good listener. That's not a boast, it's something I
learned about myself at a young age. It was reinforced after
I came to Washington. Like most people in politics, I like to
hear myself talk, but I like getting another point of view,
especially when it comes from a keen analytical or innovative mind.

Bill Steiger had that kind of mind. At twenty-eight, Bill
was one of the youngest members of Congress, but he had a
razor-sharp intelligence that cut through to the core of
things and the intellectual honesty to follow wherever logic
led him—even if it ran counter to whatever cant or conventional wisdom was going the Washington rounds.*

Bill and Janet Steiger, along with Supreme Court Justice Potter Stewart and his wife, Mary Ann, were regulars at
the informal Sunday barbecues Barbara and I had on the
patio of our home on Hillbrook Lane in northwest Washington. We'd bought the place sight unseen, over the telephone,
from retiring Senator Milward Simpson (current Senator
Alan Simpson's father). Old Milward was a good trader. We
sold the house in less than two years at a loss—possibly the
only people to achieve that distinction in Washington's
booming real-estate market.

We then moved to Palisade Lane, an ideal home and
location for our family needs. It was comfortable, and convenient to the kids' schools.

The barbecues were one way Barbara and I had of
holding onto the lifestyle we—and our children—knew back
in Houston. George was twenty, but the other kids were still
in various stages of preadolescence; Jeb was thirteen; Neil
had just turned twelve; Marvin was ten; and our youngest,
Doro, was seven.

Barbara was the mainstay, of course, the parent who
was always there to help solve the daily problems and emer-
gencies of teen and preteen life. But it was understood at my

---

* Bill Steiger seemed destined for leadership in Congress and the national scene, but
his life was tragically cut short by illness on December 4, 1978. I am godfather to his
son, Bill, Jr., who at a young age shows the same qualities of mind and spirit his father
had.

office—and still is—that when any of the kids called, no matter what I was doing, they should be put through. On weekends we worked things out so that I'd be able to get together with them individually.

These were the most important hours I spent during the week. Life in Washington can put tremendous pressure on even a freshman congressman's family. It can be a trap. You go into public life hoping to secure the future for your children and the next generation. Then somewhere along the way, unless you're careful, you can overlook the fact that your first responsibility as a parent is to be there *now*, when your kids need you, while they're growing. Barbara and I were determined when we moved to Washington that we weren't going to forget our number one priority as parents.

A congressman is only as good as his staff, and in addition to bringing my Texas team, including Jim Allison, Pete Roussel, and Aleene Smith to Washington, one of my smartest moves after being elected to Congress was in hiring Rose Zamaria to manage my office in the Longworth Building. Rose had worked for Albert Thomas, a retired senior Texas congressman from Houston. She not only knew my constituency but understood the way things operated on Capitol Hill—the mechanics and nuances (some might say tribal customs) that make Congress a unique institution.

Was I looking for cosponsors to a resolution? "Talk to Congressman A," Rose would advise, "he's always been interested in that issue. But don't bother taking it up with Congressman B, because if it doesn't have anything to do with his district he's not interested. And when you talk to Congressman C about it, don't mention Congressman D's name, because they just had it out at a closed committee hearing and won't even agree on the day of the month."

Rose also had great sensitivity about doing the right thing at the right time. The best example of this came on Inauguration Day, January 20, 1969. Thanks in large part to the efficient way my office staff took care of constituent needs, I'd been re-elected without opposition. A special grandstand had been set aside for members of Congress to watch the inaugural parade. I was getting ready to go there when Rose had a better idea.

"You know what you ought to do?" she said. "You don't really need to go sit in the cold for three hours anyway. What you ought to do is go out to Andrews to say good-bye to President Johnson, to wish him well. He's a Democrat, but he's a fellow Texan and he's been our President."

She was dead right, of course. I headed out to Andrews Air Force Base, where members of the Johnson Cabinet, along with a handful of his friends from the Senate and House, were lined up to say their farewells. It turned out I was the only Republican there. The President went down the line, his face masking whatever thoughts he had on leaving the city where he'd spent the greater part of his life. Hard as I'd worked against the man over the years—not Johnson personally, but his policies—I couldn't help but feel the poignancy of the moment.

This was the President who not many years before had moved through crowds with outstretched hands, "pressing the flesh." He loved politics, thrived on power. He'd been in Washington since the 1930s, had patterned himself after his idol, Franklin D. Roosevelt, and no doubt hoped to go down in history with FDR as one of the revered American leaders of the twentieth century. But because of Vietnam, the cheering had stopped, and he was going back to Texas a defeated man.

I shook his hand and wished him a safe journey. He nodded, took a few steps toward the ramp, then turned, looked back at me, and said, "Thanks for coming."

A few minutes later he was headed home, his last trip aboard Air Force One.

There was one senator conspicuous by his absence at Andrews that afternoon—Ralph Yarborough. I hadn't noticed it, but it seemed LBJ did. Democratic friends told me that over the next twelve months, Yarborough wrote two long letters to Johnson to explain why he hadn't been there.

The senator had reason to be worried. He was up for re-election in 1970 and couldn't afford to antagonize Johnson.

The former President had retired to his spread on the Pedernales River. Word came to me through a mutual friend, Oveta Culp Hobby, that he'd appreciated my having shown up at Andrews. Then, at a public function we both attended in Houston, he invited Barbara and me to pay a visit to the ranch. We flew down for a day and experienced what had become the legendary ranch tour LBJ gave all visitors. That meant moving over dirt roads in a white Lincoln Continental at seventy-five to eighty miles an hour, with our host at the wheel and a Secret Service van struggling to keep pace.

We talked politics, but only in general terms. He inquired about my dad. They had served together in the Senate and respected each other from across the political aisle. There was also some general talk about how things were going for the Nixon administration. But nothing specific. Not that trip.

On another occasion, however, we did talk specifics. Word was circulating around Texas that the White House wanted me to take on Ralph Yarborough again. President Nixon and other party strategists, including Texas Republican leaders like Peter O'Donnell, saw Yarborough's Senate seat as one we could pick up in an off-year national election. The feeling was that the only reason I hadn't beaten Yarborough in 1964 was his riding in on Lyndon Johnson's coattails. Six years later he seemed more vulnerable than ever. Speculation about my making the Senate race started coming up in interviews when I visited back home. *Was I interested? Would I give up my House seat to run for the Senate?*

The truth was that I hadn't made up my mind. On the one hand, Yarborough's liberal record still went against the grain of a large number of Texas Democrats. *But . . .*

It would be an off-year election—never good for the party that held the White House—and the economy was suffering—two big factors that would work in favor of Democratic candidates in 1970.

LBJ and I shared many mutual friends. One suggested

it might be a good idea to ask the former President's advice on whether I should run. I knew better than to think that Johnson, no matter how much he disliked Yarborough, would ever back a Republican candidate for office, but the opportunity to get his thinking on the subject was too good to pass up. Jack Steel, a Houston friend and supporter ever since I first entered politics, and I flew to the ranch.

This time the visit didn't include the grand tour because Johnson was waiting on some other visitors to arrive, including one of my Democratic colleagues in the House, Jake Pickle. I got right to the point. Our host said that yes, he'd heard rumors about my running, but (as I expected) he was a Democrat and would always support the Democratic candidate in any campaign. Of course, he did have friends who were free to do whatever they wanted.

"Mr. President," I said, "I've still got a decision to make and I'd like your advice. My House seat is secure—no opposition last time—and I've got a position on Ways and Means."

LBJ agreed it was a choice spot for a young congressman to be in.

"I don't mind taking risks," I said, "but in a few more terms, I'll have seniority on a powerful committee. I'm just not sure it's a gamble I should take, whether it's really worth it."

"Son," said Johnson, speaking slowly, deliberately, "I've served in the House." He paused. "And I've been privileged to serve in the Senate, too." Another pause. "And they're both good places to serve. So I wouldn't begin to advise you what to do, except to say this—that the difference between being a member of the Senate and a member of the House is the difference between chicken *salad* and chicken *shit.*" He paused again. "Do I make my point?"

Jack Steel and I flew back to Houston. I was leaning toward getting into the race, though it could never be said that LBJ had advised me to run against an incumbent Democratic senator. But the trip had been worth it anyway. It clarified my options. Given a choice, if the right kind of campaign could be put together, I'd take chicken salad.

GEORGE BUSH
HE CAN DO MORE
—Republican campaign theme,
Texas Senate race, 1970

LLOYD BENTSEN
A COURAGEOUS TEXAN WITH FRESH
IDEAS
—Democratic campaign theme,
Texas Senate race, 1970

From the Houston *Chronicle,* November 2, 1970:

TUESDAY FOCUS ON BUSH, BENTSEN

Texans decide Tuesday whether they will take the advice of President Nixon or former President Lyndon Johnson in electing the state's next U.S. Senator.

About 2 million voters, maybe more, will choose between Rep. George Bush, 46, R-Texas, and Democrat Lloyd Bentsen, 49, both wealthy Houston executives with conservative political tastes.

The winner takes the place of Texas' longtime liberal leader, Sen. Ralph Yarborough, 67, D-Texas, who was upset by Bentsen in the May 2 Democratic primary.

Bentsen started the general election campaign a decided favorite because of his unexpected defeat of Yarborough, but all indications point to a neck-and-neck finish, with Bush closing fast. . . .

Voters will also spend considerable time trying to figure out the wording of seven proposed constitutional amendments on the ballot. One, No. 2, proposes "repeal of the prohibition against open saloons." If approved by voters it means the legislature could legalize the sale of liquor by the drink on a local option basis. . . .

Excerpt, Western Union Telegram, November 5, 1970:

FROM PERSONAL EXPERIENCE I KNOW THE DIS-
APPOINTMENT THAT YOU AND YOUR FAMILY
MUST FEEL AT THIS TIME. I AM SURE, HOWEVER,
THAT YOU WILL NOT ALLOW THIS DEFEAT TO
DISCOURAGE YOU IN YOUR EFFORTS TO CON-
TINUE TO PROVIDE LEADERSHIP FOR OUR PARTY
AND THE NATION.

                                    RICHARD NIXON

The best-laid plans . . . and political risks.

"Who would have thought," wrote Reid Beveridge in the Houston *Chronicle* after the votes were in, "that Bush could get 1,033,243 votes and still lose?"

There are some things, I explained to the kids the morning after, that just aren't meant to be.

First, we had figured Ralph Yarborough was vulnerable, and we were right. So vulnerable that the conservative Democrats, pushing the right candidate (backed not only by Lyndon Johnson but former Governor John Connally) got to him before I even had a chance. Second, we carried the urban areas—Harris and Dallas counties by a combined total of 100,000 votes—but the liquor-by-the-drink proposal brought the rural counties out in record numbers. All Democrats in those days, and all voting against "open saloons" and for the straight party ticket.

So I would go back to Washington and serve out the last weeks of my term as a member of the House. But before that there was a news conference at my district office in the Federal Building in Houston. The first question, of course, was how I felt and what the future held.

"After you get over the initial hurt, the blow of losing, it's not so bad," I replied. "The future doesn't look nearly as gloomy as it did eight hours ago."

Five

HERE YOU ARE, WITH YOUR THREE WINES . . .

New York City/1971

NEW MAN AT THE U.N.

President Nixon's nomination of George Herbert Walker Bush as United States Representative at the United Nations will be greeted by two predictable reactions. Eyebrows will be raised by U.N. watchers around the world, and questions will be raised on Capitol Hill.

And why not? The appointment of a political loser—a lame-duck Congressman with little experience in foreign affairs and less in diplomacy—would seem to be a major downgrading of the U.N. by the Nixon administration. And the senators who sit in judgment of the nomination are certain to question the appointment of a conservative Republican Texas oil millionaire to the nation's highest ambassadorial post.

First impressions can, at times, be deceiving. And with any luck at all, this will prove to be one of those times. . . .

Editorial, The Washington *Star*
December 14, 1970

It had been twenty-two years since Barbara, little George, and I lived in a shotgun house on a muddy street in Odessa, while I worked overtime to prove myself at Ideco. *Could a Yale man make it as an oil equipment salesman in West Texas?*

Now "little" George was flying jets in the Air Force. Barbara, the other kids—Jeb, Neil, Marvin, Dorothy—and I were in a Waldorf suite overlooking the East River. Otherwise, nothing had changed. I was still working overtime to prove myself in a new job. *Could a Texas oilman-politician make it as U.S. ambassador to the United Nations?*

There are two things to be said for going into a job with skeptics all around doubting you can do it and asking why you were ever appointed.

First you have nowhere to go but up. A "lame-duck Congressman with little experience in foreign affairs and less in diplomacy" won't be expected to launch any great peace initiatives.

But having said that, why *was* I picked for what the *Star* called "the nation's highest ambassadorial post?" For the same reason most U.S. ambassadors to the U.N. before me were picked—political reasons that weren't likely to raise any eyebrows among experienced "U.N. watchers" or on Capitol Hill.

It's always been understood that the U.N. is a diplomatic pulpit, and every President since Harry Truman has wanted his own foreign-policy sermon delivered by his ambassador there. During the early days of the Cold War, Truman's man at the U.N. was Warren Austin, one of the President's friends and former colleagues in the U.S. Senate.

President Eisenhower named one of his original political backers, Henry Cabot Lodge, Jr., who'd lost his Senate seat to John F. Kennedy, as his U.N. spokesman. To upgrade the job, Ike gave Lodge Cabinet status.

When Kennedy became President, he viewed the U.N. job as a means of solving a political problem. Kennedy named an articulate spokesman in Adlai Stevenson, but JFK's real purpose was to deny Stevenson the job he really wanted, Secretary of State. Kennedy, wrote Arthur Schlesinger, Jr., "privately questioned Stevenson's capacity for decision and no doubt also did not want a Secretary of State with whom he feared he might not feel personally comfortable."*

The politics behind my appointment began with President Nixon wanting me to run for the Senate against Ralph Yarborough in 1970. In our first conversation on the subject,

---

* Schlesinger, *A Thousand Days: John F. Kennedy in the White House.*

he said he recognized that I'd have to give up a safe House seat to do it, but after the election he planned some Cabinet changes, and if I lost the race I'd be considered for a high post.

My answer was that if I decided to run against Yarborough it would be because I wanted to do it, and the President wouldn't be obligated, regardless of the outcome. What's more, I told him, I didn't plan to lose to Yarborough. And, of course, I didn't, losing to Bentsen instead.

Not long after the election, H. R. Haldeman, the White House chief of staff, telephoned my Longworth Building office and asked me to come by the White House. Haldeman was a strong chief of staff, who precisely reflected the thinking of the man he worked for. When he talked, you knew you were listening to the President. He told me Nixon was moving forward with some major Cabinet changes. My name had come up in connection with the United Nations job.

Nixon was looking for someone to replace U.N. Ambassador Charles Yost, a holdover from the Johnson administration. Yost had run a low-profile U.S. diplomatic mission in New York. But going into the last two years of his term—and gearing up for his 1972 re-election campaign—the President wanted his own people around at Cabinet meetings. Yost ran a nonpartisan office but was a Democrat. I had the feeling that he wasn't entirely happy with Nixon's policies, and I knew that Nixon wasn't happy with Yost's handling of the U.N. job.

Sitting in Haldeman's choice office in the west wing, the chief of staff and I discussed what the White House would be looking for in a U.N. ambassador. Obviously someone who didn't overestimate his role: the U.S. ambassador to the United Nations, while working closely with the White House and State Department, doesn't make policy, he carries it out. I commented that even if somebody who took the job didn't understand that, Henry Kissinger would give him a twenty-four-hour crash course on the subject. But I added that a U.N. ambassador should have input into policy and access to the President in order to be effective. Haldeman agreed.

The question of my lack of professional diplomatic experience came up. If I were to replace Yost, a career diplomat, there was sure to be criticism. But the fact was that most U.S. envoys up to that point, like Austin, Lodge, and Arthur Goldberg (and since that time, Pat Moynihan, Andrew Young, Jeane Kirkpatrick, and Vernon Walters) hadn't been diplomatic careerists.

My reading from the meeting was that having no diplomatic experience—other than overseas contacts as a businessman—wouldn't stand in the way of my being considered for the job. Nixon viewed the U.N. as a forum for world opinion. To him, the U.S. ambassador's job was as much a political as a diplomatic assignment. That made my political experience an asset, not a liability in his eyes.

The announcement of my appointment came December 11, 1970. Reaction started coming in immediately. The news was well received on Capitol Hill (with one exception, Senator Adlai Stevenson III, who waited three months, until the day before I took office, to say I was "totally unqualified" and my appointment "an insult" to the U.N.).

Editorially, most response was favorable. The Pittsburgh *Post-Gazette* liked it ("In naming [Bush], President Nixon has done more than provide for a lame-duck Congressman. He has also found a man with the interest and capacity to fill an important job with distinction.") But the *Star* and New York *Times* didn't ("[T]here seems to be nothing in his record that qualifies him for this highly important position.")

Which leads to the second thing to be said for going into a job with skeptics doubting you can do it: It gets my competitive instincts going. They laid down a challenge. I was determined to prove them wrong.

Like most Americans who had idealistic hopes for the United Nations when it was created in 1945, I'd undergone a sea change in attitude by the early 1970s. As "the last best hope for peace" the U.N. was another light that failed.

What many Americans find hard to accept is that even if it doesn't live up to its original expectations, the U.N. still serves a valuable purpose. It may be largely ineffective—and sometimes counterproductive—in the political area. But U.N. peace-keeping forces have performed well, from Korea in the early 1950s to the Middle East in the 1970s and '80s. And the organization's efforts in science, medicine, agriculture, and space technology—not to mention its humanitarian work providing for refugees and feeding the hungry— have been indispensable.

Nevertheless, when I reported to work as U.S. ambassador in early March, 1971, after intense briefings, I had no illusions about the U.N.'s limitations or my role as America's chief representative at the "glass palace." I was there as an advocate—not an apologist—for my country's policies. As I told Houston *Post* reporter Fred Bonavita at the end of my first full day on the job, "I've hit the ground running."

And I had . . . right into a stone wall named Yakov Malik.

I'd remembered Yakov Malik as the poker-faced, unbending Soviet spokesman at the United Nations Security Council during the Korean war years, when Security Council debates were regularly shown on television. Malik was one of the early Cold War Russian diplomats who made the word "nyet" known to the English-speaking world. He continually used a Big Power veto to block any U.N. action opposed by the Soviets.

It was Malik's walkout at the U.N. in 1950 that allowed the organization to pass the resolution—without veto —that made the defense of the Republic of Korea an international, not just an American undertaking.

More than twenty years later, Malik was once again at the U.N., his hair now white but the man himself unchanged, as I learned at our first official meeting.

The Russians have a predictable style of greeting newcomers to the international scene, whether U.S. Presidents or ambassadors. They test the newcomer, sometimes deliberately provoking a confrontation to see what reaction they'll get.

I'd hardly settled into my office after presenting my

credentials to U.N. Secretary U Thant when my deputy, Christopher Phillips, came in to report that Malik had called for a special meeting of the Big Four ambassadors— Sir Colin Crowe of Britain, Jacques Kosciusko-Morizet of France, Malik, and me—to take up the issue of immediate Israeli withdrawal from Arab territory occupied during the 1967 Six-Day War. The issue was already on the U.N. emergency agenda, but Malik chose this particular time to push for quicker action.

No sooner had the session begun than Malik launched into a harangue, accusing the United States of taking orders from Israel on the withdrawal question. I said that the charge was too ridiculous to deserve an extended reply, adding that the Soviets couldn't be too serious about wanting a Middle East peace settlement if that was the way they went about it.

It was my initiation ceremony, Malik's way of saying "Welcome to the world of diplomacy."

As chief representative of the host country, I'd get more than my share of Soviet-style diplomacy during my years as a U.N. ambassador. Malik was on the phone constantly with some protest about the Russians being inconvenienced or harassed by U.S. citizens.

Sometimes, even when the complaint was legitimate, the Soviets had a way of pushing their point too far.

For example, there was an ugly incident when a shot was fired into an apartment in the Soviet mission. I was at a dinner with the Belgians when a call came in from our mission, reporting what had happened. Together with Dick Combs, one of our Soviet experts, I headed for the scene. We were greeted by one of their KGB people. He rushed us to the eleventh floor, then into the room, where he showed us the damage. A window was shattered, the bullet having creased the refrigerator and entered the wall. A hard-bitten New York City detective was closely examining the bullet hole in the wall.

Then, after showing me the terrified family that lived in the apartment, the person in charge—it wasn't Malik, but someone down the line—tore into me, claiming that this was a deliberate provocation that couldn't possibly have happened without our complicity.

By that time I'd adopted a routine policy of taking the offensive in dealing with outrageous Soviet charges. "That's untrue and you know it," I said (though he probably didn't, since "incidents" don't happen in Russia without government knowledge). Then, pointing to the detective taking fragment samples from the wall, I added, "You see that officer there? He's America's best ballistics expert. We've assigned him to the case because we intend to find out who did this and bring whoever it is to justice."

That seemed to placate the Russian. It couldn't have displeased the New York City detective, either, though I'd never seen him before in my life.

But the essential fact was that the New York police were on the case. Not long after, they made an arrest, charging a member of the Jewish Defense League with possession of the rifle used in the shooting.

In that case the suspect was released by the courts, but the Jewish Defense League was involved in other violent incidents during my term at the U.N. I could sympathize with their cause—protesting the persecution of Soviet Jews —but made it clear to the JDL's leader, Rabbi Meir Kahane, that I didn't think he served that cause well.

Kahane had appeared at the U.S. Mission one day, demanding to see me. I was about to leave for the U.N. building. Some members of my staff, noting that Kahane was an expert at provoking headline-making confrontations, suggested we go out the back way. I decided against it.

As I moved toward the front door, Kahane, waiting in the reception area, stood up to block my way.

"Why won't you talk to me?" he demanded. "All I want is a dialogue."

"Because I've seen your idea of a dialogue—those shots fired into the Soviet embassy," I told him as I headed toward the street, "and I don't condone your group's violence any more than violence directed at Jews by Arab terrorists."

One of the worst of these Arab terrorist acts, the murder of Israeli athletes at the Munich Olympics, led to my casting the second American veto in U.N. history, against a

1972 Security Council resolution that condemned Israel for attacking Palestinian bases in Syria and Lebanon but failed to condemn the Munich atrocity that led to the attack.

It was a one-sided, irresponsible resolution, typical of what was happening to the U.N. As Third World countries attained a majority in the General Assembly, baiting the West—particularly the United States—became the order of the day. Meanwhile, this country continued to pick up nearly one third of the total U.N. budget, a fact that President Nixon never failed to note when some new incident of U.S. baiting occurred.

In the fall of 1971, the United States suffered its most serious setback in the General Assembly—up to that time— when the Third World majority voted to expel our Taiwanese allies from the United Nations. As U.S. ambassador I led the lobbying effort to permit Taiwan to keep its U.N. seat as part of what was called the "Dual Representation" plan.

The plan originated when it became clear that the United States could no longer muster the votes needed to keep the General Assembly from recognizing the Beijing (then Peking) government as the official representative of the Chinese people. Our "Dual Representation" policy was a fallback position. It accepted the inevitable—Beijing's entry into the U.N.—while still maintaining our country's commitment to our friends in Taiwan.

The actual vote came on a procedural question. Our lobbying was intense among U.N. delegates from Latin American, African, and Asian countries. On the other side, Communist and other anti-Western states lobbied equally hard in favor of Taiwan's expulsion. For a while our delegate head count showed we had the votes to win; but in the event, on October 25, 1971, what we thought were committed votes turned into abstentions. Some delegates who'd promised their support didn't show up. The final count was 59–55, with 15 countries abstaining. To this day I still remember the countries that promised to vote with us, then broke their word.

After that procedural vote, the General Assembly went on to admit the Beijing government and expel Taiwan by a sizeable margin. It was a turning point in the history of the U.N., the first time the anti-Western bloc (including Communist countries) had defeated the U.S. when American prestige was on the line. For some delegates—who literally danced in the aisles when the vote was announced—Taiwan wasn't really the issue. Kicking Uncle Sam was.

The mark of the professional diplomat is never to let personal feelings affect the way one looks at the job. I wasn't a professional, however. Sitting there in the U.S. ambassador's chair, I could feel not only bitterness but disgust at the scene taking place. One of the governments that had helped found the U.N.—the Republic of China—had been expelled from the international community, and the event was being celebrated on the floor of the General Assembly. If this was "the Parliament of man, the Federation of the world," then the world was in deeper trouble than I thought.

A short while before, when it became apparent that Taiwan's days at the U.N. had run out, I let personal feelings take over as I saw Liu Chiegh, the Taiwan ambassador, walk out of the hall with his delegation for the last time. Leaving my chair, I caught him before he reached the door, put an arm on his shoulder, and expressed regrets for what had happened. He felt he'd been betrayed by the organization his country had helped found and supported over the years.

From Liu's perspective, the United States hadn't done all it could to support the Taiwan government. America's position regarding his country's status was changing. The U.S. delegation had worked hard to get a "Dual Representation" policy through the General Assembly, but in the end it was a different kind of "Dual Representation" policy—Washington's ambivalence on the question of recognizing Beijing—that had undercut the case we tried to make to save Taiwan.

In the summer of 1971, Henry Kissinger had made the secret visit to Beijing that first signaled the change in U.S. policy. Then, not long before the debate on Taiwan's status in the General Assembly, Washington announced that President Nixon would visit China in 1972.

The news was seen in the White House and State Department as a historic breakthrough. But at the operational level of U.S. policy in the U.N., we were asking neutral nations to stand firm against Beijing, while softening our own policy toward Mao's regime.

Despite my personal feelings about Taiwan's expulsion, the long-range wisdom of having the People's Republic of China in the U.N. and of opening diplomatic contacts with Beijing was obvious. I understood what the President and Henry Kissinger were trying to accomplish. What was harder to understand was Henry's telling me he was "disappointed" by the final outcome of the Taiwan vote. So was I. But given the fact that we were saying one thing in New York and doing another in Washington, that outcome was inevitable.

The delegation from the People's Republic of China arrived in New York City in their drab gray Mao jackets* on November 11. It was my first direct exposure to the Communist Chinese. I was in for some geopolitical surprises.

It came as no surprise when the P.R.C.'s Deputy Foreign Minister, Qiao Guanhua, denounced the United States in his first formal address to the U.N. General Assembly. But while knowing that the two Communist powers had serious differences, I didn't appreciate the antagonism the Chinese felt toward the Russians, until he spent an equal amount of time denouncing the Soviet Union. A cartoon appeared in the next day's paper showing Malik and me at our desks, grimacing while Qiao dumped a bucket of rice over both our heads.

Qiao's speech was only the beginning of my education into the true state of Chinese-Soviet relations, however. The

---

* Actually, "Sun" jackets, after Sun Yat-sen, the father of modern China. A few years later, when I was U.S. envoy to Beijing, I made some mention of "Mao jackets" and was corrected by a Chinese, who quickly informed me that Sun, not Mao, was the first to wear them. The fact that both the Taiwan government and Beijing government claimed Sun as the founder of their movements points up the complexity of Chinese politics and the danger of trying to jump to easy conclusions about Chinese policy and intentions at any given time.

real surprise—that they merely disliked us, but despised the Russians—came when China's U.N. ambassador, Huang Hua, attended his first informal session of the five permanent members of the Security Council.

The session took place at the apartment of the French ambassador, Jacques Kosciusko-Morizet. Huang Hua and I had already met in one of those carefully planned scenarios laid out by State Department protocol experts. Because the United States didn't formally recognize the Beijing government, my meeting with representatives of the P.R.C. would have to appear casual, not preplanned.

I seated myself in the U.N. delegate's lounge, at a place where Qiao Guanhua and Huang Hua would have to pass on their way in. Then, as they came by, I rose, extended my hand, and introduced myself—cordially but not effusively.

They each shook my hand, cordially but not effusively. The "spontaneous" introductions over, we went our ways; but it was important that the Chinese ambassador and I talk to each other occasionally, because our two countries, despite having no formal diplomatic relations, had areas of common interest.

Now Kosciusko-Morizet, having greeted Huang Hua at the door of his apartment, was ushering him into the living room, where Sir Colin Crowe, Yakov Malik, and I were waiting. Huang was introduced to Sir Colin, shook his hand, then to me, and shook my hand. Then Malik held out his hand. I saw Huang Hua put his hand forward; but on hearing the words "Soviet ambassador," he jerked it back, pivoted, and walked away.

The insult couldn't have been more calculated. Huang knew before he came that Malik would be there. He was giving the Russian a strong taste of the medicine Malik liked to dish out on meeting newcomers—except that the Chinese weren't merely probing to see how far they could push the Russians. I realized Huang's act was a deliberate, open display to the other major powers that the Chinese considered Soviet "hegemony"—even more than American "imperialism"—the greatest threat to their country's security.

Malik, his hand extended in midair, turned a livid shade of purple. It was as if Huang had struck him with the back of his hand. At that moment—it couldn't have been more than a few seconds, though it seemed longer—the tension in the room was impossible to describe. Not a word, just heavy breathing. Then our French host, in full flap, moved rapidly toward the dining room, waving and calling out, *"Allons, allons,* let's begin the meeting."

The five of us took our places at the table—the two Communist ambassadors seated a safe distance from each other—and we went on to have a relatively civil discussion. But years later, when I was sent to Beijing as U.S. envoy, the impact of that meeting stayed with me.

The last time an ambassador had refused to shake hands with a Soviet diplomat had been when Henry Cabot Lodge turned away from Foreign Minister Andrei Vishinsky in the 1950s, at the height of American-Russian Cold War tensions. What I learned in the French ambassador's living room was that no matter what the state of détente between the United States and the Soviets, there was another Cold War taking place in the world—one between the world's two biggest Communist powers.

Dad had been on vacation in Maine when he developed a cough that he didn't seem to be able to shake. He was finally persuaded to go to Sloan-Kettering's Memorial Hospital in New York for a thorough checkup. The diagnosis was lung cancer. He didn't despair, but the disease spread rapidly.

Mother stayed with us at the ambassador's residence in the Waldorf-Astoria, spending most of her time at Dad's bedside. He died October 8, 1972. It was a real blow for me, for all his children. We had lost a best friend.

I served as U.S. ambassador to the United Nations until January 1973. On leaving to return to Washington, I was asked by a reporter whether my experience there had changed my opinion of the organization.

My answer—then and now—was yes. It made me more critical of the U.N. than I'd been before, seeing its flaws and limitations firsthand, but also more supportive, because I'd seen what the organization can do in humanitarian, social, and other areas, where ideological differences can be held to a minimum.

Politically the U.N. is and always will be a reflection of, rather than a solution to, the tensions that exist in the world. I remember the most compelling speech made to the Security Council during the 1971 session. It was delivered by Zulfikar Ali Bhutto, then the Deputy Prime Minister of Pakistan, who'd flown to New York City to ask for U.N. action to stop the Indian invasion of East Pakistan.

Bhutto made an impassioned appeal, but it was futile. What I was watching reminded me of the dismal scene at the League of Nations in 1936, when Haile Selassie flew to Geneva to ask for help when his country had been invaded by Mussolini's Italy.

The members of the League of Nations had sat on their hands in 1936. Now, in 1971, the members of the United Nations, called on to stop a war between two member states, were sitting on their hands.

"Here you are," said Bhutto as he concluded his speech, "here you are with your three wines and your grand dinners, and your *'Oui, monsieur'* and *'Non, monsieur,'* while my country is being ripped asunder by war." And with that he dramatically picked up the yellow sheets he'd been reading from and tore them to pieces, letting the paper shreds fall onto the table—at which point Israel Byne Taylor-Kamara of Sierra Leone, the presiding officer of the Security Council, as if to underscore Bhutto's message, stirred awake to say, "We thank the distinguished gentleman from Pakistan for his most helpful remarks."

Clearly, the United Nations has much to be said for it, but it still has a long way to go before it can ever achieve its early promise as "the world's last best hope for peace."

The President wanted to see me at Camp David. When the call came in, I knew our days in New York City were drawing to a close.

Following the landslide victory over George McGovern in November 1972, rumors out of the White House were that big changes were shaping up for the second Nixon administration. It wouldn't be the usual Cabinet reshuffling that came after an election, but something the President had been thinking about a long time: a major restructuring of the executive branch.

What Nixon envisioned was a "Super Cabinet" of top-level officials, working closely with the White House. One of the "supers" would be Treasury Secretary George Shultz, who'd leave the actual running of his department to a Deputy Secretary.

On the day I was scheduled to meet the President, I flew to Washington and went by the White House. John Ehrlichman, who was working with Nixon on the restructuring plan, had said that Shultz wanted to meet with me before I went to Camp David.

George was his usual unflappable self. He came straight to the point, with no wasted time or motion: *Would I like to help him run Treasury as his deputy?* I told him the offer was flattering, but I'd first have to see what the President had in mind for me.

On the chopper ride from the Pentagon helicopter pad to Camp David, I thought about George's offer. My preference—and Barbara's—would have been to stay at the United Nations, but if the President's idea was to shake things up, to move people around, the Treasury offered a new and different opportunity.

At Camp David I was met by a military aide and taken to the President's weekend home, "Aspen," a well-appointed cabin tucked away in the lush greenery of the Catoctin Mountains. There's an aura of history about the place, almost as strong as you feel on going into the White House. FDR called it Shangri-La, after the mystic Tibetan retreat in James Hilton's *Lost Horizon*. I could understand why. The quiet, especially after the heightened noise of my chopper ride from Washington, had an eerie feel to it.

The President was relaxed—at least, more relaxed than during the campaign. Even with a thirty-point lead in the Gallups, Nixon's competitive instinct had kept him on edge.

"George," he said as soon as we were settled in, "I know that Shultz has talked to you about the Treasury job, and if that's what you'd like, that's fine with me. However," he continued, "the job I really want you to do, the place I really need you, is over at the National Committee running things. This is an important time for the Republican Party, George. We have a chance to build a new coalition in the next four years, and you're the one who can do it."

So that was it. I told the President I'd like a little time to think it over. He agreed and told me to call Ehrlichman or him when I made my decision.

As soon as I got back to Washington, I called my good friend Rogers Morton, who was Secretary of Commerce. When it came to the inner workings of the White House, I valued Rog's judgment more than anyone else's. He advised that if I accepted the party chairmanship, I should make sure I got to sit at the Cabinet table and was allowed to restructure the committee. Senator Hugh Scott, a former RNC chairman, seconded Rog's advice. "Insist on it," he told me.

After talking options over with Barbara and the kids, I called Ehrlichman the next day and told him I'd take the RNC job, if given access to Cabinet meetings and a free hand. Ehrlichman said he was sure the President would agree, but would have to check. He was back on the phone within an hour and I had a new assignment.

We were on our way back to Washington and life in the political lane.

Dear Mr. President,

It is my considered judgment that you should now resign . . . [G]iven the impact of the latest development, and it will be a lasting one, I now feel that resignation is best for the country, best for this President. I believe this view is held by most Republican leaders across the country. This letter is much more difficult because of the gratitude I will always feel toward you. If you do leave office, history will

*properly record your achievements with lasting re-
spect. . . .*

*Excerpt, letter to President Richard Nixon,
August 7, 1974.*

It was the hardest political statement the chairman of a
national party would ever have to make, but the letter had
to be written and delivered—just as Barry Goldwater had to
lead a delegation of Republican leaders to the White House
that same afternoon, to tell the President he ought to resign
in the interests of his country and his party.

I owed Richard Nixon a great deal and, as a matter of
fact, I still do. He came to Texas to campaign for me when I
first got into elective politics, then gave me the rare opportunity to represent my country on an international level. But
my letter asking him to resign was written because a political party and the country is bigger and more important than
any one person, even a President.

Watergate was taking this President down, but it was
the White House that was responsible for the cover-up that
led to Nixon's fall; and it was the independent Committee to
Re-elect the President, not the official Republican National
Committee, that had served as the base of operations for
G. Gordon Liddy and the others who planned and executed
the break-in that led to the cover-up.

From the party's standpoint, it was important, even vital, that the public understand the difference. If it didn't, not
just the administration but a party would face political ruin.

The Watergate scandal broke only a few months after I
went to the RNC. From the spring of 1973 until President
Nixon's resignation on August 8, 1974, little else took up my
time as national committee chairman.

I was able to change some committee operations, em-
ploying much the same management practices as I'd used
during my Zapata days. Budget cutbacks, for example—
beginning with an order deep-sixing the chairman's limousine for more modest transportation. Major personnel re-
ductions were made and "Happy" hours during the work-
day—a habit a few employees had fallen into—were also

stopped by a directive making the RNC off-limits for alcoholic beverages during working hours.

But these were routine housekeeping changes, hardly the sort of thing the President had talked about at Camp David. Building a new majority coalition? It was an idea whose time hadn't come. As each new landmine went off, shaking the foundations of the Nixon presidency, it became clear that we'd be lucky to save the coalition we had.

Most national party chairmen, Republican or Democrat, visit state and local party workers in the role of cheerleader. My job was to serve as a bandage carrier, traveling the country to wrap up party wounds.

After our meeting at Camp David, I had only two other private sessions with the President concerning party matters. There were the Cabinet meetings, but as Watergate absorbed more and more White House time, their importance diminished.

But if I was disappointed in the White House, the President's staff had to be equally disappointed in me. What Haldeman, Ehrlichman, and Chuck Colson had wanted at the RNC was a chairman who'd be point man in a counterattack against investigators leading the Watergate charge.

Colson once sent a letter over from the White House, drafted for my signature under the national committee's letterhead. It attacked the President's partisan critics in what some White House staff members called "hardball" terms. As I read it, the language wasn't just hardball, it was beanball.

My feeling was that the RNC chairman's job wasn't to be a rubber stamp for wild political charges drawn up by White House staffers. Told that signing letters like the one Colson sent had been "routine" in the past, I said it wasn't anymore.

I was ready to defend the President against unfair criticism, but drew the line on how far the RNC would go in launching political broadsides. It wasn't the White House staff's ends I objected to, but their means: the more serious the situation got, the wilder the countercharges they wanted to make under the committee's name.

My own measure of the impact of Watergate on Nix-

on's presidency wasn't the Gallup Poll but the volume and
tenor of the letters coming into my office. These were letters
from Republican leaders and party members across the
country. At first, nine out of ten supported the President
and wanted me to do more to defend him. But the revela-
tions of Senator Sam Ervin's Watergate investigating committee started taking effect. Soon letters started coming in
criticizing me for not putting more distance between the
party and the Watergate scandal. By early August, when I
wrote my letter asking the President to resign, there was
widespread concern that Nixon, by staying in office, would
bring the party down with him.

The final turning point came when ideological divisions
in the party blurred. After Jim Buckley, one of Nixon's
strongest Senate supporters, phoned to tell me he was scheduling a news conference to ask the President to step down, it
was clear that whatever the legal outcome, a political consensus had already been reached in the Watergate case.

The last Nixon Cabinet meeting was held August 6, the
day before I delivered my letter to the President. It was—as
Dean Burch, then a counsellor to the President, described it
—"a surreal event."

Nixon entered the room, his usual neat, well-tailored
self, but his face looked puffed and tired, the look of a man
who'd been spending sleepless nights. The meeting pro-
ceeded, with the President going around the table, asking
for updated reports on a variety of problems facing the Administration.

Bill Saxbe, the Attorney General, was the Cabinet
member who mentioned the Administration's greatest problem. But it was clear that Nixon wasn't interested in discussing Watergate that day. With his presidency coming down
around him, impeachment no longer even a probability but
a certainty, demands for his resignation growing by the
hour, the President conducted his last Cabinet meeting as if
the Watergate issue didn't exist. He seemed to be a man
beleaguered, worn down by stress, detached from reality.

When his presidential helicopter lifted off the White
House south lawn three days later, my own emotions were
mixed. As chairman of the Republican National Committee,

I felt a tremendous load had been taken off my shoulders; but as a person who owed Richard Nixon a great deal—as a friend not only of the President's but of his family—I was saddened by what I saw as not merely a political disaster but a human tragedy.

Six

I HAVE ALREADY RECEIVED AN INVITATION FROM GOD

After only a month on the job, I was facing my first major diplomatic challenge as chief of the U.S. Liaison Office in Mao's China: Henry Kissinger was coming to town.

In the mid-1970s, if you were a member of the Ford administration and uttered the word "China," you knew that wherever he was at the moment—Cairo, Jerusalem, Paris—Henry Kissinger's antennae would quiver. China was Henry's private diplomatic domain, the scene of his greatest diplomatic exploit.

Four years had passed since Kissinger's surprise trip to Beijing, the first step in President Nixon's historic China initiative. Nixon was gone, but his Secretary of State was still guiding U.S. foreign policy in general and China policy in particular.

I quickly learned that after taking over David Bruce's job as United States envoy to the People's Republic.

The appointment came when President Ford invited me to the Oval Office to talk about what role I might play in his new administration. The first role I'd been considered for— Vice President—had gone to Nelson Rockefeller. Before announcing his choice of Rockefeller, Ford had phoned to give me the news. At that time, he mentioned our getting together as soon as possible to "discuss the future."

The future. As far as Barbara and I were concerned, the best "future" we could imagine was one that took us as far as possible from the immediate past. Serving as Republican National Committee chairman during the last months of the Nixon administration had been a political nightmare.

---

* Called Peking at the time Barbara and I were there, but to avoid confusion contemporary spelling of Chinese proper names is used here.

Much as we liked Washington, this seemed a perfect time to get away from the city, if the right job offer came along.

When I visited the Oval Office, the President thanked me for the service I'd given the party as RNC chairman, then mentioned the fact that two key diplomatic posts were about to open up. Ambassador to Great Britain and Ambassador to France.

But I had something else in mind. David Bruce was planning to leave his post as head of the U.S. Liaison Office (USLO) in China. Given a choice, I told the President, that was the job I wanted.

Ford finished tamping his pipe, then looked up. "China?" he said, obviously surprised.

I repeated: China—if and when it was available.

Barbara and I had talked it over. We'd come to a decision much like the one we made in 1948. Back then we decided not to do the traditional thing, but to head for the West. We now agreed that if the President gave me a choice of overseas assignments, the thing to do was head for the Far East. An important, coveted post like London or Paris would be good for the résumé, but Beijing was a challenge, a journey into the unknown. A new China was emerging, and the relationship between the United States and the People's Republic would be crucial in the years to come, not just in terms of Asian but of worldwide American policy.

The United States didn't maintain formal diplomatic relations with the People's Republic at the time, so my appointment wouldn't need Senate confirmation.* But it would need Henry's cooperation, because nothing in the U.S. Government that touched on China passed without his inspection and approval.

Henry was so apprehensive about the possibility of "leaks" concerning the Sino-American relationship that the State Department and National Security Council briefings for my new job were conducted in a lock-and-key atmosphere.

Some of the most important papers I needed to know

---

* Because I'd been ambassador to the United Nations I carried the title "ambassador" to China.

about—fundamental documents like Nixon's conversations with Mao that led to the Shanghai Communique of 1972—were closely held by Henry's staff. So closely held that I could read them only inside the private office of Richard Solomon, senior staff member of the National Security Council and one of our top China experts.

Kissinger's academic specialty was European, not Asian, affairs, but he viewed United States–China relations in a context of global strategy and security. The word was out that China policy was to be handled only by him and his closest aides: Solomon; Philip Habib, then Assistant Secretary of State for East Asian and Pacific Affairs; and Winston Lord, director of the State Department's Foreign Planning staff.

Henry assured me before I left for China that I'd be kept fully informed by him and his staff on everything that transpired between the United States and China. Most of the action along this front came not in Beijing but Washington, where he met frequently with Ambassador Huang Zhen, my counterpart in the Chinese Liaison Office. I'd learn, as had David Bruce, that it took a bureaucratic battle with the State Department to get any information about the Secretary's private talks with the Chinese.

My briefings ended in mid-September, 1974, and Barbara and I headed toward our new assignment, with a new member of the family in the airplane hold, C. Fred Bush.

C. Fred was named after our Midland, and later Houston, friend, C. Fred Chambers. When Barbara had asked Ambassador Huang whether it would be all right to bring our new family dog with us to Beijing, we got our first hint of the culture shock we were about to meet in our new assignment.

"A dog?" said Huang, nodding. "Yes, of course, bring him." Then: "He isn't a *sleeve* dog, is he?" This, we learned, is the Chinese expression for the small pekinese that the old Manchu mandarins used to carry in their sleeves. Pre-Revolutionary "sleeve dogs" weren't appreciated in Mao's China.

C. Fred passed that test, but after our arrival in China he turned out to be something of a culture shock to the Chinese. Dogs have been a rarity in China, ever since the

People's Republic began a canine extermination program after the civil war of the 1940s to check the spread of disease. When we'd take Fred for walks, some Chinese were confused, pointing to him and saying, *"Mao!"*, the Chinese word for cat. Others were simply curious, and a few were terrified. Practically the first sentence Barbara learned to say in Chinese was "Don't worry, he's only a little dog and he doesn't bite."

Not that dogs are entirely unacceptable in modern China. At a dinner we attended shortly after our arrival, an item was described on the official menu as "fragrant meat." After we came home and showed the menu to a staff member familiar with Chinese culture, he explained that what we'd just eaten was "the upper lip of a wild dog."

The Kissinger visit was coming after a month of settling into my new post and getting acquainted with the thirty-member USLO staff, headed by John Holdridge, deputy chief of mission. John, a onetime college athlete who stood well over six feet, was an impressive presence at diplomatic functions. He was a China scholar who later became U.S. ambassador to Singapore, then Assistant Secretary of State for the Far East. Other top-level staff members included Don Anderson, our expert in Chinese political affairs, the head of our economic section—first Herbert Horowitz, later Bill Thomas and my executive assistant, Jennifer Fitzgerald.

Anderson's job had to be one of the most frustrating diplomatic assignments in the U.S. foreign service. He was supposed to figure out what was going on politically in a country with a centuries-old tradition of secrecy in government. Don and his deputies searched for the slightest clue that some Chinese leader was rising or falling in status. They were experts in the protocol of Chinese leadership. *Was some leader not mentioned in a news story about the dedication of a new building in his city of birth? Was a Chinese deputy minister sent to an international conference, instead of his boss? Why hasn't so-and-so been heard from in over three months? Who's up, who's down?*

Being briefed by Don and his political section on the subtlety of Chinese politics, I couldn't help thinking what a field day Evans and Novak, Sam Donaldson, and other American political pundits would have if they could cover Beijing the way they cover Washington.

After getting to know the USLO staff, my next assignment had been to start meeting some of the Chinese leaders Don Anderson's department told me about. The first high-ranking Chinese official I called on was one I'd known from my days at the U.N.—Qiao Guanhua.

Qiao was then the vice minister of foreign affairs who'd led the first People's Republic delegation to the U.N. in 1972. He'd introduced his country to the world body with a speech that impartially ripped into the United States and Soviet Union. He was the figure shown in the following day's newspaper cartoon, emptying a rice bowl over both my head and Yakov Malik's.

That was Qiao the tough diplomat. Later, I found out there was a Qiao the quiet diplomat, who was interested in pursuing his country's policy of improved relations with the United States. We got to know each other over informal dinners.

Qiao, who had since risen to become Foreign Minister, remembered those U.N. days when I made my first official call on him as head of the U.S. Liaison Office. Not long after that, he hosted a family-style dinner for Barbara and me. Political experts in other foreign embassies in Beijing, particularly the Soviet embassy, probably took note and started drawing conclusions. No doubt Qiao had that in mind when he planned the dinner

Educated in Germany, Qiao spoke excellent English. He was married to Zhang Hanzhi, a high-level official at the Chinese Foreign Ministry, a brilliant, attractive woman who wore a Western-style hairdo, unusual in Mao's China. Unlike many other Chinese leaders, Qiao was at ease when he talked to foreigners. He could be gracious, but also blunt, and was frequently compared to Premier Zhou Enlai.

Later, both Qiao and his wife would lose power for a combination of reasons. He sided with the anti-Deng faction during a period of upheaval. She was too close to Jiang Ging, Mao's wife and later a leader of the "Gang of Four." When the "Gang" was purged in the autumn of 1976 and

Deng returned to power, Qiao and his wife went the way of all Chinese leaders who back the wrong faction.

But when I arrived in Beijing two years earlier, in the autumn of 1974, Qiao was a rising power in China, a man Western diplomats wanted to see and talk to because of his own brilliance and frankness.

We discussed Kissinger's coming visit, and I could tell by the way Qiao talked about Henry that the Chinese held the American Secretary of State in high esteem. From what I gathered, the Chinese leaders felt that Henry had a better understanding of them—and the Russians—than any other top-level Western diplomat. When the huge blue-and-white Kissinger jet bearing the Seal of the United States touched down, the Beijing airport couldn't have been more crowded if the President of the United States himself had been arriving.

For a split second, when the door to the jet opened, I thought it was the President who'd arrived. The first people off the plane were Henry's security men. I stopped counting after half a dozen.

"So many," commented Nancy Tang, the official Chinese Government interpreter, as the Kissinger Secret Service team fanned out across the tarmac. The number did seem excessive in a country so tightly controlled that the American Secretary of State's security was virtually guaranteed by his hosts.

Now Henry himself was climbing down the plane ramp, accompanied by his wife Nancy and his two children, David and Elizabeth. There were warm greetings at planeside, after which the Kissinger party climbed into an official black car and moved off, in a cloud of dust, to the government guesthouses on the eastern outskirts of Beijing.

Literally in a cloud of dust. For all Beijing's historic grandeur, a month there had reminded Barbara and me of life on East Seventh Street in Odessa, Texas, in 1948. Like Odessa, the Chinese capital lies in the center of a great plain. Unpaved side streets make for limited visibility when the winds kick up. C. Fred's color had already been altered from bright natural gold to dull gray. I had a cold—if not actually triggered by dust, then aggravated by it.

We arrived at the guesthouses where the Kissingers were staying. Henry was in an expansive mood, trading pleasantries with his Chinese hosts. I'd seen him like this on other occasions. Whenever he was center stage, the Secretary seemed to come alive, like a political candidate working a crowd back home.

To save commuting time—traveling through and around the million bicycles that operated between the USLO and the Kissingers' quarters—Barbara and I were temporarily staying at a nearby guesthouse. One of our Chinese hosts pointedly reminded us that we'd been assigned quarters in Guest House 18, the same quarters President Nixon had stayed in during his first visit to China, in February 1972.

The guesthouses were comfortable, though not lavish. Like most hostelries in China, they came provisioned with everything a foreign traveler might need: pens, ink, writing paper, bathrobes, slippers, cosmetics, even toothbrushes and toothpaste. In the lull before our first official function, Barbara sat down to write a letter home. When she'd finished addressing the envelope and got ready to apply the Chinese stamps—which seldom come with glue on the back side—she looked around, then commented, "Everything's here but the glue."

There were only two other people in the room at the time: John Holdridge and I. The next day a bottle of glue was in place on the desk.

The Kissinger visit included top-level talks with Vice Premier Deng and Foreign Minister Qiao, meetings that gave me a rare opportunity to pick up information about the latest developments in Sino-American relations. Information, I'd come to realize after four weeks on the job, was hard to come by for an ambassador to China.

It wasn't my problem alone—the fact that Henry's staff in Washington was reluctant to share what they knew. That was true, but other diplomats in Beijing proved to be equally hungry for facts, speculation, even rumors about what was going on. A veil of secrecy surrounded diplomatic life in

China, and after Kissinger left, my appointment book was filled with visits from other ambassadors scrambling for any inside information they could get.

According to one theory held by the ambassador from Nepal, there were certain advantages to being a new envoy to Beijing. A fresh perspective, he said. "I've been here ten years," he remarked, "and I think I actually know less about the Chinese than when I arrived."

Foreign ambassadors soon learned that Chinese diplomacy transforms the cryptic phrase into an art form. Send in a request to see a high-level Chinese official and you may be rejected in one of three ways—all polite.

First, you might be told that such a meeting was "not convenient." That meant, you would see the official when hell freezes over.

Second, your request might be accepted "in principle." That meant, don't hold your breath.

Third, you might be told such a meeting was "possible, but it might take a while." Since Chinese measure time differently than impatient Westerners, "a while" might mean anything from five to twenty years.

Like other ambassadors stationed in Beijing, I soon discovered that there was more than one kind of Chinese Wall. It was impossible to pick up a phone and ask a Chinese official for a meeting to discuss some international issue. The rule was: Don't call us, we'll call you.

The Wall got particularly frustrating at times for someone who had arrived in China eager to learn about the country and its people. If diplomacy means anything at all, it's establishing contact. But the Chinese bureaucracy saw it differently.

Not long after our arrival in Beijing, for example, a team of medical experts arrived from the United States. The team was interested in the tropical disease bilharzia, or snail fever. Since the disease was prevalent in China, anything the experts learned about it was bound to help the Chinese. So it seemed to me as U.S. ambassador.

The Chinese greeted members of the delegation warmly. They gave them the full treatment of special sightseeing tours and succulent banquets. Days passed, with the

American experts sightseeing and gaining weight from eating well. But the purpose of their visit had hit a snag. They could see the Great Wall and the Forbidden City but not the one thing in China they'd come to see. Only after numerous requests—and finally complaints—did the Chinese bureaucracy break down and permit the Americans to examine their native snails.

As far as the Chinese were concerned, foreign visitors were in their country to learn only what their hosts wanted them to learn. Their usual technique was simply to limit visitors' access to information; but there was a Potemkin village variation reserved for special visitors like the Kissingers.

Toward the end of the Kissinger family's five-day visit, a trip was arranged to the city of Suzhou, a place famous for its embroideries, located halfway between Beijing and Shanghai. We all took off from Beijing airport in two British-built Trident jets furnished by our hosts. Lynn Pascoe of the USLO had been to the city only a week before, escorting a group of American university presidents. He reported that it was as cluttered with bicycle and truck traffic as Beijing.

But not on the day we came to Suzhou with the Kissingers. As we drove down empty streets, there were no vehicles, no pedestrians. Under similar circumstances, Bill Buckley, visiting China with a group of journalists, asked his guide where all the people were. "The what?" asked the guide. "The people," replied Bill. "You know, as in *People's* Republic of China."

As the Kissingers and Bushes drove down the main boulevards of Suzhou, I could see masses of people huddled on side streets, held back by barricades. Whatever the Chinese Government's reason for clearing the streets during our visit, it was an eerie, even frightening demonstration of how a totalitarian government can control its population.

The Potemkin variation came at one of Suzhou's parks, where we saw a group of small children playing, laughing, and singing in what was obviously a well-rehearsed, choreographed scene. Our suspicions were confirmed when, after we returned to our cars, the park suddenly fell silent. The scene was over; the kids had done their duty for Chairman Mao.*

Two days later the Kissingers were flying back to Washington and life around the USLO compound returned to normal. Under my predecessor David Bruce, that meant acting simply as a United States observer and point of contact on the Beijing diplomatic scene. He felt that the lack of formal relations between the United States and the People's Republic called for a low-key operation.

Kissinger obviously agreed. When Henry heard I'd turned down the ambassador's posts in London and Paris in order to go to Beijing, he was baffled. "There'll be some substantive work from time to time," he said, outlining my duties as chief of the USLO, "but for the most part you'll be bored beyond belief."

Considering the strictures that Chinese authorities put on the diplomatic community, that might have proven true under "normal" conditions. But after examining the job's limits and potential, I set out to redefine what "normal" conditions would be around the USLO.

The compound itself, located in a section of Beijing set aside for embassies, is built in a style reminiscent of Southern California architecture in the 1920s: Sunset Boulevard— one part Spanish, one part Oriental. Two green-uniformed soldiers of the People's Liberation Army stood guard at the gate.

Inside the compound is a small consular building and next to that the residence of the chief of the mission. The house itself is open and well lighted, with reception and

---

* It was only the first of many such scenes Barbara and I were to witness during our stay in China. Regimentation and dogma permeate the Chinese educational system. On one trip to a provincial school, we were guests at a kids' performance featuring songs like "I'm Longing to Grow a Pair of Industrial Hands" and "I Want to Hurry and Grow Up So I Can Fight for the Revolution." Popular adult songs while we were in Beijing—a period when Mao's wife was in charge of cultural affairs—were "Baritone Solo to Be Loaded with Friendship and Carried Abroad by Sailors in Chinese-Made Ships" and "The Red Sunshine Lighted Up the Platform Around the Steel Furnace." Fortunately for the Chinese, cultural restrictions were relaxed after the fall of the Gang of Four. They can now balance their ideological diet with music from other parts of the world. And their talented artists are enjoying more freedom.

dining rooms on the ground floor. Our private quarters were upstairs.

There was a six-member house staff—two cooks, two attendants, two cleaning women. The head of the staff was Mr. Wong, a young man in his twenties, pleasant but with a rigid sense of order. Our head cook, Mr. Sun, was a culinary artist, said to be one of the best in Beijing. Other embassies weren't as lucky. One ambassador's wife constantly complained to the Chinese protocol office about how poor their cook was. Eventually the Chinese got around to removing him—but not happily. They didn't send a replacement for weeks, leaving the ambassador's wife to do her own cooking.

For transportation, the chief of mission was provided a Chrysler sedan, and at first Barbara and I used it. But within a month I took my first step in breaking the mold on what was expected from a U.S. envoy to Beijing. Not a major diplomatic move, but one that would help prove Henry wrong in his prediction that my new job would be boring.

When in China, I figured, why not travel as the Chinese do? By the time my mother arrived for a Christmas holiday visit, Mr. Wong had informed me that among his friends Barbara and I were known as "Busher, who ride the bicycle, just as the Chinese do."

Christmas of 1974 was the first time since Barbara and I had married that we'd spent the holiday apart. She'd gone back home to be with the children, who were still in school. But I didn't have to spend Christmas alone. My mother and an aunt, Marjorie Clement, had come to visit. After church we bicycled around the embassy district, paying a call on the British ambassador, Ted Youde.

We also called Washington, where Barbara and the kids had gathered for Christmas. Jeb had made Phi Beta Kappa, Neil was getting good grades, Marvin was gearing up for the basketball season.

On Christmas night Mr. Sun outdid himself with his first Western holiday meal: turkey, cranberry sauce, the trimmings; however, instead of a pumpkin or pecan pie dessert, he prepared a spectacular Chinese specialty called Bei-jing Dust: a light pastry with a mountain of whipped cream, topped by ground chestnuts (the "dust").

But the main part of the day was spent underground. During the Kissinger visit, when Henry and I visited Vice Premier Deng, he'd asked whether I'd had an opportunity to see "the caves." When I said no, a special Christmas Day tour was arranged.

"The caves" were the tunnels beneath Beijing. To get there, I met a cadre from the People's Liberation Army and a neighborhood commune at a specified intersection. They led me to a nearby clothing store. In the store we ap-proached some racks that concealed a button. When the button was pushed, a trap door slid open. We walked down about twenty-five feet, through a honeycomb of tunnels, and through what appeared to be large rooms. There were also lavatories, and though there was no sign of a ventilation system, my hosts assured me there was good air and drain-age—and space enough to house thousands of people in this one neighborhood.

What I was seeing were underground bomb shelters—civil defense "caves" the Chinese were digging in every ma-jor city. "Dig tunnels deep," Chairman Mao had instructed, "store grain everywhere." Why? In the event, I was told, that the Soviet Union ever decided to wage war against China with nuclear weapons rather than by conventional means.

After my visit to "the caves" was over, I thanked my guides and bicycled back to the compound. When Mother asked how I enjoyed the tour, I told her what I'd seen. Her comment was that it was an odd Christmas gift: an invita-tion to visit a bomb shelter on a day dedicated to the spirit of peace on earth.

By that time, however, I'd been in China long enough to know that my hosts left little to chance or accident in dealing with foreigners. The Chinese were out to make a point—that they are vigilant against the Soviets, and ready for any turn of world events, even the worst.

I agreed with Mother that arranging the tour for Christmas Day was odd timing. But it was timing guaranteed to make my visit to "the caves" one I wouldn't soon forget.

There was an incidental note about that Christmas that left me shaking my head as to whether, like the ambassador from Nepal, I'd end up feeling that the more you learn about the Chinese, the less you really understand them.

Before leaving Beijing, Mother told Mr. Wong, the chief of our house staff, how much she and Aunt Marge appreciated what had been done to make their visit comfortable. In the spirit of the season, she offered him and members of his staff small gifts, explaining that was the custom of our country. When Wong said, "No, thank you," Mother persisted, feeling he was just being modest. But he still refused, and nothing could budge him.

The reason, a member of my USLO staff explained, was that in Mao's China, taking a gratuity of any kind for doing one's job is considered bourgeois—or worse. It would have been risky for Wong to accept the gifts. Under the strict revolutionary dogma that governs Chinese life, he would have felt compelled to stand up at a so-called "self-criticism" session in his neighborhood and confess that he had accepted a gift from foreigners.

When it was explained to me, I nodded as if I understood. But I really didn't—at least not completely. It turned out there was a way around the no-gift rule. So long as our houseguests specified that the items were "to help you in your work," Wong and the others would accept them—which was the way the impasse between Eastern and Western, Communist and capitalist custom was solved during our time in China. Or so we thought.*

---

* When our stay in China ended, as we prepared to return to the United States and a new assignment, Mr. Wong suddenly appeared one day, bearing gifts—every gift that the house staff had received from every guest we'd had.

"Why?" I asked. Mr. Wong explained: the gifts had been given "to help us in our work" in the Bush household. But now there would be no Bush household in Beijing, in which case, he told me with perfect Chinese logic, there was no more reason to keep them.

• • •

While "the Bushers" bicycling around town was one
way to break out of the diplomatic cocoon of Beijing's foreign embassy district, it still didn't solve the problem of
being isolated from contact with Chinese government officials. Other members of the diplomatic corps at least met
these officials at various receptions held in honor of each
country's national holiday. Some Chinese government representative and his coterie would always show up at these
open-house social events.

David Bruce hadn't attended these receptions. He
strictly defined his role in terms of being U.S. liaison to the
Chinese Government, not a full-fledged diplomatic representative. However, I thought that in bypassing these events
we were missing an opportunity to make our presence felt in
Beijing, and adopted a policy of accepting national holiday
invitations.

The first invitation we accepted was from the Algerian
embassy. There was a flurry of animated conversation
around the room when we walked in with the Holdridges.
Americans at a diplomatic reception at Beijing! But things
soon returned to normal. The diplomatic ice had been broken; from then on, our appearance at these events was considered routine.

Henry Kissinger didn't think much of my policy of
being an active liaison officer. "It doesn't matter whether
they like you or not," he once told me. I disagreed. My
purpose wasn't to win popularity contests in Beijing but to
get to know the Chinese—and to get them to know Americans—at a personal level. Henry, of all people, knew the
value of personal relationships in world affairs. It was his
warm relationship with Anwar Sadat that helped break
down barriers of distrust in the Middle East.

But there was one period during our stay in China that
had me second-guessing myself as to whether David Bruce
wasn't right in staying away from diplomatic events. That
came in the spring of 1975, as the military situation for the
United States and our South Vietnamese ally deteriorated.
This turn of events seemed to sharpen the anti-American

instincts not only of our country's adversaries in the world, but of some of our friends as well. Whenever I walked past groups of diplomats, I could sense their hostility and, in some cases, satisfaction that America's policy in Southeast Asia was failing.

The worst of these days was April 30, the eve of Beijing's May Day celebration. Barbara and I were at the Netherlands embassy, at a reception commemorating the birthday of Queen Juliana. As the guests gathered, word was spreading that Saigon had fallen. Ordinarily the atmosphere at these events was restrained, but that night the room was charged with anticipation. Then, suddenly, the representatives of the Provisional Revolutionary Government of South Vietnam, about half a dozen in all, rushed from the room. Cheers went up in the street outside.

Barbara and I stayed until the end of the reception, then returned to the U.S. compound to the sound of firecrackers going off throughout Beijing. The next day, May Day, revolutionary music played through loudspeakers in the streets. The music continued for several days, celebrating not only May Day but the "Vietnam people's victory." Display cases outside the Vietnamese embassy carried photographs of U.S. leaders—though interestingly enough, not Nixon or Kissinger, but former President Johnson and his Secretary of Defense, Robert McNamara.

It was a difficult time for the small contingent of Americans inside the People's Republic of China. Knowing that, some of my colleagues from friendly nations approached me to underscore how important it was for the United States not to abandon its commitments in the Far East, especially in South Korea. The most interesting of these comments came not from the representative of a Western ally but a high Chinese official some weeks later. Speaking in a tone that suggested his remarks were authorized, he told me, "The United States has a useful role to play in Asia."

The Chinese can be oblique in their diplomatic relations, but at times they say exactly what they mean. What the official was telling me was that regardless of our opposing interests in Vietnam, we had a common interest in dealing with the Russians. We could be "useful" to each other.

• • •

Four of our five children were with us during the summer of 1975. The fifth, our second oldest son Jeb, then twenty-two, and his wife Columba, had to stay in Houston, where Jeb held a job with the Texas Commerce Bank. But George was there, at age twenty-nine just out of Harvard Business School and about to go into the oil business in Texas; along with Neil, twenty, an undergraduate at Tulane; Marvin, nineteen, about to enter the University of Virginia; and Dorothy, who celebrated her birthday that August 18, 1975, in a special way. She was christened at our church in Beijing.

The ceremony was overdue, but for good reason. Over the years we kept trying to get the entire family—grandparents, uncles, aunts—together for it, but were never able to bring the reunion off. Finally, Doro had reached age sixteen, and it was clear that we'd waited long enough. The occasion would be unique in itself, something she'd always remember —being christened in China by not one but three Chinese Christian clergymen, an Episcopalian, a Presbyterian, and a Baptist, in the church used by the Beijing diplomatic community.

Because Dorothy's godparents—my sister Nancy Ellis; Betsy Heminway's husband, Spike; and our family friend from Houston, Mildred Kerr—couldn't be present, her brother Marvin acted as their surrogate.

In the ceremony itself, questions and answers concerning Dorothy's faith had to be translated by a militant atheist interpreter, who didn't seem too happy about repeating the religious terms. Nevertheless the ceremony went off without any major problem, and when it was concluded the ministers told Dorothy she was now a lifelong member of their small church in a Communist land where, they said, "we will love you and always miss you."

Henry was back. The Secretary of State arrived October 19, this time with a high-priority agenda. He was in Beijing to lay the groundwork for President Ford's official visit to China later in the year. As always, the Secretary's schedule was hectic—three long meetings with Vice Premier Deng in two days to work out the details of a communique that would be issued after the President and Chairman Mao met.

Not that anyone could program what two of the most powerful leaders in the world would say in their meetings. Only that when chiefs of state sit down to talk, the common practice is to have an outline, if not the text, of their conclusions already prepared, before the visiting leader arrives. This defines the agenda of the talks and minimizes the risk of misunderstandings on major issues.

On the Chinese side, Foreign Minister Qiao sat in on the Kissinger-Deng talks; on the American side, the Secretary's staff, plus Assistant Secretary Phil Habib, and I. I'd met Deng several times before. He was the ascending power in China, likely to succeed to the top position after Mao and Zhou were gone. An incessant chain smoker and tea drinker, he was a man who projected himself as a grassroots rural man-of-the-people, a rough-hewn soldier from Szechuan Province in Southwest China.

Deng had the ability to balance toughness and affability in perfect proportions in his meetings with foreign leaders, but his mood during his sessions with Kissinger was notably tipped toward aggressive, tough talk. His complaint—incredible as it might sound—was that the United States was showing weakness in the face of the Soviet threat to world peace. Except for the difference in language, I might have been listening to a speech by Barry Goldwater in 1964.

Deng, like Mao and other Chinese leaders, was concerned about the direction taken by the U.S. policy of détente with the Soviets. He charged that American policy toward the Russians was similar to British and French policy toward Hitler at Munich in 1938—a policy of "appeasement," said Deng. Kissinger bridled, but kept his poise. "A country that spends $110 billion for defense cannot be said to be pursuing the spirit of Munich," replied the Secretary. "Let me remind you that we were resisting Soviet expansionism when you two were allies, for your own reasons."

It was a sharp exchange, a good example of why presidential summits need to be advanced through preliminary discussions. Finally, with the air cleared concerning U.S.-Chinese differences, Kissinger said, "I do not feel that the President's visit should give the impression that our countries are quarreling." Deng agreed. "There is still time for further concrete discussion," he said.

The big unanswered question of the Kissinger advance trip, however, was whether he'd be invited to visit the Chairman. The Chinese approached his question, as always, in a circuitous way.

During lunch on October 21, Vice Foreign Minister Wang Hairong pointedly mentioned that former British Prime Minister Edward Heath had seen Mao during a recent visit. Wang, who was Mao's grandniece, added that Heath had specifically requested the meeting. Kissinger got the message. "If this is an official inquiry as to whether I would like to meet with the Chairman," he said, "the answer is yes."

A few hours later, Kissinger was in his third and final meeting with Deng and Qiao at the Great Hall of the People, when I saw Deng handed a paper with a few large Chinese characters on it. Deng read the message, then interrupted the discussion to announce, "You will meet with the Chairman at six-thirty."

Mao lived in a secluded enclave for high-ranking officials not far from the Great Hall of the People. We entered through an elaborate gate, drove past a lake and through several courtyards before pulling up to the house. A Chinese television crew was waiting. They followed us through several rooms of the villa, right into Mao's sitting room.

Mao, then eighty-one, was sitting in an armchair. He was helped to his feet by two women attendants. This was my first meeting with the Chairman since coming to China, and I was shocked by his physical condition, observed from a distance. When he opened his mouth to greet Kissinger—who had been ushered in first, in order of rank—only guttural noises emerged.

I was ushered in next. At closer range, the Chairman's

physical appearance seemed to improve. He was tall, tanned, and still fairly husky, with a strong handclasp. He was wearing a well-tailored suit of the style that bears his name, brown socks, and a pair of black slippers with white rubber soles, the kind worn by millions of ordinary Chinese.

Kissinger asked him how he was feeling. Mao pointed to his head. "This part works well," he said, "I can eat and sleep. These parts"—he tapped his legs—"these parts do not work well. They are not strong when I walk. I also have some trouble with my lungs." He paused. "In a word, I am not well." Then he added, smiling, "I am a showcase for visitors."

I was seated to the left of Kissinger, who was seated to Mao's left. Glancing around the room, I saw that it had built-in TV lights along one wall. There was a book of calligraphy on the table in front of us. Across the room were several tables with medical tubes of some sort and a small oxygen tank.

Mao was in a philosophical mood. "I am going to heaven soon," he said, words that were stunning when spoken by the leader of the world's biggest Communist country. "I have already received an invitation from God."

"Don't accept it soon," replied Kissinger with a smile.

Mao, unable to speak coherently, was laboriously writing out characters on a pad of paper, to make himself understood. He'd write; then the two women at his side would leap to their feet, study the words, and try to make sense out of what he was trying to say. "I accept the orders of the Doctor," Mao wrote. It was a pun on the title the Chinese used when referring to Henry Kissinger, Ph.D.

Henry nodded, then changed the tenor of the talk. "I attach great significance to our relationship," he said. Mao responded by holding up a fist and the little finger of his other hand. "You are this," he said, pointing to the fist, "and we are that." He held up his finger. "You have the atomic bomb and we don't." Since China had had nuclear weapons for over a decade, Mao apparently meant that the United States was stronger militarily.

"But China says that military strength is not the only thing," Kissinger said. "And we have common opponents."

Mao wrote his reply; then one of his assistants held it up for us to see. It was written in English: YES.

There was an exchange between the Chairman and the Secretary on the subject of Taiwan. Mao said the issue would be resolved in time, possibly in "a hundred" or even "several hundred" years. The Chinese use such expressions, I'd concluded, to impress foreigners with the fact that their history dates back several thousand years. They see time and their own cultural patience as allies in dealing with impatient Westerners.

Like Deng and most other leaders of the revolution, Mao had a rustic background and often used Chinese barnyard expressions in the normal course of diplomatic conversation; as when, on another topic, he described a particular problem in U.S.-Chinese relations as no more important than a "fang go pi," which one of his women assistants dutifully translated as "a dog fart."

That was one even Harry Truman didn't have in his barnyard vocabulary.

As the meeting went on, Mao seemed to become stronger, more alert. He gestured frequently, moved his head from side to side and appeared stimulated by the conversation. And he continued to refer to the Almighty, once remarking, "God blesses you, not us. God does not like us because I am a militant warlord, also a Communist. No, he doesn't like me. He likes you three." He nodded toward Kissinger, Winston Lord, and me.

The meeting was coming to a close when Mao drew Winston and me into the conversation. "This ambassador," he said, gesturing toward me, "is in a plight. Why don't you come visit?"

"I would be honored," I replied, "but I'm afraid you're very busy."

"Oh, I'm not busy," Mao said. "I don't look after internal affairs. I only read the international news. You should really come visit."

I saw Mao once again, for the second and last time, when President Ford made his state visit to Beijing five weeks later. By then, my new assignment as Director of the Central Intelligence Agency, had been announced. Talking to USLO staff experts after the Kissinger meeting, I mentioned what he'd said about coming to visit and said that I might just try to take him up on it. Their impression was that the Chairman was just being diplomatic, so I didn't follow up. A year later, however—after Mao had died—Barbara and I visited China, and I mentioned the Chairman's remark to a Chinese government official.

"You should have followed your instinct," he told me. "I can assure you the Chairman would never have made such an invitation unless he meant it."

Seven

THE PRESIDENT ASKS . . .

Langley, Virginia/1976

> TO: AMBASSADOR BUSH
> FROM: HENRY A. KISSINGER   NOVEMBER 1, 1975
> THE PRESIDENT IS PLANNING TO ANNOUNCE
> SOME MAJOR PERSONNEL SHIFTS ON MONDAY,
> NOVEMBER 3, AT 7:30 P.M., WASHINGTON TIME.
> AMONG THOSE SHIFTS WILL BE THE TRANSFER OF
> BILL COLBY FROM CIA.
> THE PRESIDENT ASKS THAT YOU CONSENT
> TO HIS NOMINATING YOU AS THE NEW DIRECTOR
> OF THE CENTRAL INTELLIGENCE AGENCY.
> THE PRESIDENT FEELS YOUR APPOINTMENT
> TO BE GREATLY IN THE NATIONAL INTEREST
> AND VERY MUCH HOPES THAT YOU WILL AC-
> CEPT. YOUR DEDICATION TO NATIONAL SERVICE
> HAS BEEN UNREMITTING, AND I JOIN THE PRESI-
> DENT IN HOPING THAT YOU WILL ACCEPT THIS
> NEW CHALLENGE IN THE SERVICE OF YOUR
> COUNTRY. . . .

"It is all very shocking," the young Chinese guide told a British journalist after word of my appointment as Director of the CIA became known in Beijing. "Mr. Bush has been here a year, and before that he was at the United Nations. And to think he's been a spy all along!"

The guide's shock was only a little less than my own after I received Henry's cable. Director of the CIA? I handed the wire to Barbara and from the expression on her face knew we shared the same thought: New York, 1973. In Yogi Berra's phrase, it was déjà vu all over again.

Watergate was the problem then, with President Nixon calling me to Camp David to ask that I become Chairman of

151

the Republican National Committee to handle the political mess spilling over from the west wing. Now I was being asked to leave another diplomatic post we both enjoyed, to return to Washington and take charge of an agency battered by a decade of hostile Congressional investigations, exposés, and charges that ran from lawbreaking to simple incompetence.

I reread the opening line of Henry's cable:

THE PRESIDENT IS PLANNING TO ANNOUNCE SOME MAJOR PERSONNEL SHIFTS. . . .

Then the last line:

REGRETTABLY, WE HAVE ONLY THE MOST LIMITED TIME BEFORE THE ANNOUNCEMENT, AND THE PRESIDENT WOULD THEREFORE APPRECIATE A MOST URGENT RESPONSE.

There was no point cabling for further information—answers to questions like WHO'S GOING WHERE, HENRY? or WHAT'S GOING ON? Like the language of diplomacy, the language of politics has its nuance. The tone of the Secretary's wire suggested that they wanted a quick reply, no questions asked.

Colby was leaving. Wholesale changes were underway. Would I take the CIA, *yes* or *no?*

The key words were THE PRESIDENT ASKS. Barbara read the cable, handed it back, and said, "I remember Camp David." That's all. Just "I remember Camp David."

What she specifically remembered about my trip to Camp David in 1973 was that she hadn't wanted me to take the national committee job. But when I returned that night, she knew, even before I'd taken off my coat, what had happened. The President had asked, and as long as what he'd asked me to do wasn't illegal or immoral, and I felt I could handle the job, there was only one answer I could give. Now, two years later, she knew there was only one answer I could give this President. We'd soon be leaving Beijing for Washington.

Barbara had grown fond of China in our thirteen months there, throwing herself into the study of Chinese history, art, and architecture. She also had another, more personal concern about our leaving to return to Washington. She was worried about the effect the change of jobs would have on our kids. We both still remembered the Watergate days, the grief they'd taken from some of their classmates at school. If that was bad, what would life in Washington be like for the children of the head of the CIA?

For that matter, what would the future in Washington hold for the head of the CIA himself? Once past the impact of Henry's cable on our personal lives, I had two instinctive reactions to what it meant professionally.

First, politics was still my first interest. In the best of times the CIA job wouldn't be considered a springboard to higher office, if only because the director of the agency has to be nonpolitical. Anyone who took the job, would have to give up any and all political activity. As far as future prospects for elective office were concerned, the CIA was marked DEAD END.

(Could *that* be what was happening? Bury Bush at the CIA? George, living in the Byzantine political atmosphere of a Communist capital is starting to get to you. The idea that anyone in Washington—not the President or Henry, but somebody else—might have that in mind was absurd. . . . But how did Henry once put it? "Even paranoids," he told a reporter, "have real enemies.")

My second reaction was concern over what it might mean diplomatically. For over a year, I'd worked—*we'd* worked, because Barbara had put as much into the job as I had—to develop a climate of mutual respect and friendship between China and the United States, a people-to-people approach that could transcend ideological divisions. In a low-key, informal way, we'd made progress breaking down some of the barriers of suspicion and distrust that existed between our two countries. What would the Chinese government think? That Bush the diplomat had been Bush the spy all along?

When I expressed this fear to a friendly Western diplomat, he reassured me with a story about another "CIA ambassador," Richard Helms: A reception took place in Tehran the evening in 1973 when Helms's nomination to be

U.S. ambassador to Iran was announced. The Soviet ambassador, himself a veteran of the KGB, walked up to an Iranian government official and asked, "Well, Mr. Minister, what do you think about the Americans naming their number one spy ambassador to your country?" Taking a sip of champagne (this was pre-Khomeini Iran), the pro-Western Iranian replied, "Well, your Excellency, I think it is better than what the Soviet Union did. They sent us their number ten spy."

My friend's optimistic view of how the Chinese would react to my becoming CIA director was close to the mark. However suspicious the Chinese might be about U.S. intentions, their distrust of the Russians is greater. When word of my appointment reached Beijing, Chinese officials, far from being appalled, were openly pleased. As one of them confided, they felt they'd spent a year "teaching" me their views on the Soviet threat and now, as America's chief intelligence officer, I'd be able to "teach" them to the President.

In fact, when President Ford visited China one month later—before Barbara and I had left—Chairman Mao greeted me with the remark, "You've been promoted," then told the President, "We hate to see him go."

But the most significant indication that the Chinese weren't upset by my appointment came when Vice Premier Deng invited us to a private luncheon where he assured me I'd always be welcome in China—then smiling—"even as head of the CIA."*

So my concern about the diplomatic repercussions of Henry's cable proved 180 degrees off course. In the long run, that would also be true of its effect on my political future. But in the immediate weeks and months ahead that was by no means clear. After a round of farewell functions, Barbara and I left Beijing with mixed feelings: warm memories of our thirteen months in China, but glad to be going home; satisfied with the job we'd done, but looking down what apeared to be a political dead-end street.

---

* Two years later, we did return on a private visit. By then, Deng was running the government.

• • •

The Washington press corps called it "the Halloween Massacre," inviting comparison to the Watergate era's Saturday Night Massacre. The major personnel shifts mentioned in Henry's cable were a mixed bag of resignations, retirements, and one outright firing: Some moved up, some down, some laterally. It was as if the Ford White House had been on a political shakedown cruise its first year and a half and was gearing for battle as election year approached.

Jim Schlesinger, the CIA director once removed—he held the job before Bill Colby—had been removed again, this time involuntarily, as Secretary of Defense. Don Rumsfeld, the White House chief of staff, was moving over and up to the Pentagon, replacing Schlesinger.

Secretary of State Kissinger, who had been wearing two foreign-policy hats, was voluntarily taking one off, allowing his White House deputy, Air Force Lieutenant General Brent Scowcroft, to move up as the President's national security adviser.

Colby was leaving and Bush was moving laterally to the CIA—assuming I could be confirmed by the Senate.

And simultaneously with all this Cabinet shuffling, Nelson Rockefeller had suddenly announced he wouldn't be a candidate for the vice presidential nomination at the Republican convention in Kansas City. This was the political move, I was told by Bill Steiger and Tom Kleppe, that led to my being offered the CIA job.

According to Washington speculation, the scenario went like this: With Reagan contesting Ford for the Republican presidential nomination, the President needed to protect his right flank. This meant that Rockefeller—poison to conservatives since his bitterly fought campaign against Goldwater in 1964—had to go. Having lost out to Rockefeller as Ford's vice presidential choice in 1974, I might be considered by some as a leading contender for the number two spot in Kansas City—but not if I spent the next six months serving as point man for a controversial agency being investigated by two major Congressional committees.

The scars left by that experience would put me out of contention, leaving the spot open for others.

Reflecting on that scenario, I recalled something Rog Morton had told me before I left for China. "I don't plan on staying at Commerce much longer," he confided. "What you ought to think about is coming back to Washington to replace me when I leave. It's a perfect springboard for a place on the ticket."

When I received the cable in Beijing, however, there was no mention that Rog was leaving as Secretary of Commerce, to be replaced by Elliot Richardson. The odd thing was that Richardson's experience as a former Attorney General would have made him an ideal choice to head the CIA, while my business background would have fit in well at Commerce. Rog suspected the switch had been deliberately arranged to keep me off the ticket. He wasn't my only friend to come to that conclusion.

"I think you ought to know what people up here are saying about your going to the CIA," another former House colleague told me shortly after we returned to Washington. "They feel you've been had, George. Rumsfeld set you up and you were a damned fool to say yes."

White House chief of staff Don Rumsfeld—"Rummy," as his friends call him—had a reputation as an able administrator and a skillful political in-fighter. It was inevitable that he'd be singled out in any rumor having to do with the Halloween Massacre and engineering my move to the CIA. In a meeting in his office, Rumsfeld vehemently denied the rumor. I accepted his word. But even if the rumor were true there wasn't any way I could refuse when the President asked me to take on this assignment, no matter how difficult.

Since the initial surprise of Henry's cable, I'd also had a chance to think things through. After thirteen months of duty in China, I liked the idea of heading a worldwide organization, a job that would require 110 percent effort from early morning to late night. As for "being had," I told my former colleague, doing something this important had to take precedence over personal ambitions.

My ex-colleague listened, then shrugged. "You're still a

damned fool," he said, "but if there's any way I can help, let me know."

"Give Frank Church a call," I replied, as we shook hands at the door. "Tell him I'm a tame elephant."

Senator Frank Church, the Idaho Democrat and chairman of a special investigating committee, had labeled the CIA a "rogue elephant out of control" during 1975 hearings into the agency's operations. But my reference had a double meaning. Church had also been among the first to oppose my nomination because, he said, as former chairman of the Republican National Committee, he said, I was too "political" for the CIA director's job.

Other Senate Democrats, along with influential media voices, echoed that view. Anthony Lewis of *The New York Times* wrote that the one thing the Central Intelligence Agency didn't need was "an ambitious partisan figure" like George Bush running it. The Baltimore *Sun* asked, "Who will believe in the independence of a former national party chairman?" Robert Keatley of *The Wall Street Journal* called me "another upward-striving office-seeker."

Ironically, having agreed to take a job that led to a political dead end, I was now getting criticized for being too political.

Some surprising support came my way, however. Breaking partisan ranks, Senator Walter Mondale—who fifteen months later would become Vice President—told an interviewer that perhaps "a politician" would be good at the CIA job because he'd be more sensitive to the dangers of the agency's abusing its power. And while conservative columnist George Will was questioning the wisdom of my appointment, liberal columnist Tom Wicker of *The New York Times* suggested that my political experience, as well as my nonpartisan service at the U.N. and in China, might even be an asset to the CIA in its effort to regain credibility.

As the controversy over my nomination grew in the days leading up to the Senate hearings, I also received a letter of support and advice from San Clemente, California.

Dear George,
What you have been through before will look like
a cakewalk compared to what you will now be
confronted with. I only have one bit of advice: You
will be tempted greatly to "give away the store" in
assuring members of the Senate Committee that
everything the CIA does in the future will be an
open book. This, of course, is the surest way for
you to be confirmed and to reduce the number
who will vote against you. It will also be the surest
way to destroy an agency that has already been
terribly weakened by the irresponsible attacks that
have been made upon it by both the Senate and
House investigating committees.

　　　　　　　　　　　　　　　　　Richard Nixon

Nixon's mention of giving away the store was an
oblique reference to the policy of the man I'd replace at the
CIA, Bill Colby. As CIA director, Colby had been criticized
by agency professionals and others in government for what
they perceived as his "open book" candor whenever he testi-
fied before a Congressional committee. Colby quoted Kissinger as once having told him, "Bill, you know what you do
when you go to the Hill? You go to confession."

But Colby was walking the same tightrope I'd have to
walk as CIA director. The question is where does Congress's
and the public's right to know end and the need for secrecy
in intelligence operations begin? Under the best of circumstances it's the question that troubles all intelligence operations in a free society and it defies any single, arbitrary answer. In the large, undefined gray area known as "national
security interests," one government official's idea of TOP SE-
CRET may be another government official's idea of UNCLAS-
SIFIED.

In Colby's case, he was serving as CIA director in a
period when the agency's credibility on Capitol Hill—and
since Congress controls the government purse strings, that
meant the agency's ability to function—was at an all-time
low. The Vietnam and Watergate years had seen the term

"national security" both abused and overused. When reaction set in, the Central Intelligence Agency—by the nature of its work, the most secretive of government agencies—was especially hard hit.

Colby was like a general with an army disorganized and in retreat. He was trying to hold it together so that it could fight another battle, another day. The last thing the CIA needed in the early 1970s, thought Colby, was a director who might be charged with stonewalling Congress and the public.

Not that Colby's "open door" policy fully satisfied the agency's outside critics. Just as there were closed-minded government officials who wanted everything, down to the last memo, stamped TOP SECRET or CLASSIFIED, there were opportunists on Capitol Hill and in the media who viewed CIA bashing as a vehicle for their own ambitions. What the country's intelligence community faced in the 1970s wasn't just the loss of public confidence in government institutions. There was also the loss of restraint on the part of some politicians and journalists—a failure to recognize that while the term can be misused, real "national security" interests do exist and have to be protected in today's world.

Nixon's letter to me dealt with this problem:

> In any period of détente, the danger of war goes down but the danger of conquest without war goes up geometrically. We can expect that the covert activities of those who oppose us and our friends around the world will be enormously stepped up in the months and years ahead. The United States must not adopt the philosophy of our communist opponents, particularly those in the Soviet Union, of using any means to an end. On the other hand, we must find an effective way to combat and thwart the communists if they start to use a period of détente for purposes of conquest.

Enclosed with the letter from San Clemente was a list of "Meditations from Sun Tzu," the Chinese von Clausewitz, who lived around 500 B.C. Nixon had circled one particular maxim that summed up the point of his letter: "The acme of excellence," wrote Sun in his meditations on war, "is not the winning of a hundred victories in a hundred battles, but rather to subdue the armies of the enemy without fighting."

December 1975 wasn't the best of times for a Republican to come up for Senate confirmation as Director of the CIA. President Ford's honeymoon period with Congress had long since passed, and it seemed as if one out of every three Democratic senators was running for President. The other two were jockeying for either Vice President or a Cabinet position in the next administration.

But partisan jockeying was only part of the problem the Ford White House faced in trying to put the CIA's house in order. As the year drew to a close, the controversy surrounding the agency grew more heated each day.

On November 20 Senator Church's select committee had released a report charging that during the 1960s the CIA instigated assassination plots against Fidel Castro in Cuba and Patrice Lumumba of the Congo.

On December 4, Church alleged that the CIA was involved in the overthrow of President Salvador Allende of Chile two years before, in 1973.

Eleven days later, the House select committee, chaired by Congressman Otis Pike of New York, demanded that the Ford administration explain covert United States involvement in the civil war in Angola. Seventy-two hours later the Senate cut off funds for all military supplies to the pro-Western side in that war.

It was a signal, if any were needed, that Congress was no longer deferring to White House leadership in foreign affairs. We read the signal in Washington. Unfortunately they also read it in other capitals of the world. Overseas, in friendly capitals, the question was whether President Ford was really in charge of U.S. foreign policy. In Washington, the question was whether he could get a controversial nomination through the Senate.

Two days before Christmas, on December 23, Richard

S. Welch, the CIA station chief in Greece, was assassinated after his name and job description had appeared in a letter to the English-language Athens *News.* He was murdered as he stepped out of the door of his home in Athens.

It was a sobering tragedy, one that pointed up the constant danger that agency personnel face overseas. But given the mood of Washington, that wasn't the lesson some people drew from Richard Welch's death. Instead, Senator Gary Hart of Colorado, a member of the Church committee, told of a lunatic letter he had received accusing the committee of causing Welch's death. Hart, in the spirit of the times, publicly speculated that the CIA was behind the letter.

All this set the tone for my two days of hearings before the Senate Armed Services committee. Bryce N. Harlow, a Republican specialist in Congressional affairs going back to the Eisenhower years, had been called in by the Ford White House to round up votes for my confirmation. Bryce was one of the most astute head counters on Capitol Hill. After a quick reading of the mood of the committee, he came back with word that the Democratic majority planned to make an issue not only of my political past but my political future.

"They want a blood oath you won't be on the ticket next fall," he said. "Otherwise I don't think we've got the votes."

Reflecting on it even a decade later, the request was odd. A Sherman-like statement about the *vice* presidency? Something like "I will not run if put on the ticket, I will not preside over the Senate if elected?" It was also pointless. The CIA, I reiterated to Bryce, was no springboard to high office.

He nodded in agreement. "They still want it," he said.

"I won't do it," I replied. Enough was enough. Being at the service of the President was one thing, but catering to partisan demands to be confirmed was asking too much.

And that's where matters stood, until a compromise was suggested: no blood oath on my part, but a statement from the White House.

> Ambassador Bush and I agree, that the nation's immediate foreign intelligence needs must

take precedence over other considerations and there should be a continuity in the CIA leadership. Therefore, if Ambassador Bush is confirmed by the Senate as director of Central Intelligence, I will not consider him as my vice presidential running mate in 1976.

> Gerald Ford

That satisfied the committee, which then voted 12–4 in my favor. After Christmas recess the full Senate approved the nomination by a 64–27 vote, and three days later my friend and neighbor, Supreme Court Justice Potter Stewart, swore me in as CIA director at the agency's headquarters in Langley, Virginia, just across the Potomac from Washington.

It was January 1976, the beginning of a presidential election year. President Ford and Governor Reagan were already going head to head in the New Hampshire primary. But coverage in the Washington press was also being given to two new, unheard-of phenomena on the national political scene: the Iowa caucuses and Governor Jimmy Carter of Georgia.

One of the lessons I'd learned in two diplomatic assignments, at the United Nations and in China, was never to underestimate the importance of symbolism. Not image— that's something else entirely. Image has to do with appearance, how you look to the world. Symbolism has to do with messages, what you want to tell the world.

On taking over as DCI—Director of Central Intelligence—the first message I had to send was to the agency's employees, not only at Langley headquarters but overseas. How I looked on Capitol Hill was important; how I came through in the media was important; but my number one priority was to head America's intelligence operations, and popularity on the Hill or with the press was secondary to gaining the confidence of the people who worked for the CIA and the intelligence community.

In the mid-1970s, the morale of U.S. intelligence employees was at an all-time low. Some were risking their lives; all were applying their skills to jobs they saw as vital to their country's interests, even its survival. But there had been laws broken and excesses committed by some CIA personnel. Mistakes had been made, some far-fetched and aborted plots exposed. As a result the entire agency had been put into the dock and all its employees and projects placed under suspicion. When agency employees weren't being pounded in the press, they were being pilloried by the politicians.

That was the way most CIA employees viewed the situation facing their agency in January 1976. And now Bill Colby, a professional in the intelligence field, was being replaced by a nonprofessional outsider—and a politician to boot.

I needed to send a message that would tell CIA employees they hadn't been given a new director who, in former President Nixon's words, would give away the store. The message had to say, "I'm on your side, we're in this together."

My chance to do that came with the first decision I had to make as DCI. On its face it wasn't too important—just a matter of logistics.

"Where do you want to locate your main office?" I was asked. "At the Old EOB or Langley?"

The Old EOB is the Executive Office Building, a huge, gray, turn-of-the-century structure on Pennsylvania Avenue that once housed the State and War departments but since the end of World War Two has served as a White House annex. The Vice President, the OMB, and other top-level executive agencies have offices there. If I was located in the Old EOB, I'd have convenient access to the White House west wing and the Oval Office. That was on the plus side. Going through the southwest gate of West Executive Avenue every morning, with a reserved White House parking place, would be good for the image. But it would also send a message that the new director was a politician more interested in playing the Washington power game than running the agency.

So locating in Langley, on the seventh floor of the CIA building, would be my first message. It was a decision made easier because I'd already made sure that wherever I located, I'd have direct access to the President.

That was one of two conditions I set in accepting the job of DCI. After replying to Kissinger's cable, I got in touch with Brent Scowcroft, the President's national security adviser, to make sure that along with the responsibility of my new assignment, I also had the means to carry it out. First I'd need to be able to reach the President directly, without having to go through anyone else in the west wing bureaucracy; second I wanted to name my own deputy and staff.

Scowcroft cabled back word of top-level approval on both points, which meant I wouldn't have to be near the Oval Office in order to get through to the President.

Locating in Langley also reflected my view that the CIA director should go out of his way to avoid even the appearance of getting involved in policy making. The agency's sole duty, outlined in its 1947 charter, is to furnish intelligence data to the President and other policy makers. I was determined to operate the agency within its charter, not only regarding policy but politics. As DCI, I would turn down invitations to all partisan events, including the 1976 Republican Convention in Kansas City.

The second important message I sent to agency personnel came through my choice of deputy director, a job being vacated by my friend, General Vernon Walters. To replace Walters, I named E. Henry Knoche. A former college athlete who stood about six-four, Hank Knoche was a well-known presence around the seventh-floor corridors at Langley, widely respected by his colleagues as a professional with hands-on knowledge of how the CIA operated.

There was a third message to send, one that wouldn't be as popular in certain parts of the agency as my first two. Some career officers in key positions didn't impress me as much as Hank Knoche did. They'd have to go.

Within six months, eleven of fourteen top administrators had been changed. Some were promoted. Others retired, resigned, or were discharged—but in every case, by direct personal contact, not by impersonal notices or pink slips.

No school or instructor can teach anyone how to be a congressman or a Cabinet officer—or a President—because each of these jobs makes unique demands. Experience in other jobs can be helpful, but it's no guarantee you'll succeed. There are things you can't know until you've been there. Taking over as DCI was that kind of challenge.

I'd come to the CIA with some general knowledge of how it operated. My diplomatic experience had made me aware of the role intelligence operations play in the conduct of foreign affairs, such as: You're negotiating with another ambassador regarding his country's position on an issue. He tells you something about political conditions in his country which, if true, means he doesn't have much bargaining room. Be reasonable, he asks. But you've been given an intelligence briefing just before the meeting and know that the situation in his home country isn't the way he describes it. You hold firm. He reports back to his government for further instructions and discovers he has more bargaining room than he originally stated. You resolve your differences in line with the original U.S. proposal.

Then, a few days later, you pick up the morning paper and read a scathing report on some alleged CIA foul-up, complete with demands from congressional critics that the agency clean up its act. You'd like to call the reporter and the critics and let them know about at least one CIA success, but that's out of the question; where intelligence work is concerned, talking about past achievements precludes future ones. As President Kennedy said when he dedicated the new CIA headquarters in 1961: "Your successes are unheralded; your failures are trumpeted."

One of the first things I discovered as part of my education as DCI was that press coverage of the CIA was almost universally negative. After a round of press interviews that kept me on the defensive with questions coming out of the Church and Pike committee hearings, I asked my public affairs assistant, Angus Thuermer, if he could develop a list of CIA successes that *could* be heralded.

Angus came up with a lengthy report, beginning with the CIA's role in bringing off the Kennedy administration's finest moment.

Ask most people what they know about the CIA's involvement in Cuba during the Kennedy administration and the answer generally is "They fouled up at the Bay of Pigs." But how many remember that it was CIA aerial surveillance of Cuba that uncovered Soviet missile bases there eighteen months later? When President Kennedy told the American people and the world that the Soviets had "lied" about not having bases in Cuba, he had the proof in hand because of advanced U.S. intelligence capabilities. And eight years after that, when the Russians made still another run at covert base building in Cuba—constructing facilities for missile-firing submarines at Cienfuegos—it was a CIA analysis of aerial photographs that enabled President Nixon to pressure the Kremlin into stopping the project.

The failure at the Bay of Pigs became the CIA's failure, but resolving the missile crisis of 1962—which wouldn't have been possible without CIA intelligence efforts—became Kennedy's success.

I was beginning to understand why Hank Knoche and his colleagues at Langley had adopted a stoic, hunker-down philosophy about the agency's public image. And why some of my friends on Capitol Hill were against my becoming CIA director; they saw it as a no-win job for an agency with a no-win image.

My day as CIA director would begin when a gray Chevrolet arrived in front of our home in Northwest Washington promptly at 7:30 A.M. In addition to the driver there was an agency security officer whose primary mission wasn't so much to protect me as the classified papers we carried on our fifteen-minute drive across the Potomac to CIA headquarters at Langley.

When the weather was bad, the driver would drop me off at a private elevator that shot directly to the director's office on the seventh floor. But most days I'd go to the front entrance, show my laminated plastic badge to the security guard, and head through the main lobby, past marble walls with rows of stars—one for every CIA employee killed in the line of duty.

The director's office was long, narrow, blandly furnished, a dark wood desk at one end, a rectangular conference table at the other, with a panoramic window view of a northern Virginia countryside that became spectacular in the autumn months.

I'd usually be at my desk around seven-fifty and spend the next half hour or so reviewing a summary of overnight cable traffic from CIA stations around the world. Hank Knoche, whose office adjoined mine, would join me with other executive assistants for a brief conference before the heads of various agency directorates began arriving for our regular nine A.M. meeting.

These meetings, informal but fast-paced, usually involved going around the table for an update on agency affairs. On days when I was scheduled to go before a congressional committee—I made fifty-one appearances on Capitol Hill in less than a year—we'd take time to go over some aspect of my upcoming testimony.

Once a week, either Thursday or Friday, I'd report to the White House for an early-morning briefing session with President Ford. NSC chief Brent Scowcroft would sit in at these meetings. When highly technical subjects were on the agenda, I'd bring along one or two CIA specialists, in case the President wanted additional data.

It was about this time, having passed age fifty, that I got into regular jogging. Some lunch hours I'd be joined by one or two other fitness types from the agency on a three-mile run along nearby sideroads. On bad-weather days we'd use an indoor track set up in the basement corridor.

My office day would generally end around seven P.M., winding down with informal staff meetings and signing papers. Only when there was a presidential briefing or important Congressional hearing the next day did I take the office home.

There were two aspects to my term as CIA director that made it different from our previous stays in Washington, however. The first was that there were fewer social events to attend, since I regarded anything that had political overtones as off-limits. The second was that Barbara and I spent a lot more time at home talking about family, friends, and personal matters: for the first time in our married life, we couldn't speak freely about how things were going at the office.

Like most outsiders—although I'd served in government and should have known better—whenever the CIA came up in conversation, I automatically thought in terms of spying, counterspying, and covert actions. But I quickly learned that very few CIA personnel are in the Directorate of Operations—the division responsible for foreign intelligence, counterintelligence, and carrying out covert actions.

Most CIA employees work for one of three other directorates—either Administration, Science and Technology, or Intelligence.

Administration is the housekeeping division. It pays the checks, maintains employee records, and, among other things, handles personnel recruitment.

Science and Technology is the James Bond/"Mission Impossible" division involved in developing electronic and other devices for advanced intelligence work. This is the branch that captures the imagination of outsiders, to the extent that some people have seriously suggested technology may replace humans in foreign intelligence work one day in the not-too-distant future.

The flaw in this theory is that nobody has yet invented a machine to assess human intentions thousands of miles away. Science and technology can give us an accurate assessment of how many warships a particular country has and where they're located; but whether that country's leaders intend to use those warships is something only human judgment can gauge.

That's where the Directorate of Intelligence comes into

play. In the CIA, an intelligence officer isn't a "spy" in the popular cloak-and-dagger image, but an analyst in some special area—foreign politics, economics, military affairs, agriculture, to name a few. At the time I was director, the CIA had over 1,400 employees with master's and doctoral degrees. When specialists at that level got together around my office conference table, the conversation sounded more like a university seminar than a chapter out of Ian Fleming.

One morning about three months after I became DCI, a meeting was held in my office to discuss the upcoming 1976 Italian elections. I don't know what I expected when the topic appeared on the agenda, but what I didn't anticipate was a heated academic debate, with four different analyses going around the table.

That particular argument was resolved, but when intelligence officers couldn't reach a consensus on an issue, it was up to me as DCI to decide what to tell the President and his National Security Council.

The most important intelligence estimate I ever brought before the President and the NSC concerned the situation in Beirut in the summer of 1976. On June 16 of that year, Francis E. Meloy, Jr., the U.S. ambassador to Lebanon, was assassinated while going to a meeting with Lebanese President-elect Elias Sarkis. Two other Americans, the embassy's economic counselor and the driver of the car, were killed with him.

President Ford called an emergency meeting of the NSC in the White House Situation Room, located on the ground floor of the west wing. The question before the group was whether the crisis was serious enough to evacuate Americans living in Lebanon.

The answer looked simple on the surface. Wasn't the murder of an ambassador proof enough that events were getting out of control?

Not necessarily. The ambassador's murder could have been an isolated act. There was also the possibility that the purpose of the assassination was to undercut the new Lebanese Government. If that were the case, would an evacuation play into the terrorists' hands?

As DCI, my job was to furnish an up-to-the-minute

intelligence estimate on what was happening and likely to happen in Beirut. No frills, just the data coming in from CIA personnel and other segments of the U.S. intelligence community.*

Seated around the rectangular table in the small room were the President, Secretary of State Kissinger, Deputy Defense Secretary Bill Clements, and National Security Adviser Brent Scowcroft. There was also a chair for the CIA director, though I spent most of the meeting on my feet, going through charts—including intelligence aerial photos showing overland escape routes—and answering questions.

It isn't the job of the Director of Central Intelligence to get involved in policy-making, but the data made it clear that the Meloy assassination signaled a new, more dangerous level of terrorist activity in Beirut—enough to warrant instructing the U.S. embassy there to advise all American nationals in Lebanon to leave the country. The President also ordered a Navy task force sent in to aid the evacuation. Hundreds of Americans and citizens of other countries boarded the ships, while others left Beirut in three convoys headed toward Damascus, Syria.

Other Americans, for their own reasons, chose to stay in Beirut, playing the odds that the violence and terrorism they saw around them wouldn't touch their lives directly, that the warfare between Christians and Muslims would soon come to an end and Beirut would again become one of the most beautiful, civilized cities in the world.

It was—and more than a decade later remains—a dangerous gamble, not only for themselves but for their country.

---

* Contrary to widespread impression, the CIA and the U.S. "intelligence community" aren't the same thing. The "community," as it's called, is made up of all the various intelligence services in the U.S. Government—e.g., Defense, State, Treasury, Army, NSA, Navy, Air Force. Following a 1975 recommendation made by an investigative commission headed by Vice President Rockefeller, President Ford gave the CIA director budgetary control over all segments of the "community," minimizing the risk of bureaucratic in-fighting among U.S. intelligence agencies.

• • •

It was during the 1976 Lebanese crisis that I was able to observe at close range the way Brent Scowcroft carried out his duties as the President's national security adviser. A tall, scholarly Air Force lieutenant general, Scowcroft possessed not only the experience but the even temperament needed for the job. Little more than a decade later, millions of television viewers would get to know him as a member of the three-man Tower Commission looking into the Iran-Contra affair.

As chief of the Ford White House NSC, Scowcroft operated under the same law that created the Central Intelligence Agency in 1947. His job, under the original NSC congressional charter, was to "advise the President with respect to the integration of domestic, foreign, and military policies relating to the national security."

Like the CIA, the NSC was never intended to be in the policy-making loop of government—much less the operational end of American foreign policy. Scowcroft understood that. As a Tower Commission member, he reflected that understanding when he made the point that it wasn't the NSC process that failed during the Iran-Contra affair but the way some members of the NSC staff abused that process.

I agreed with Scowcroft. For years the NSC, by slow degrees, had been inching away from the intent of its original charter to advise on and integrate policy.

Under Presidents Truman and Eisenhower, the original charter was scrupulously followed. With strong personalities like Dean Acheson and John Foster Dulles heading the State Department—two secretaries with close ties to the Presidents they served—it wasn't likely that an NSC head could stretch the limits of his mandate in the foreign-policy field.

That changed under Presidents Kennedy and Johnson, however. Kennedy, according to Arthur Schlesinger, Jr., was still President-elect when he announced he wanted to use the NSC "more flexibly than in the past. "When Kennedy's national security chief, McGeorge Bundy—and later

Lyndon Johnson's NSC chief Walt Rostow—began exercising the power that came from easy access to the Oval Office, it didn't take long for the Council to begin influencing rather than simply advising on foreign policy.

What Kennedy had created, along with a more flexible NSC, were the conditions for a policy rivalry between his Secretary of State, Dean Rusk, and his NSC adviser, Bundy. That institutional rivalry continued between Rusk and Rostow. Then, during the Nixon years, came Henry Kissinger to contend with William Rogers (until he replaced Rogers at State). The fight to control foreign policy also went on during the Carter years, with only the names changed: Zbigniew Brzezinski vs. Cyrus Vance.

The Reagan years saw a continuation of the fight in a different form. President Reagan has had five NSC heads, from Richard Allen to Frank Carlucci. None had the kind of power and influence exercised by Kissinger or Brzezinski. But an NSC staff apparatus was in place, operating far outside the agency's original charter. In 1985–86, it took the ultimate step of not only shaping but operating an independent covert action in the foreign-policy area.

This couldn't and wouldn't have happened under Brent Scowcroft. His conduct as NSC chief was a model that every future American President ought to follow in choosing and properly using a national security adviser. Scowcroft scrupulously adhered to the NSC charter, seeing to it that the views of all Council members were accurately and objectively reported to the President. He didn't try to make the NSC into a policy-making agency. He knew that the United States didn't need two secretaries of State and two secretaries of Defense.

When I took over as DCI, there were daily messages from CIA stations on my desk every morning, reporting that we were losing valuable sources of information as a result of worldwide publicity caused by leaks from irresponsible investigators on Capitol Hill. Some examples:

14. Campaigning in Miami during my run for the presidency in 1980. I started off as an "asterisk" candidate who wasn't given much chance, but thanks to dedicated campaign workers I became Ronald Reagan's leading challenger for the nomination that year.

15 & 16. With Mother and Dad. Their teaching and example had a lasting influence on all their children. Dad died in 1972. Mother makes her home at Walker's Point, in Kennebunkport, Maine.

17. The President and I going over a report at a meeting in the Oval Office. What began as a political alliance at the 1980 convention in Detroit soon developed into a warm personal friendship.

18. U.S. Supreme Court Justice Potter Stewart, a family friend, conducted the swearing-in ceremony when I took the oath as Vice President for the second time, in January 1985. Barbara is holding the family Bible also used in the ceremony held four years before.

19. Tip O'Neill and I had our political differences when he was Speaker of the House, but I got along with him fine when we discussed subjects we could agree on, like the Boston Red Sox. We're seen here talking just before the President arrives to deliver a State of the Union message to Congress.

20. Mikhail Gorbachev was a rising power in the Soviet Union when I visited Moscow for the funeral of Yuri Andropov.

21. At the Thatchers' country residence, Chequers, where Barbara and I met with Prime Minister Margaret Thatcher and her husband Denis, during a vice presidential visit to England.

22. One of my best overseas trips as Vice President was a return visit to China, where I served as American envoy in Beijing in the mid-1970s. Here Deng Xiaoping and I renew acquaintance before getting down to the subject of U.S.–China relations.

23. Three generations of the Bush family on vacation at Walker's Point, Maine. Though scattered from Colorado (Neil) to Texas (George) to Washington, D.C. (Marvin) to Massachusetts (Dorothy) to Florida (Jeb), the kids stay in close touch with Barbara and me, as well as with each other.

24. Piloting my powerboat, the *Fidelity,* in the waters off Maine. I learned my love of the sea from my grandfather, George Walker.

• The intelligence services of four Latin American countries drastically reduced their contact with the CIA, citing press leaks.

• A ranking East European official and U.S. secret agent since 1972 stopped cooperating with us, out of fear of publicity and exposure.

• A Communist-bloc diplomat who had agreed to provide information about his government broke off all contact after saying he couldn't risk working with an intelligence agency whose internal affairs were in the news every day.

Still new on the job, I read these reports with growing frustration as demands came in from Capitol Hill and the press for even greater exposure of CIA operations. I believed in cooperating with Congress and the press, but unless CIA sources were protected, the agency couldn't carry out its national security assignment.

My biggest fight to protect CIA sources came during the final days of the Ford administration, however, and it wasn't with a hostile Congressional committee or the press. It was with the Justice Department and involved the bizarre case of Edwin Gibbons Moore.

Moore was a former CIA employee who left the agency in 1973. Three years later, at about eleven P.M. on December 21, 1976, he threw a package over the fence of the Soviet embassy's residential complex in northwest Washington. The Soviet guards thought it was a bomb and called in the U.S. Secret Service. What the U.S. authorities discovered were copies of CIA documents dating from Moore's days with the agency, plus a note promising more material for $200,000. The exchange was to be made the next evening.

At this point the Federal Bureau of Investigation stepped in. Moore, the Inspector Clouseau of volunteer spying, had pinpointed his own neighborhood as the site of the exchange. The FBI drove past the spot and dropped a package. Adding to the absurdity, a child ran over to pick it up. But Moore, who had been raking his yard a short distance away, charged across the street, chased the kid off, and grabbed the package. He expected $200,000. What he got was an indictment for espionage.

At that point, the Justice Department entered the act. To prove their case, Justice attorneys wanted the papers Moore had tossed over the Soviet embassy fence. The CIA cooperated by furnishing some, but not all the papers. The papers withheld included the names of undercover agency personnel and the identity of private citizens who had aided the CIA while traveling overseas.

From Langley, we pointed out that if Justice used these papers as evidence in an open trial, it would be giving the Soviets, free of charge, what Moore wanted to charge $200,000 for. We wanted Moore convicted, but we couldn't risk releasing those undercover names. What's more, we told Justice, there was enough material already furnished to make a strong case.

Justice didn't agree. Attorney General Edward H. Levi insisted on not just some, but all the papers. We refused. CIA and Justice were stalemated, and the issue still wasn't resolved going into the last month of the Ford administration. It would come down to a confrontation between the Attorney General and the CIA director in the Oval Office, with the President making the final decision.

Levi and I were in Brent Scowcroft's office, waiting to see the President. We started talking about the case, coolly at first, until the Attorney General tried to drive his point home by arguing that the CIA's refusal to turn over all the documents, "smacked of a Watergate cover-up."

Blame it on the fact that we were both putting in overtime, winding up our work as we got ready to leave office, or the fact that Levi hadn't been in Washington during the Watergate years and didn't know how deeply his words cut. But after a year of hearing "Watergate cover-up" used by every cub reporter in town and every junior staff investigator on Capitol Hill, my patience snapped.

"We'll be talking to the President in a few minutes," I said, my voice rising. "Why don't you tell *him* that—*in just those words.*"

At this point, Scowcroft broke in to bring the temperature down a notch before we went into the Oval Office. Levi and I had always been friendly, and he now realized he'd hit a raw nerve. Perhaps, he said, there wasn't any need to bother the President in these last hours of his administration. There might be some way we could settle our differences.

There was. Levi cooled down, I cooled down, and our lawyers worked the problem out. In December 1977 Edwin Gibbons Moore was convicted and sentenced to a twenty-five-year prison term—without use of the documents the CIA didn't want to release.

For the second presidential campaign in a row I was watching a race for the White House as a close but outside observer. During the 1972 Nixon-McGovern race I was serving as ambassador to the United Nations. Now, from my seventh-floor office at Langley, I watched the Ford-Carter campaign as a strictly nonpartisan (though not dispassionate) public official.

There were two roles I had to play in the campaign, however—one minor, the other functional. The minor role was to serve as as a one-day target for Jimmy Carter in a speech he made to the American Bar Association in the summer of 1976. Carter told the ABA that both Presidents Nixon and Ford had used important government posts as "dumping grounds for unsuccessful candidates, faithful political partisans, out-of-favor White House aides, and representatives of special interests." He specifically named me, citing my U.N. appointment in 1971.

All of which didn't make my second, functional role any easier. As CIA director I was expected to give intelligence briefings to the candidates. That meant flying to Plains, Georgia, several times, accompanied by agency officials who could fill the Democratic nominee in on specialized subjects.

We would meet Carter in the living room of his home in Plains, he the courteous but distant host, we the courteous but slightly ill-at-ease guests. After the campaign, Carter would call the briefings "professional, competent, and most helpful." That was good to know, because in the time I spent with him, I wasn't able to gauge his reaction too well. It wasn't the ABA speech that threw me off. I pegged that for what Wendell Willkie once called "mere campaign rhetoric." It was only a one-time shot.

Carter's attacks on the Central Intelligence Agency, on the other hand, were frequent and vituperative. He called the agency one of Nixon's two scandals—Watergate being the other. Whatever Carter's reason—because he didn't really understand the agency, its expertise, or the dedication of its people—I felt that beneath his surface cool, he harbored a deep antipathy toward the CIA.

At the briefings, however, he was all concentration, soaking up data. Sitting in a straight-back chair, he would listen for long stretches without asking any questions, only perfunctorily saying "okay" or "I understand" when he thought he'd heard enough on a particular topic. He seemed to have an index-card mind, filing everything away for recall whenever he might need it.

What really came through about Carter, however, was that he was a loner, suspicious of strangers and their motives. Someone would say something, and he'd react with a look that conveyed, "I hear you, but think you've got some angle you're hiding."

He was a man, in short, who always seemed to have his guard up. Jimmy Carter might have been the European foreign minister who, on hearing that Prince Metternich had just died, asked, "I wonder what he meant by that?"

My last visit to Plains came in mid-November, 1976, not long after the election. This time I'd be briefing not candidate Carter but President-elect Carter, and his running mate, Vice President-elect Mondale. It would be one of my last official acts as DCI. Before leaving on an early morning flight, I'd visited President Ford and Vice President Rockefeller, to tell them I was headed for Plains. On the trip down I told Hank Knoche that before the briefing started I planned to tell the President-elect I was resigning so that he could name his own DCI on taking office.

The session lasted five full hours. Halfway through the briefing, one of my deputies, Dan Murphy, began outlining long-range national security problems facing the country. He mentioned a particular problem, due to come to a head around 1985—at which point the President-elect, who'd been quietly listening, held up his hand.

"I don't need to worry about that," he said, half smiling. "By then George will be President and he can take care of it." Then, nodding toward the Vice President-elect sitting across the room, Carter added, "Either George or Fritz Mondale there."

George will be President? It was an odd statement, coming from Jimmy Carter. I wondered what he meant by that.

Eight

WE'LL BE THERE

Cleveland/Autumn 1979

Cleveland's Stouffer Hotel is on Public Square, not far from where I interviewed for my first job with Dresser Industries. I pointed out the old gray building to Pete Teeley on the way to the hotel. He nodded glumly; as press secretary to an asterisk candidate* for President, Pete had other things on his mind.

"Don't expect a mob scene at your news conference," he cautioned, looking out our car window at deserted downtown streets. "We'll be lucky to turn out a stringer on a day like this."

It was Sunday and drizzling. Baltimore and Pittsburgh were playing a World Series game on one TV channel, while the Cleveland Browns were playing on another.

Question: With that kind of competition, why were we holding a news conference?

Answer: Because presidential candidates are expected to hold news conferences when they come to town, even on a wet Sunday.

Follow-up Question: With the presidential election still thirteen months away, why were we out campaigning fulltime?

Answer: Because an asterisk candidate either starts early or doesn't get started at all. The old idea that "the office seeks the man" doesn't apply anymore. There are no true presidential "draft" movements, no "dark horse" candidacies able to sweep a national convention at the last minute.

We had just endured a long, choppy flight from Des

---

* An "asterisk candidate" is one whose national poll numbers are so fractional that he or she doesn't rate being listed by name, only by asterisk, under the group heading, "All Others."

Moines in a small plane. No greeting committee had met us at Hopkins International. No crowds lined our route into the city. There were no bands, no balloon drops. When we arrived at the hotel, our preregistration cards had been misplaced.

"George Bush," the advance man repeated to the young woman at the check-in desk. "He's here to speak to the National Conference of Christians and Jews."

"Bush?"

"B-u-s-h."

"I don't believe . . . Oh yes, here it is. The Bush party. Ambassador Bush, Mr. Bates, Mr. Teeley. Sorry for the mix-up, Mr. Bush."

"I'm Teeley," said Pete.

"Well, welcome to Cleveland, Mr. Teeley."

Welcome to presidential politics its own self, from the bottom, looking up.

For months, Pete, David Bates, and I had been sky-hopping from Houston to Iowa; then from Iowa to New Hampshire; then back home to Houston for a change of laundry; then back to Iowa, retracing the circuit.

Pete was a quick-witted media expert in his mid-thirties, prematurely gray from having handled press relations for two United States senators and the Republican National Committee before joining our campaign staff. He was also the wordsmith who would author the one memorable phrase from my campaign that made it into *Safire's Political Dictionary*.

David, my chief traveling aide, was a young Houston attorney with an unflappable manner and the ability to separate urgent problems from minor flaps. Before the year was out, we would travel 250,000 miles in 329 days, covering more than 850 political events. The numbers would grow as we went through the cycle of preconvention primaries and caucuses: New England, the Southeast, and Midwest in midwinter; Pennsylvania and Texas in early spring; as the snows thawed and summer approached, Ohio, New Jersey, and the Far West.

By June, under the new rules, the presidential nominee would be picked, with enough delegate support to make the actual vote at the convention a formality. It had been a long time—going back to the Eisenhower-Taft race in 1952—since a real convention fight for the nomination had taken place at a Republican Convention. The Democrats hadn't had one since the Kennedy-Johnson contest in 1960.

But before June there were still miles to go and events to make. Occasionally we'd visit our national campaign office in Alexandria, Virginia. It was a low-rent district headquarters, across the Potomac from the Washington offices of the high-rent district candidates. At other times, campaign manager Jim Baker and Margaret Tutwiler, my chief scheduler, would recommend a speech or fund-raiser in some state other than Iowa or New Hampshire. Margaret was from Birmingham, a soft-spoken Deep Southern dynamo still in her twenties. On a given day, she could come up with anywhere from five to fifteen events to choose from, with recommendations. A Rotary Club meeting in Michigan, a strawberry festival in Florida, a state party convention in New England . . . the panorama of American presidential politicking.

But wherever we might go in these early campaign days, the trail always led to Iowa, then on to New Hampshire.

Until Jimmy Carter made them headline news in 1976, the Iowa caucuses had been America's best-kept political secret. For the public, presidential campaigns had traditionally begun (and for some candidates, ended) in New Hampshire. But Carter's early victory in Iowa—while his opponents were concentrating their time and resources in New Hampshire—made him a known, viable candidate.

Whatever history has to say about his presidency, Jimmy Carter was quicker than others in understanding the new dynamics of presidential campaigning. In 1976 Carter proved that the old political establishments—the state and local hierarchies and machines—don't control the presidential nominating process anymore. Before that, in 1972, there had been McGovern, organizing a grass-roots movement in the Democratic Party to upset the favorites at the Miami Beach convention. But McGovern had been a nationally known figure. Carter showed that even a little-known candidate can get nominated, if he understands how the new rules work.

The new rules say that nominations aren't brokered at conventions by political leaders controlling big blocs of delegates. Nominations are won in the field, campaigning for delegates in primaries, caucuses, and at state conventions. Under the old system, political leaders passed the word about a candidate. Under the new rules, the word is given out by the media. The smoke-filled room has been replaced by the klieg-lit room.

Some candidates who thought they understood the new rules were sold on the idea that all it took to get their message across to voters and delegates was national media attention. The professional political managers call this "wholesaling" a candidate—trying to reach mass audiences through major media events. But national media exposure is only one part of the new dynamics—and for an asterisk candidate, not the most important part. At least, not at the beginning of the 1980 campaign. Jim Baker explained to a *Newsweek* magazine writer early in the campaign how he got phone calls every day from supporters complaining about my not taking advantage of national media opportunities. They'd say that an unknown candidate ought to be spending more time in major media markets, getting his face on the evening news. "I'd argue that that wasn't the way someone like George Bush could ever get nominated," said Jim. "To cure the name-identification problem when you're running for President, you have to win early—the same way Jimmy Carter did—and you can't win those early ones by standing in the lobby of the Waldorf-Astoria in New York."

Winning early meant winning in Iowa. That couldn't be done by standing in the lobby of the Fort Des Moines Hotel either. It meant long campaign days: up at six A.M. or earlier, on the move until ten P.M. or later, meeting people individually and in small groups. And doing the little things, like staying with the schedule, being on time, and sticking with commitments, no matter how small. One of my favorite stories of the 1980 campaign had to do with how I ended up getting the vote of an elementary school teacher in Exeter, Iowa. "Hearing Bush talk didn't influence me," she told a reporter. "He promised to be there at seven and speak at seven-thirty—and he did!"

Not that we ignored the major rallies in Iowa. As Rich Bond, our thirty-year-old field director, described the scheduling process, "The state committee sent out a Republican calendar every week, and we'd check for the events, call the country chairman, and say, 'We'll be there.' "

My feeling was and is that nothing beats personal, eye-to-eye contact in a political campaign—not just talking to (or at) people, but listening to what they have to say.

That was our Iowa game plan: start early, campaign person to person, outwork the opposition. It wasn't drawing attention in Washington, but more than a year of "retail" campaigning had begun to produce results. Just before we left Des Moines for Cleveland, a straw poll was taken at a gathering of Iowa Republicans. I led the field. That alone guaranteed that the poll wouldn't be taken seriously, either by the national press or the opposition. They'd write it off as a random, unscientific survey, proving nothing—which was fine as far as we were concerned, because the first principle of campaign strategy in a primary or caucus state is McCarthy's Law of Minimal Expectations.

When Gene McCarthy did better than expected against President Johnson in the 1968 New Hampshire primary, the fact that Johnson actually came in first didn't prevent the media from calling the results a McCarthy victory. All it would take for me to "win" in Iowa was to do better than the media had projected. I was campaigning to come in ahead of the field, but even if I ran a close second—ahead of the better-known candidates, Howard Baker, John Connally, and Bob Dole—it would break me out of the pack as Ronald Reagan's chief competitor for the nomination.

Iowa had been the Democratic campaign surprise of 1976. Our game plan was to make it the Republican campaign surprise of 1980.

Money alone can't win a modern presidential campaign; if it could, Nelson Rockefeller would have been elected in 1964 and 1968, and John Connally might have won the Republican nomination in 1980—or at least run stronger than he actually did. But given the marathon nature of modern campaigns, the candidate who enters a presidential race without financial backing faces insurmountable odds.

By the time they were over, my Iowa campaign would cost $462,388 and my New Hampshire campaign $264,857. And that was only the beginning of the high cost of running for President.

The key to financing a winning presidential race wasn't just raising money, but knowing how, where, and when to spend it. Obvious enough in theory, but in practice a political campaign is like a federal government agency: unless held in check, it takes on a financial life of its own. Most campaign organizations tend to become top-heavy and bloated with professional staff. The more top-heavy they get, the more people there are with the authority to spend—and, without strong direction from the top, to overspend. I'd heard all the horror stories about presidential candidates whose campaigns ran up huge debts because they spun out of control. The Bush for President organization would be run with a tight—literally tight—hand on the campaign budget.

All through 1978 and 1979, I held a series of number-crunching sessions with Jim Baker and my chief national fund raisers, Bob Mosbacher and Fred Bush (no relation, but like Bob a longtime friend). After consulting with our state campaign leaders, George Wittgraf in Iowa and Hugh Gregg in New Hampshire, we developed some best-case/worst-case estimates on what it would take to get through the early races. By "get through," I mean either win them outright or run well enough for the campaign to survive.

There were no illusions about what would happen if George Bush was still an asterisk coming out of Iowa and New Hampshire. The first wave of contributions in a political campaign comes from friends, relatives, and the candidate's true believers. After that, the campaign has to do well enough to attract contributors whose enthusiasm for the candidate, while sincere, is tempered by a desire to be with a winner.

The 1980 Republican presidential race was going to come down to a two-man contest between the front-runner, Ronald Reagan, and whichever other candidate did well in its early stages. If I won or ran second in Iowa and New Hampshire, the money would come; if I didn't exceed the media's minimal expectations, I'd balance my campaign books and take a seat in the grandstands as a spectator.

Cleveland had originally been scheduled for a fund-raising reception at a private home the evening of Monday, October 15. The month had been booked solid, with just one twenty-four-hour stopover in Houston. That was supposed to have been on the fourteenth—the gray Sunday that now found me unpacking my bags at the Stouffer.

But Jim Baker called me in Des Moines on the thirteenth. He had another event to add to the schedule. I'd suddenly been invited to address the Cleveland chapter of the National Conference of Christians and Jews. Experience told me that being invited to address a black-tie dinner on short notice meant that the group's original speaker had to cancel out for some reason. Who would I be subbing for? Henry or Zbig? No matter. It was a golden opportunity to get a foreign-policy message over to a prestigious audience of 1,200 community leaders.

So much for my one day of R & R at home. But as Jim pointed out, what difference did one more night in a hotel bed make?

There's a story told about Ed Muskie being over-scheduled and blowing up at his staff at one point during his 1972 presidential race. Finally, with the candidate's face turning beet red, one of his staffers, Mark Shields, is supposed to have leaned across Muskie's desk and said, "Senator, I know it's a tough campaign, but just remember, *we're* the ones on *your* side."

I kept reassuring myself of that as the small plane carrying us into Cleveland heaved and tossed through miles of mid-autumn air turbulence: Jim Baker was one of the ones on *my* side.

Pete Teeley had been too pessimistic. My news conference drew more than a string correspondent. We had two
local TV crews and three print reporters. Still, the session
was a disappointment.

I'd hoped to take questions on foreign policy, since that
was the theme of my upcoming speech. But with two excep-
tions—a question on steel imports and a second on the CIA
—all the assembled press wanted to know was how the presidential race was shaping up. Could Reagan win on the first
ballot? What about Kennedy's run against Carter?

It was the same media horse-race syndrome that Jimmy
Carter had complained about four years earlier. Carter said
then that the only thing his traveling press seemed interested
in was the tactical part of the race—who was ahead, who
was behind. He'd make a speech on the state of the economy, only to be asked afterward about some poll result that
had nothing to do with his remarks. When he answered the
question, the media played that up and ignored his speech;
then, adding insult to injury, he'd be editorially roasted for
not addressing the issues.

Jimmy Carter and I didn't have many areas of political
agreement, but that was one of them. It took months for me
to realize that answering questions about the process of the
campaign drew attention away from its substance. But worst
of all, before finally catching on, I compounded the problem, telling Iowa audiences and the press that my campaign
was picking up *momentum*. That produced one of the two
campaign catch phrases that would later come back to taunt
me. "Voodoo economics" was Pete Teeley's brainchild; but I
had only myself to blame for borrowing Don Meredith's
phrase from "Monday Night Football"—"Big Mo" as
shorthand for what I thought was campaign momentum.

That mid-October Sunday in downtown Cleveland,
however, "Big Mo" hadn't arrived on the scene yet. After
the news conference, I returned to my room for a few hours'
rest before the NCCJ dinner. The scheduling term for that
sort of pre-event rest break is "down time," and it fit my
mood perfectly. I put in a call to Barbara to report we'd

arrived in Cleveland safely and told her about the good news from the Iowa straw poll. She could tell from my voice that I was bone-tired. After two straight weeks on the road and nearly a half year of hard campaigning, I'd reached a point where one hotel room was beginning to look like another.

In every political campaign there come periods when a candidate—even a confirmed optimist—goes through down cycles. Not just in the polls, but within himself. Sometimes these cycles last only a few hours; at other times they last days. Sometimes they pass after a good night's sleep or a thirty-minute jog; at other times they hang on, affecting the way the candidate delivers a speech, handles a TV interview, and looks at the campaign generally.

He may begin to have second thoughts about the all-out commitment required by the campaign, asking himself —as I did, after calling Barbara—*What am I doing here on a Sunday afternoon when I could be at home?* Or he may even ask the basic question: *Why am I in this race?*

Early in the 1980 campaign Roger Mudd surprised Ted Kennedy during a televised interview by asking *Why do you want to be President?* Kennedy was faulted for not coming back with a quick, articulate reply; but any presidential candidate honest with himself had to wonder: *What would I have said if Roger Mudd surprised me with that question.*

There are the shorthand answers, off-the-cuff and perfectly fitted to a thirty- to sixty-second television time frame. During the 1960 campaign John F. Kennedy explained that if you get into politics it's because you want to achieve something, and if you want to achieve something big, the White House is where the action is. Hubert Humphrey said that he ran for President for the same reason he did everything else, because it was "in my glands." Teddy Roosevelt might have told Mudd that he was a man with a mission, to save America's soul, and the White House was "a bully pulpit" (though his cousin Franklin, according to one contemporary columnist, wouldn't have been able to answer the question, because FDR—so wrote Walter Lippmann—was merely a "pleasant man who, without any important qualifications for the office, would very much like to be President"

—proving that candidates aren't alone in committing election year gaffes).

Jimmy Carter said that after he became governor of Georgia, he had a chance to meet some national leaders—Nixon, Ford, Ted Kennedy, Humphrey—and concluded, "What do they have to offer the country that I don't?"

Something along that line occurred to me after I returned to Houston in 1977 and settled into private life. By that time I'd served in government for more than a decade. My experience near the center of action—Congress, the United Nations, the Republican National Committee, China, the CIA—had been extensive. I'd seen the inner workings of the White House during two administrations and developed my own ideas about how it ought to run—at least, how I'd run it if given a chance.

Looking over the field of presidential candidates mentioned for 1980, I saw prospects whose qualifications were no better than mine and whose experience in government and business wasn't as extensive.

I saw something else, too. Jimmy Carter was beginning to look like a one-term President. In 1976 his slogan had been "Why not the best?" He campaigned on the theme that the American people deserved better than the leadership they were getting in Washington.

But what Carter the candidate had promised, Carter the President didn't deliver. Toward the end, he blamed the failure of his administration on the country. In a televised speech delivered in late 1979, he traced the country's problems—double-digit inflation, high interest rates, unemployment, a stagnant economy—to what he called a national "crisis of confidence" and "a malaise of the spirit."

It was an incredible speech coming from an American President. Listening to it in Houston, I became more than ever convinced that neither Carter nor the Democratic Party could meet the problems facing the country in the 1980s—that new blood was needed in the White House, someone who believed in the system and had confidence in the people.

The generation that came of age during the Depression and World War Two was infused with that kind of confidence. Bad as things looked for the country, we never doubted for a moment that America's political and economic institutions—but most of all, our national spirit—would see us through. Whether or not you approved of his New Deal programs, that was the genius of Franklin Roosevelt's leadership in the 1930s and '40s. And of Dwight Eisenhower's leadership in the 1950s. As President, both FDR and Ike had faith in the system; they had confidence in the people; they were optimistic about the future of the country, and their optimism, in wartime and peace, was contagious.

This to me was the essence of presidential leadership—in the 1930s, 1950s, or 1980s. America needed someone in the Oval Office who could restore the people's faith in our institutions, a leader who could revitalize the national spirit.

By May 1, 1979—the day I announced my candidacy—if Roger Mudd had asked why I was running for President, my answer would have been: first, because I didn't see any Roosevelts or Eisenhowers running; second, because we needed a great deal better than Jimmy Carter's best to solve the serious problems that faced our country both at home and overseas; and finally, because I believed that by experience in government and business, as well as philosophy and temperament, I was the best-qualified candidate on the scene to lead America in the 1980s.

My mid-October campaign swing through Cleveland was important not only because of the NCCJ dinner and Monday night fund-raiser, but for a personal reason. I had family ties in Ohio. Both Barbara's father, Marvin Pierce, and my father were native Ohioans. Grandfather Sam Bush had even been active in state party affairs. Wrong party—he was a Democrat—but the personal attachment was still there.

Another state with that sort of link to the past was Maine, where the Republican State Convention was scheduled for Portland on Saturday, November 2. It was there that Howard Baker planned to kick off his own presidential campaign with a media splash by winning a poll of conven-

tion delegates. Not only had Baker's staff been working
Maine, but John Connally's operatives had also been active
there.

Only a straw vote was involved, but my coming in a
poor fourth at a gathering of Maine Republicans—behind
Baker, Reagan, and Connally—would be bad news at three
levels: first, it could establish Baker as Reagan's leading
challenger, the goal I was working toward in Iowa; second,
since asterisk candidates live on the political edge, it could
reverberate in Iowa, affecting the morale of our volunteer
field workers (not to mention financial contributors); third,
because of my family link to Maine. Texas was home and
had been for more than thirty years, but I'd spent some of
the happiest days of my boyhood at Walker's Point, where
Mother still lived and the family still visited every summer.

We had a late organizational start in Maine, so it didn't
seem possible I could come in first in the straw vote. Baker
appeared to have that locked up. But Bush for President
volunteers from nearby colleges headed to Portland to work
the streets outside the convention, as well as the galleries.
They'd make up in enthusiasm what the other candidates
had in nuts-and-bolts organization.

On my arrival in Portland Saturday morning, Ron
Kaufman, one of our New England field directors, filled me
in on late developments: Baker supporters were in control of
the convention agenda. Obviously, they'd given Howard an
optimistic report on his strength among the eight hundred
delegates. He was so confident of the outcome of the straw
poll that he'd invited a planeload of Washington political
reporters and TV crews to travel with him to Portland. Saturday being a slow news day, that meant the convention
would get heavy coverage.

Kaufman's second bit of news was that Baker would be
the final speaker before the vote. The convention's planners
had arranged what the media calls a "beauty contest" appearance by each candidate. We'd all get to address the delegates before the poll was taken—with Howard getting the
last word.

The bottom line was that with Baker and Connally better organized for the event, my chances for a creditable

showing—third place was our best hope—depended on how well I did in my appearance at the convention.

Waiting backstage before my turn to go to the rostrum, I went over the notes to my Speech—capital *S*. Every presidential candidate develops a basic Speech, one that he shapes and polishes through the course of the campaign. It's the all-inclusive message that sums up his campaign theme, his stand on the issues, his appeal for support.

The best-known Speech in recent American political history has been Ronald Reagan's. It was first delivered to a national television audience during the Goldwater campaign of 1964. It went through several political cycles between 1964 and 1980, but its central theme—that America was "the last best hope of man on earth," and Americans had arrived at "a time for choosing between individual freedom and statism"—didn't change.

The style was uniquely Reagan's. My own style varied, depending on whether I was delivering a written speech or extemporizing. Staff speech writers naturally want a candidate to stick to a text, but going back to my days of campaigning in Texas, I was always more comfortable working from general notes, responding to the audience and the occasion.

In Portland that day there was a convention-like atmosphere. The eight hundred delegates on the floor were flanked and backed by seats of spectators, and despite being out-organized in other areas, the Bush campaign, with its vocal student supporters, was well represented in the bleachers. As my speech went along, I felt that the spontaneous enthusiasm of our young supporters was having an impact on the delegates.

The speech itself addressed the issue of national leadership and the failure of the Carter administration—a domestic economy out of control and a lack of direction and focus in foreign policy. I hit the post-Vietnam guilt syndrome that seemed to afflict the Democratic Party and the Carter White House, coming up with a line that I found effective throughout the campaign—that I was "sick and tired of hearing people apologize for America."

My theme wasn't original—every candidate appearing

that day catalogued the failure of the Carter White House.
But knowing that a special effort was needed to get through
to the delegates, I delivered my remarks in stump-speaking
style, as if addressing an outdoor rally rather than a seated
indoor audience.

There was a rousing ovation when I finished—though
how much came from the Bush bleacher brigade and how
much from the delegates was hard to tell. As I left the rostrum, I did notice that some of the delegates were on their
feet, applauding—a hopeful sign that we could get enough
votes to finish a respectable third.

Howard Baker followed me to the rostrum, wrapping
up the program. Then came the balloting and the vote
count. In true beauty-contest style, the results were announced in reverse order.

After reading off the names of the candidates who ran
sixth, fifth, and fourth, it was announced that Connally had
run third. When it was announced that Baker had run second—meaning I had run first—the Bush bleacherites ran
wild on the convention floor.

Fortunately for me, the national front-runner—who
ran fourth—hadn't come to Portland. He was then following the advice of John Sears, his chief strategist, and avoid-
ing any joint appearance with other candidates. Otherwise,
if he had shown up and delivered his Speech, the next day's
political headline might have read: REAGAN SWEEPS MAINE
CONVENTION instead of BUSH PULLS UPSET IN MAINE.

Things seemed to be falling into place. We were even
being helped by our opponents. With the heavy media coverage Howard had inadvertently given my campaign, even
George Gallup would soon have to concede that George
Bush had moved out of the asterisk stage.

When I entered the presidential race on May 1, 1979,
Jack Germond and Jules Witcover, two of Washington's
leading political forecasters, came up with a memorable line
—at least, I still remember it. George Bush's presidential
campaign, wrote Germond-Witcover on the front page of

the Washington *Star,* is the first campaign in history to have peaked before it was even announced.

Jack and Jules were wrong, by eight months. My campaign actually peaked the night of January 21, 1980, when the Iowa precinct caucuses were held. When the vote came in, it was clear that our state organization and volunteers had pulled off a major upset. Seven short weeks before, the Des Moines *Register and Tribune* had run a poll showing Reagan at 50 percent, Bush running second at 14 percent. But when the caucus vote was counted, I ran first by a little over 2,000 votes, taking 31.5 percent of the total to Reagan's 29.4 percent.

So we finally had our two-candidate race, leaving Baker, Connally, Dole, Phil Crane, and John Anderson far behind. It turned out exactly as we'd hoped. The next morning, after making the full circuit of network news shows, I flew to New Hampshire, followed by a planeload of national correspondents and TV crews.

It was heady stuff. There was the cover of *Newsweek,* with the flattering appraisal that a "combination of sweat and savvy" had "raised the serious possibility" that I "could accomplish on the Republican side this year what Jimmy Carter did with the Democrats in 1976—parlay a well-tuned personal organization and an awesome appetite for on-the-ground campaigning into a Long March to his party's Presidential nomination."

After Iowa, the polls changed dramatically. On January 13, pre-Iowa, a nationwide Gallup survey of registered Republicans reported Reagan at 45 percent, Bush at 6 percent. Eleven days later Reagan's lead had shrunk to 33–27.

There was also a sharp, volatile change of opinion among Washington political experts. Suddenly most pundits perceived Reagan as a loser. One such expert, Richard Reeves, reflected this view in a column that saw Jimmy Carter regretting my Iowa win because Carter had "lost his favorite Republican opponent."

"The former California governor was a set-up for Mr. Carter," wrote Reeves. "The President's polls showed him taking everything from Reagan but conservative Republicans."

There's a lesson there about how seriously candidates and voters ought to take political polls and pundits. In due time, Jimmy Carter was going to learn it, but I was about to learn it first, in the cold political snows of New Hampshire.

The good news about Iowa was that it turned the 1980 campaign for the Republican presidential nomination into a two-candidate race, exactly what our game plan called for; the bad news, for me, was that the other candidate was the new Ronald Reagan.

Reagan hadn't changed; but his approach to the campaign had. The governor had hardly campaigned in Iowa, following John Sears's front-runner strategy to distance himself from the other candidates. But when that strategy failed, Reagan came into New Hampshire running as if he were the underdog.

He wasn't, of course. Beneath the media glow of my Iowa success was the political reality that Reagan, without campaigning, had come within two percentage points of winning the caucuses. Now he was campaigning full speed, working from the solid New Hampshire base established when he'd run against President Ford in 1976.

Because I thought I had "momentum," I also made the mistake of overlooking New Hampshire's tradition of presidential primary surprises and gaffes. For political buffs under the age of twenty-five, a capsule history:

1964. Barry Goldwater, the Republican front-runner, is upset by Ambassador Henry Cabot Lodge, still stationed in Saigon.

1968. George Romney explaining in New Hampshire why he's changed his stand on the Vietnam war, says he was "brainwashed" into supporting the war in the first place.

1972. Ed Muskie, the Democratic front-runner, overreacts to the editorial attacks of publisher William Loeb by shedding tears in the snow in front of Loeb's Manchester *Union-Leader.*

Then came 1980. For political buffs of all ages who

keep track of New Hampshire primary incidents, the one best remembered that year took place Saturday night, February 23, preceding the Reagan-Bush debate at the Nashua High School. And the best-remembered line is "I paid for this microphone, Mr. Green."

Jon Breen, not Green, was editor of the Nashua *Telegraph,* sponsor of the two-candidate debate scheduled at the school. Mispronouncing his name was my opponent's mistake, but as coverage of the event bore out, it was the only mistake Ronald Reagan made that night.

The idea for a two-candidate debate came from the Reagan campaign staff after my post-Iowa surge in the polls. They approached my New Hampshire campaign chairman, former Governor Hugh Gregg. He liked the idea and so did I. It confirmed the fact that I was Reagan's leading challenger for the nomination.

Hugh took the idea of a Reagan-Bush debate to the publisher and editor of the Nashua *Telegraph.* They agreed to sponsor it and set the date for February 23. Meanwhile, a debate featuring all the candidates was scheduled by the League of Women Voters at Manchester, New Hampshire.

The League debate took place February 20. Like most debates featuring three or more candidates, it didn't provide enough time to shed any new light on the issues. I came away feeling I'd neither helped nor hurt myself; but neither had anybody else, with the possible exception of John Anderson.

It was in Iowa that John first staked out his position as a maverick Republican with "new ideas." Having crossed the political spectrum from right to left, he'd become a favorite among some segments of the media. I'd listened to John during those debates with two questions running through my mind: first, whatever happened to the conservative John Anderson I'd known in Congress? Second, aside from a proposal for a fifty-cents-a-gallon tax on gasoline, what "new ideas" was he talking about?

Four years would pass before Walter Mondale asked the "new ideas" candidate of 1984, Gary Hart, "Where's the beef?" But if those television commercials had been running in 1980, the line could have been applied to the Anderson

campaign. In any case, John didn't seem to be making much
headway among Republican primary voters. But at media
events like the Manchester debate, he did manage to shore
up his position as the Doonesbury candidate.

After the Manchester debate, I started blocking out
time in my daily campaign schedule to prepare for my showdown with Reagan at Nashua. But at that point, things began to get complicated.

First, the Federal Elections Commission—the NCAA
of political campaigning—came down with a ruling that a
newspaper couldn't sponsor a Reagan-Bush debate. All the
other candidates would have to be included. Then the Reagan camp, insisting on the two-candidate format, agreed to
pay for the event. So the showdown would take place, as
scheduled, at the Nashua High School Saturday night.

It was on Saturday afternoon, however, that Pete
Teeley started hearing rumors that the other candidates
planned to show up at the high school, either to come on
stage or hold a news conference.

"It's John Sears," said Pete. "He's been calling around,
trying to get them to come."

I didn't understand. It was Sears, after all, along with
Reagan's other advisors, who'd originally wanted to exclude
the other candidates. "That's the debate the *Telegraph*
agreed to sponsor," I told Pete. "We can't change the rules
now."

"All I'm reporting is what I hear," said Pete. "There's
no telling what's going to happen once we get there to-
night."

What happened was that the other candidates—Bob
Dole, Howard Baker, John Anderson, Phil Crane—showed
up, as Pete had predicted, and their surprise appearance set
off a political chain reaction.

Things got underway not long after we arrived at the
high school and went to our holding room. Jim Baker and I
were talking about what the other candidates were up to,
when John Sears came by to tell us he thought it might be a
good idea to open the debate up to everybody. Jim said he
didn't think much of Sears's idea. David Keene, one of my
key campaign aides, agreed with Baker. The audience had

turned out to see Reagan against Bush, not a recycling of the Manchester debate. I made the point that the *Telegraph* had set the ground rules and it wasn't for us to change them.

Sears left. Jon Breen, the debate moderator, was telling the press out in the corridor that his paper had scheduled a two-candidate debate and wouldn't be pressured into opening it up. That was his frame of mind when we climbed the stairs to the stage: first Breen, then me, then Reagan, followed by Dole, Baker, Anderson, and Crane.

Right away there were calls from the audience to let the other candidates participate. But Jon Breen stood firm. When Reagan started explaining his position on the issue, Breen broke in, ordering the sound technician to "turn Mr. Reagan's microphone off." It was the wrong thing to say, to the wrong person. If Breen had forgotten that Reagan was underwriting the debate, Reagan hadn't. His instinctive "I paid for this microphone, Mr. Green" made everything that followed irrelevant—including our two-candidate debate, after the others had finally given up and left the stage.

The political consensus after the incident was that I'd committed a major gaffe, not because of anything I'd said but because of what I didn't say. I felt my position was sound—that the ground rules for the debate had been set and I intended to abide by them. But the lesson I learned that night, if I didn't know it before, was that political campaigns have their own unique rules. The public perception was that it was unfair to exclude the other candidates. Afterward I realized that things would have turned out better if I'd told Jon Breen that if it was all right with Governor Reagan, it was all right with me for the other candidates to pull up chairs and join the debate.

And if I'd done that, would the outcome of the New Hampshire primary have turned out differently? Not likely. The readings we got after the vote were that Ronald Reagan was headed for a sizeable victory even before the incident at Nashua.

• • •

Reagan took 50 percent of the New Hampshire primary vote on February 26. I ran second, with 23 percent. The rest of the field lagged behind. We finally had the two-candidate contest we wanted, but as the Reagan bandwagon rolled through the southern and midwestern primaries, the press saw the outcome of the campaign as foregone: Reagan had the Republican presidential nomination locked up.

Why was I still in the race? Was I really running for *Vice* President?

That question came up at just about every news conference. Political rumor had it that I was only going through the motions of running for President, using the campaign as a bargaining chip for the number two spot on the ticket. Why else would a candidate stick with a hopeless cause?

My answer, not only to the press but to my staff, was that the cause wasn't as hopeless as it looked. We'd spent carefully, and even after New Hampshire we still had around $3 million in campaign funds. By concentrating our resources on key states, we could hope for an Iowa-like breakthrough down the line. There was always a chance that the Reagan camp would make a tactical mistake and we could bring off another surprise.

On the campaign plane Kenny Rogers's "The Gambler" was piped through our public-address system, and we'd all sing along when he got to the line, "You've got to know when to hold 'em, know when to fold 'em." To emphasize to a skeptical press that we were still holding, I borrowed another line, used by the Washington Bullets during the 1979 NBA championship play-offs: "The opera ain't over till the fat lady sings."

That wasn't just for media consumption or to keep my staff's (or my own) morale up. I meant it. Whenever anybody—press, staff, or a well-meaning but pessimistic friend —would ask why I didn't look at the race "realistically," my answer was that political "realism" isn't necessarily dictated by the media or the polls. Our going into Iowa to campaign in 1979 hadn't been realistic; for that matter, in the eyes of some experts even Reagan's getting into the race wasn't "realism." They'd all but written him off after he lost the 1976 nomination to President Ford.

I was—and am—an optimist, convinced that no matter how bad a situation might look, something good can come of it. It's ingrained, part of my nature. But if optimism is a plus in getting a person through dark moments in everyday life, I found out that it can lead to problems for a presidential candidate—not tactical, but image problems.

Optimism in my case meant, among other things, enthusiasm, talking about "Big Mo" and America's being "Up for the Eighties." Well-meaning friends tried to counsel me in that area, too. They said those were "preppy"* phrases that created an impression that my campaign lacked substance, that once I'd lost momentum, I'd lost everything.

After New Hampshire, that became the biggest criticism leveled at my campaign: that I'd failed to spell out a "vision of the future."

The criticism was off-base. My view of America's future—the direction I wanted to lead the country—had been spelled out in dozens of speeches and position papers since the beginning of the campaign.

It was (and is) a view shaped by my political philosophy—a conservative philosophy based on the idea of Amer-

---

* "Preppyism has been a charge that stayed with me during the campaign and afterward. P.R. experts offered unsolicited advice that, first, I stop wearing button-down Oxford cloth shirts, in order to blunt the media impression that I was "elitist." On learning that I hadn't worn a button-down in twenty years, they shifted their focus to my striped watchbands. There was also critical P.R. comment about my playing tennis. After it was pointed out that I did more jogging than tennis playing, one political reporter said jogging was poor political strategy (actually I thought it was exercise), because I appeared to be promoting myself "more as a candidate for the Olympics than the presidency." The same sort of reaction came when my press secretary, under questioning, revealed that my taste in popular music ran to country-and-western. Several writers concluded, despite the fact that I'd lived in Texas for more than thirty years, that I was just claiming to be a country-and-western fan in order to counter my "elitist" image.

I finally asked one media specialist why—since they'd gone to Ivy League schools —the two Roosevelts, the two Tafts, and John F. Kennedy hadn't been charged with "elitism" when they were presidential candidates. He said he didn't know why, but in my case it had something to do with "perceptions"—leading me to conclude that the charge that I was part of a preppy conspiracy to take over the government was just something I'd have to live with.

ica as a beacon of hope throughout the world, and of freedom, justice, and opportunity for all its citizens.

Overseas that translates into honoring our commitments to our friends and allies, and maintaining America's interests by a policy of peace-through-strength—in John F. Kennedy's inaugural phrase, being strong enough so that we "never negotiate out of fear" but "never fear to negotiate."

Here at home, it means viewing government as the last, not the first, recourse in solving problems. I believe, as did Jefferson and Lincoln, that the sole purpose of government is to do for people what they can't do for themselves; that political and social freedom is tied to economic freedom; and that the proper role of a President is to develop a domestic and social agenda to improve the quality of American life through a free, competitive marketplace, not only of products but ideas.

None of which means—as some liberals argue—that they alone are "compassionate" and "responsive" to the needs of the country's socially and economically disadvantaged. On the contrary, the central theme of every domestic policy speech I made during the 1980 campaign—and my record as a congressman—reflected my personal commitment to the idea that each individual is entitled to a fair opportunity to fulfill his or her God-given potential.

My "vision"—it was all there in everything I'd said as a candidate and done in nearly twenty years of public life; but somehow, along with the issues, it got lost in media coverage of the horse-race aspects of the campaign.

That problem didn't start with the 1980 campaign. In 1976 the issues that drew maximum media attention weren't President Ford's overall foreign-policy record or Jimmy Carter's stand on nuclear proliferation, but Ford's presumed debate "gaffe" about Poland, and Carter's "lust in my heart" interview with *Playboy*.

I remember watching a segment of "60 Minutes" one late summer Sunday in 1976, when Carter's P.R.-advertising man, Gerald Rafshoon, explained how he had to handle the ongoing charge that his candidate wasn't discussing the issues. Rafshoon argued that in fact every Carter speech and television spot covered one or more issues, but the message wasn't getting through. His solution, he said, was to redo his TV spots, dubbing in an announcer's voice to preface Carter's remarks with "Jimmy Carter speaks out on *the issue* of . . ."—whatever subject the spot happened to take up.

Maybe that should have been my approach to the "vision" question in 1980—prefacing every public statement with *"My Vision for the future is . . . ,"* then just stating the position I'd been stating all along. Or maybe I could have pronounced myself the candidate of "new ideas," as John Anderson did that year and Gary Hart did four years later.

My problem with that approach, however—now as in 1980—is that I'm not comfortable with rhetoric for rhetoric's sake.

Vision of the future? Why would anyone run for President of the United States *without* a comprehensive view of the world as it is, and as he (or she) thinks it ought to be, or *without* deep convictions about the course the country needs to take in the years ahead?

New ideas? Another rhetorical device. What's misleading about this phrase is that candidates who use it do so as if they've discovered a patent medicine cure-all for the country's problems—not new ideas but new panaceas. But if the experience of the past fifty years teaches anything, it's that a "new idea" on how to shape a coherent foreign policy or develop the economy isn't good just because it's new.

Jim Rhodes, the former Governor of Ohio, impressed me with that fact of political life when I met with him not long after I decided to run for President. The purpose of my visit wasn't just to ask for support, but to get his no-frills perspective on how to succeed in government and politics.

As a Republican governor of a major industrial state, Jim Rhodes was unique. To begin with, he contradicted the stereotyped idea of what a Republican governor looks and acts like. A large, dominating presence—the tag "Big Jim" was a natural fit—Rhodes made a mockery of the standard Democratic charge that the Republicans are the elitist "country club" party. Gruff-speaking and good-humored, he was unbeatable in Ohio during the 1960s and 1970s, both on the campaign stump and at the polls. His appeal was trenchant and direct, as effective with Ohio's blue-collar factory workers as with the state's farmers.

So there I was with Jim Rhodes one morning, drinking orange juice and outlining my presidential campaign and program for America—my "vision of the future." I went down the list: foreign policy, national defense, the economy. I was talking either about strengthening NATO or about macroeconomics, when my host, who'd been leaning back in his chair, suddenly had enough.

As a candidate, you can generally tell when you're not getting through to people. After a while they either start squirming in their chairs or take on a dull MEGO—My Eyes Glaze Over—look. But with Big Jim Rhodes, you didn't have to wait long.

"Cut the crap, George," he said, shoving his chair back and getting to his feet, "because if you're serious about running for President, you might as well get a few things straight. What you're talking about is dandy, but I want to show you what people vote for, what they *really* want to know."

And with that, Big Jim pulled a thick, frayed leather wallet from his pocket, slammed it on the table, and said, "That's it right there, my friend. Jobs. Who can put money in people's pockets—you or the other guy? Jobs. That's what it's all about, George—*jobs, jobs, jobs.*"

An old pol had just given me one "new idea" for the campaign trail. Discussing economic theory is all right for position papers; but from that time on, whenever I wanted to sum up my economic vision for an audience, I'd quote Jim Rhodes, pull out my wallet, hold it up, and talk *"jobs, jobs, jobs!"*

It seemed to get the message across to blue-collar audiences: after the debacle of New Hampshire, we were able to keep the campaign going with victories in key industrial states—Massachusetts, Connecticut, Pennsylvania, and Michigan. Big Jim's "new" campaign idea could have been the reason. "Big Mo" certainly wasn't.

. . .

John Anderson's strategy was to claim he was the only candidate in the race who represented an alternative to Reagan the front-runner. If you don't like Reagan's policies, he argued, you shouldn't like Bush's because, said John, "George Bush is simply Ronald Reagan in a Brooks Brothers suit."

He was wrong about the suit—I wear Arthur Adler, not Brooks Brothers—but accurate in claiming that Reagan and I weren't far apart on issues. When the race came down to Reagan-versus-Bush, however, the traveling press naturally focused on our differences. Three areas were usually mentioned: ERA, abortion, and economic policy:

• *ERA.* I supported the original Equal Rights Amendment until time ran out on its adoption. The extension bill passed by Congress allowed states to switch positions to favor the amendment, but not to oppose it. I thought that was stacking the legislative deck. The amendment was given a fair shot at approval and failed (as, in time, the extension did). Both Reagan and I believed (and still do) that the best way to secure equal rights for women is through legislation, not constitutional amendment.

• *Abortion.* I oppose abortion, except in cases of rape, incest, or when the life of the mother is at stake. Reagan and I both disapproved of the Supreme Court ruling in *Roe v. Wade;* we agreed that some form of a constitutional amendment was needed to overturn the decision.

• *"Voodoo economics"* had been a one-time "insert" to a campaign speech during the Pennsylvania primary. Reagan's economic plan called for a supply-side tax cut to stimulate the economy. I agreed with the need for a tax cut, but added that it could only be made in connection with a reduction in the size of government and federal red tape. Since Reagan also favored less government and bureaucratic overregulation, the phrase proved to be a rhetorical distinction without a difference.

"Voodoo economics" was a campaign phrase that turned out to have a long political shelf life. The Democrats tried to turn it to advantage during the general election, though without much success.

Still, given the pace of modern campaigning, there's no guarantee that any presidential candidate won't use a phrase or answer some question in a way that boomerangs. It goes with the territory.

Presidential campaigns now start the day after the previous one ends (sometimes *before* they end: my first question about the 1988 campaign came in my first news conference of the 1984 campaign). The length of the race, the number of primaries, caucuses, speeches, debates, news conferences, interviews and meetings involved—all these factors make it hard, if not impossible, for anyone to run for President without making a "gaffe" or verbal slip somewhere along the way.

I've made my share. Some were the result of misjudgment. Others were due to misunderstandings or misperceptions. Either way, to comprehend how gaffes and slip-ups can occur during a presidential campaign, it helps if you look at the process as a kind of ordeal by pressure cooker.

A presidential candidate is called on to make anywhere from a dozen to two dozen decisions a day. They may range in importance from how to react to a late-breaking foreign-policy development, to which of two events he (or she) should attend on a tight schedule. If he decides to attend Event A, a party campaign rally, one group of advisers will tell him he's not going to do himself any good preaching to the choir; if he opts for Event B, a local charity event, another group of advisers will tell him he's not doing himself any good ignoring his political base.

Meanwhile, a local television crew is waiting outside his room for an interview scheduled to begin in five minutes, and his speech writer has just shown up with a suggested speech "insert" covering the foreign-policy development. While he's looking it over, an "urgent" long-distance call comes in from a campaign field director halfway across the country to report that ticket sales for an upcoming fund-raiser would go better if the press could be told that a "major economic address" is planned for the event. The candidate says he'll get back to the field director, writes in some changes on the "insert,"* then tells his press secretary he's ready for the interview.

The TV interviewer enters with his crew. As they set up their equipment and the make-up expert tries to dull a shiny spot on the candidate's forehead, an adviser whispers one last word before the cameras roll: There's a local issue that was inadvertently left out of the briefing book. The candidate has to be aware of the issue, even if he doesn't take a position on it. Since he's running for President, he's expected to be familiar with all issues, at all levels. (In Oregon a young woman once asked my position on East Timor. When told I wasn't close enough to the East Timor situation to give an immediate answer, she said, "You *don't know?* And you want to *run* American foreign policy?")

Obviously a candidate who wants to minimize gaffes and slip-ups has to delegate responsibility. But no matter how hectic a day he's had or how much pressure he's under, when it comes to key decisions, what Harry Truman said about the presidency also applies to a presidential campaign: The buck stops with the candidate, not with his campaign advisers.

Would I change the overall process? In some ways, yes.

To begin, the cost of running for President has gotten out of hand, and the spending cap applied by the federal financing law hasn't kept some candidates from piling up huge campaign debts that take years to pay off.

Tied to the problem of skyrocketing costs is the fact that presidential races now go on for four years. To some extent this is due to the horse-race aspect of modern political coverage (the first polls on the 1988 race appeared during the 1984 conventions). But by and large it's the responsibility of the politicians and the parties, not the press, to initiate changes in the process. After all, it wouldn't be a horse race if the horses and jockeys weren't testing track

---

* For a vice presidential candidate running on a national ticket, the problem is a little more complicated. Any position taken on a late-breaking news development has to be coordinated with the presidential candidate so the ticket doesn't fly off in two directions at the same time.

conditions four years before the starting gate opened; and as a candidate who benefited from an early start in the 1980 campaign, I'd be the last to argue in favor of some arbitrary time limit on campaigning—even if one were possible under our system.

As for the candidate-selection process itself, in my opinion primaries are better than caucuses and caucuses are better than closed conventions in choosing presidential delegates. Anything that brings the process closer to the people is all to the good.

In short, our presidential selection process may be pressurized, chaotic, sometimes even unfair; but I disagree with critics who think it needs a massive overhaul—especially those who argue that television, because it can reach millions, makes it unnecessary for a candidate to travel the country "retailing" his campaign message.

For all its flaws, the virtue of the present system is that it brings presidential candidates—as well as Presidents—out of the insulated politics of television and electronic computers, into contact with the flesh-and-blood world. A candidate can go into a campaign with his own ideas about what issues concern people. But time and again I learned—from audience reaction at speeches, question-and-answer sessions, and individual or group discussions—about problems that people considered important but that didn't show up on the public-opinion polls.

Campaign messages travel both ways. President—then Governor—Reagan arrived at the number one issue of his 1976 campaign for the Republican presidential nomination as a result of a surprising audience reaction he got to a line in a speech he delivered in Sun City, Florida. The line, expressing strong opposition to the Panama Canal treaty, suddenly brought the audience to its feet. It was a sleeper issue. The governor and his campaign staff were surprised by the audience response, but they were quick to get the message: though the Canal issue hadn't surfaced in any polls it was deeply felt by Republican primary voters and became a rallying cry for Reaganites.

My own experience along the same line came during the first months of the 1980 campaign. The word inside the

Washington Beltway was that after Vietnam and Watergate, the Central Intelligence Agency was politically unpopular. A rash of Hollywood films and TV dramas depicting CIA men as the heavies supported that view. It was so widely accepted in Washington that some Democrats even saw CIA bashing as a springboard to the White House.

The advice I got from friends was that if my CIA experience had to be mentioned at all, it should only be in passing. "Don't dwell on it," one friend advised. "It's a loser." I thought it over and concluded that loser or not, it was part of my record and shouldn't be ducked. So I included my role as CIA director in my standard campaign speech, summing it up with an endorsement of the agency's achievements and a pledge that if elected I'd strengthen U.S. intelligence capabilities around the world.

The response? Whether delivered to Republican audiences during the primaries or mixed political audiences in the fall, the line never failed to get applause. It turned out to be one of those insights into public opinion a candidate doesn't get from polls, by consulting with experts inside the Beltway, or by campaigning from insulated TV studios.

Not that all flesh-and-blood campaign encounters give a candidate a true reading on the mood of the electorate. . . .

On the Saturday night before the Michigan primary of May 20, 1980, Governor Bill Milliken and I had just finished a prodigious Greek dinner, shish kebob to baklava, in downtown Detroit. We were walking it off, trailing a scattered entourage of staff, press, and TV cameramen. It wasn't a planned media event; but then again, nothing a presidential candidate does seventy-two hours before the polls open can fairly be described as nonpolitical. Even if he does nothing—flies home or relaxes in his hotel room—somebody is sure to put a political spin on it. *(Is he sulking or overconfident?)*

In any event or nonevent, Bill and I were walking along, followed by the cameras, when we were suddenly approached—more accurately, stormed—by a middle-aged couple, the man muttering something undecipherable but the woman very emphatic: "Bush, you *expletive!*" she shouted, shaking a shopping bag in my face as the Secret Service detail moved in. "I wouldn't vote for you if *Castro* was running!" Then, just as suddenly, she and her husband disappeared into a crowd of onlookers. The detail relaxed.

Bill shook his head. "What do you think, George?" he asked. "For or against?"

"Undecided," I replied. "Put her down as a firm undecided."

Three days later, we carried Michigan, by a big margin: urban, rural, white-collar and blue-collar areas. By "we" I mean Bill Milliken and I, because it was only through Bill's putting warm personal friendship ahead of political reality that the last contested primary of the campaign went my way. One of the most popular governors in Michigan history, he'd laid his prestige on the line, endorsing my candidacy even after the national delegate count showed Reagan far ahead.

Optimistically I got ready to turn in that night, thinking that Michigan might make a difference, turn the tide. But the eleven o'clock news put things back into perspective. Reagan, reported the anchorman, had picked up enough delegate votes in Nebraska to put him over the top; and, oh yes, George Bush had won the Michigan primary.

So Michigan didn't matter in terms of the presidential nomination. It would not, however, go unnoticed by those around the presidential nominee who were already thinking in terms of putting together the strongest possible Republican ticket to run against Jimmy Carter and Walter Mondale in the fall.

We shut the campaign down ten days later, at a news conference in Houston. I finally reconciled myself to the fact that we'd lost, but some members of the family and close friends were slower in coming around.

All the kids had worked overtime during the campaign. Neil went to New Hampshire, Marvin to Iowa, and George was all over the country, as was our youngest, Dorothy. Jeb, who speaks fluent Spanish, and his Mexican-born wife, Columba, were active among Hispanic voters during the Puerto Rico, Florida, and Texas primary races. Along with my longtime friend and staffer Don Rhodes, Jeb was one of the last diehards arguing in favor of an Alamo-style campaign finish, with guns blazing until the ammo ran out.

The problem was, we were already out of ammunition. Despite our best efforts—cutting back on advertising and travel expenses in the last month—the campaign had finished $400,000 in the red. This included the salaries of dedicated workers who went on volunteer status as the race wound down. As it happens—at least, as old hands at political finance told me—$400,000 isn't much of a shortfall for a losing presidential campaign by today's standards. Still, I was determined to pay it off in full, including back salaries, as soon as possible.

So it was back to work for a last swing of fund-raisers. In a way it was the most heartening campaign trip of all, because greater loyalty and friendship has no man or woman than to contribute to a campaign that isn't just losing but has already lost. The last stop was at Clint Frank's home in Illinois, the day before the convention began. It wiped the ledger clean. We went to Detroit without a debt in the world—except the one that couldn't be paid back in dollars.

Nine

ONLY THE PRESIDENT LANDS ON THE SOUTH LAWN . . .

WELCOME ABOARD
FLIGHT INFORMATION

From <u>Austin, TX</u>   To <u>Andrews AFB, MD</u>
Distance <u>1,370</u> Statute Miles
Flight Time <u>2 Hours 29 Minutes</u>
    Please Set Your Watches Ahead <u>1 hour</u>
    For A <u>6:40 P.M.</u> Arrival
Our Route Will Be Over <u>Washington</u>
The En Route Flight Conditions Will Be <u>Good</u>.

DESTINATION WEATHER FORECAST
Temperature <u>65</u>° F.   Precipitation <u>Showers</u>
Wind <u>West 20 M.P.H.</u>   Clouds <u>Overcast</u>

                    MAJOR ORCHARD
                    Aircraft Commander

    It started as a routine vice presidential trip, though after only two months and ten days on the job, I still hadn't settled into thinking of anything as "routine." The plane itself was awesome, and not just because of its size and designation as "Air Force Two."*

    This, we were told, was one of the Boeing 707s that Lyndon Johnson had used when he was President. The sliding panel that separated the staff section of the front cabin from the President's private quarters opened and closed electronically. LBJ, they said, loved that sort of thing in his aircraft: sliding panels, furniture that magically appeared

---

* A word here about a widespread misconception: there is no single plane called "Air Force One" or "Air Force Two." The designation is given any aircraft the President or Vice President is aboard.

and disappeared. Most of the electronics were gone now, except for a kidney-shaped conference table that could be raised or lowered at the touch of a button, and a small black-and-white TV set behind a couch on the starboard side of the staff cabin.

On the Air Force books, the plane was officially listed as Aircraft #86970. It had seen a lot of Texas sky in its days with LBJ, flying the same flight pattern we'd followed that morning, from Washington to Fort Worth.

We'd boarded the plane—staff, guests, press, Secret Service—at 8:45 A.M. That was another "routine" part of the vice presidency I hadn't grown accustomed to—the size of my traveling party. Since my days of trimming costs at Zapata Off-Shore, I'd always preferred traveling lean, with only one or two staffers along, on business trips. Now, in addition to staff, there were a dozen reporters and cameramen, seven guests, and a Secret Service detail—not to mention an officially assigned doctor, a White House communications specialist, and a military aide.

My schedule stayed lean, however, fast-paced with no wasted motion. The trip would be a twelve-hour turnaround, leaving Washington in the early morning, returning that night. There would be two stops—Fort Worth and Austin—that included three speeches, a meeting with Governor Bill Clements, and two "press availabilities" (what in previce presidential days I'd known as a news conference).

Schedule
THE VICE PRESIDENT'S TRIP TO TEXAS

Monday, Marach 30, 1981

8:55 a.m. E.S.T.	Depart Andrews A.F.B. en route Fort Worth, Texas
10:45 a.m. C.S.T.	The Vice President arrives Fort Worth, Carswell A.F.B.
10:50 a.m.	The Vice President departs Carswell A.F.B. en route Hyatt Regency Hotel.
11:10 a.m.	Unveiling of plaque on the new Hyatt Regency, formerly the Old Hotel Texas.

The hotel, a well-known Texas landmark, was being recognized by the Department of Interior as a national historic site. There would be brief remarks before we moved on to my major speech in Fort Worth.

12:00 noon	*Address the Texas and Southwestern Cattle Raisers Association Luncheon— Tarrant County Convention Center*
1:20 p.m.	*The Vice President departs Convention Center en route Carswell A.F.B*
1:45 p.m.	*Air Force II departs Carswell A.F.B. en route Austin, Texas.*

The main event scheduled for Austin was an address to the Texas state legislature. Joining me on the trip were House Democratic Majority Leader Jim Wright of Fort Worth, and Congressmen Bill Archer of Houston and Jim Collins of Dallas, both Republicans. Bill had succeeded me as congressman from the Seventh District in 1970.

Flying time to Austin was forty-five minutes, a "routine" flight. But as the plane was taxiing down the runway at Carswell, Ed Pollard, the agent in charge of my Secret Service detail, came to my front cabin with word from Washington that an attempt had been made on President Reagan's life. The first report was that the President was all right, but "two agents were down."

"Where did it happen?" I asked.

"Outside the Washington Hilton," Ed replied. "I'll let you know when we get more information."

A few minutes after Ed left the cabin, I got a call from Secretary of State Haig in Washington. Phone calls in flight are transmitted by radio signal, which meant our conversation could be picked up anywhere in the world. Al spoke guardedly.

"There's been an incident," he said. "The feeling is you ought to return to Washington as soon as possible." He finished by adding that a coded message would be teletyped to the plane in a few minutes.

The message had just started coming over the teletype when the cabin phone buzzed again. It was Don Regan, urging that I scrub my Austin schedule and fly back to Washington. As Secretary of the Treasury, Don was responsible for Secret Service operations. Any attempt on the President's life alerts the Service to the possibility that it might be part of a larger plot.

Moments later the teletype message came through and was decoded. Ed Pollard's earlier report was only part of the story. The President had been shot. Even as we started our descent to the Robert Mueller Airport in Austin, he was undergoing emergency surgery at George Washington University Hospital in Washington.

It had to occur to me, but I didn't want to think about it. . . .

The Old Texas Hotel, where I'd unveiled the national historic plaque a few hours before, had been the place that John F. Kennedy spent the night of November 21, 1963, before his visit the next day to Dallas.

Even the plane we were on had played a part in that tragic trip. It was the "Air Force Two" used by then-Vice President Johnson as he accompanied President Kennedy to Texas on November 21, 1963. . . .

By the time we touched down in Austin, the enormity of what had happened was just beginning to sink in, reinforced by the sight and sound of what came over the plane's small black-and-white TV set: the President smiling and waving before he stepped into his car, the crack of gunfire, people hitting the pavement, Secret Service agents struggling with the suspect, the President's car speeding away.

I made the decision to cut my schedule short and head directly back to Washington. We were in Austin only to refuel. Once on the ground I called the White House. My chief of staff, Dan Murphy, told me what had happened at the Washington Hilton. There were three men wounded, in addition to the President: Tim McCarthy, a Secret Service agent; Tom Delahanty, a District of Columbia police officer; and White House press secretary Jim Brady.

Ed Meese filled me in on President Reagan's condition. At first, the President hadn't known he was wounded. Only the alert work of Secret Service agent Jerry Parr, who re-routed the car to nearby George Washington University Hospital, prevented a tragedy. As it was, the President was still in the operating room and there was no word about his condition. Nancy Reagan was at the hospital, waiting. It might be a long wait, several hours, before we knew.

I hung up the phone. The governor and Rita Clements were coming aboard the plane, along with George Strake, the Texas secretary of state. I got ready to greet them. But before that I closed myself off in the plane's front cabin to collect my thoughts. And to say a prayer not simply for the President of the United States but for someone I'd come to know and respect.

Eight months had passed since the night I got the call at the Pontchartrain Hotel in Detroit and heard the voice on the other end of the line say, "Hello, George . . ." When Ronald Reagan offered me the vice presidential spot on his ticket, I was under no illusion that George Bush was his first choice as a running mate. I knew that Reagan had reservations about me before Detroit, and while they weren't personal, they made him think twice before giving me the call.

Still, from the standpoint of national ticket unity, things could have been worse. The political alliance between John F. Kennedy and Lyndon Johnson in 1960 brought together two political leaders with a history of personal differences, going back to Kennedy's days as a junior senator who didn't defer to Johnson, the Democratic majority leader. As Vice President, Johnson was cut out of the White House inner circle.

My relations with Ronald Reagan started out on a different footing. There was never a hint of negative feeling left over from our fight for the presidential nomination because Reagan's instinct, I learned, is to think the best of the people he works with. It was clear that once he'd made his decision on the vice presidency, he viewed the Reagan-Bush ticket not simply as a convenient political alliance but as a partnership. We would run and serve together as a team.

Not that there was any doubt who was the senior partner. But as President, Ronald Reagan—more than any President before him—broke down the barriers between the nation's two highest elective offices. Jimmy Carter deserves credit for giving Walter Mondale office space in the White House, upgrading the prestige of the vice presidency. Carter and Mondale even had a written agreement on how their offices would work together. But Carter seemed to keep his Vice President—as he did most members of his Cabinet—at a distance, politically and personally. One Carter administration official told me that Mondale's White House office was more symbol than substance.

As Vice President, I was given the same White House space that Mondale had occupied, down the corridor from the Oval Office. But Ronald Reagan did more than that: he disproved Harry Truman's dictum that "a President, by necessity, builds his own staff, and his Vice President remains an outsider, no matter how friendly the two may be."

President Reagan had built his own staff; but since we'd taken the oath of office on January 20, he had gone out of his way to bring his Vice President inside the White House circle, and our trust and friendship had grown each passing day.

"There might be a crowd at Andrews. If you don't mind, sir, we'd like to bring the plane into the hangar and disembark there."

Ed Pollard and the Secret Service were still uncertain about whether the person who shot the President was acting alone or as part of a conspiracy. Under ordinary conditions Andrews Air Force Base would be considered a secure area, but for the Secret Service there are no "ordinary conditions" when an attempt has been made on the life of the President. The word from Washington was that the would-be assassin had worked his way into the press area outside the Washington Hilton. Ed had been trained to expect the unexpected, and an "ordinary" disembarkment on the open tarmac seemed to be taking unnecessary chances.

News from Washington was sketchy and some of it unreliable. Gathered around the flickering television set in the front cabin, we tried to piece together what was happening in the capital. There was a television report that Jim Brady had died. A few minutes later, word came through that the report was untrue. Jim was alive but in critical condition.

Meanwhile, the President was still in the operating room and there was nothing to do but wait—wait and stay calm. In the passenger cabin, Deputy Press Secretary Shirley Green was making a valiant effort to keep traveling reporters informed on what was happening. They wanted to talk to me, but I told Shirley it was no time to be talking to the press. Not until we had more information.

We were heading east, into the dark. Air Force Two began its descent, though we were still some distance away from Andrews. My contact on the President's staff was Ed Meese. It was agreed that as soon as we landed, I would head for the White House to meet with members of the Cabinet and National Security Council. Though we still had no word on the President's condition, it was vitally important that a signal be sent, to our friends as well as our potential adversaries around the world, that the United States Government wasn't paralyzed.

Waiting. Then, at 6:08 P.M.—Chase Untermeyer, a member of my staff, checked his watch after I hung up—the call we were waiting for finally came through.

It was Ed Meese on the line with the news that the President is out of the operating room. They had recovered the bullet. Everything was going well.

The President was out of danger, but there was still work to do, beginning with my meeting with members of the Cabinet and NSC. After that, I'd go before the White House press corps to make a statement and answer questions.

Forty-five minutes before we were scheduled to land at Andrews, Ed Pollard and Lieutenant Colonel John Matheny, my Air Force military aide, came to the front cabin to go over the logistics of our arrival. We were joined by members of the traveling staff. About half a dozen people were crammed into the cabin as we made our slow descent.

It was late dusk. Through the cabin window, lights from the Virginia countryside flickered on the horizon.

Matheny had a point to make. Ordinarily I'd board a Marine helicopter at the end of a day-long trip and be flown to a landing pad near the Vice President's residence on Massachusetts Avenue. But these weren't ordinary circumstances, said the colonel. Flying to the residence, then taking a car to the White House, would waste valuable time. It would be simpler to fly directly to the White House.

There were two things that argued in favor of taking this suggestion. First, members of the Cabinet, press, and NSC were waiting. Second, our ETA at Andrews was 6:40 P.M. By going straight to the White House, we'd get there in time for the 7 P.M. network news. What better way was there to reassure the country and tell the world the executive branch was still operating than to show the Vice President, on live TV, arriving at the White House?

It made sense, logistically and in other ways. But something about it didn't sit well with me. *The President in the hospital . . . Marine Two dropping out of the sky, blades whirring, the Vice President stepping off the helicopter to take charge. . . .*

Good television, yes—but not the message I thought we needed to send to the country and the world. I told Matheny to scrub his emergency arrival plan, that we'd follow customary procedure.

"We'll be coming in at rush hour," he pointed out. "Mass Avenue traffic will add anywhere from ten to fifteen minutes to your arrival time at the White House."

"Maybe so, but we'll just have to do it that way."

Matheny nodded. "Yes, sir," he said, moving toward the cabin door. He looked puzzled. I felt I owed him an explanation.

"John," I said, "only the President lands on the south lawn."

John Matheny was doing his job as he saw it, and I was doing mine as I saw it.

Not landing the Marine helicopter on the south lawn of

the White House was simply applying rule number one in the ground rules I'd adopted on how to be a functioning, useful Vice President. It's the most basic of all the rules. It says that the country can only have one President at a time, and the Vice President is not the one.

I'd been on the job only seventy days when the President was shot, but I'd already learned that some people don't seem to understand that principle. The modern vice presidency is the most misunderstood elective office in our political system. People either make too little or too much of it.

Those who make too little of it see the office in premodern terms, as it existed before President Eisenhower upgraded the vice presidency, including Richard Nixon in the Cabinet and NSC meetings. Before Nixon, Vice Presidents weren't included in the White House decision-making process. Their office was on Capitol Hill, and when thought of at all by the White House inner circle, they were considered in strict constitutional terms: the Vice President's job, as long as the President was alive, was to preside over the Senate. Period.

The idea that this wasn't much of a job dates back to the country's first Vice President, John Adams. George Washington received $25,000 annually to serve as President and Adams received $5,000 a year to serve as Vice President. Not much salary for the nation's second-highest elective officer, even by eighteenth-century standards. But it was too much, as some people saw it: a bill was introduced in Congress to trim the federal budget by eliminating the Vice President's salary and putting him on a per-diem basis.

Although the bill failed, the view that inspired it is still widely accepted nearly two centuries later. The perception of the vice presidency as a useless appendage persists in some quarters. Arthur Schlesinger, Jr., for one, has argued in favor of a constitutional amendment to abolish the office.

At the other end of the spectrum are those people who hold what might be called a "surrogate President" view of the vice presidency. Because modern Vice Presidents have offices in the White House–Executive Office Building complex and attend Cabinet and NSC meetings, it's thought that

they have constitutional and political power which they
don't actually possess.

During my first term as Vice President, I was constantly urged by friends to staff my office as if it were a
campaign operation, with an eye toward expanding my political base. I went out of the way to do just the opposite,
pointing out that the last thing any President needs is a Vice
President with his own agenda, grinding his own political
ax.

Some members of the news media also reflect this "surrogate President" view of the vice presidency, though in a
different way. One of the recurring questions I've had from
reporters, almost from the day I became Vice President, has
been: "Well, we know that's the official Administration position on the issue, but what's *your* position?

My answer has always been the same: a Vice President
can hold a different opinion from a President on an issue
and express it while the White House decision-making process is going on. But once the President makes his decision,
the matter is settled.

That answer doesn't always satisfy inquiring reporters
and columnists, but consider the alternative: A President
takes a position on a foreign-policy objective. Unhappy with
that position, the Vice President goes public with his views
in a major speech or interview. Here at home he may become a hero to those opposed to the President's policy. He
may even be editorially praised (by the President's editorial
opponents) for his "independence." But overseas, any division at the highest level of American government can only
be perceived by potential adversaries as a vulnerable area to
exploit, through diplomacy and propaganda.

It's fundamental that the country can only have one
President at a time. On the day a disgruntled, self-serving
Vice President declares civil war on the White House by
publicly challenging a President, our system of government
will be in serious trouble.

Early on, I recognized that the most important ingredi-
ent in an effective vice presidency is mutual respect between

the President and Vice President, based on mutual confidence. To gain and keep the President's confidence, I adopted five ground rules. In addition to the rule about knowing the limitations of my job—who lands and doesn't land on the south lawn—the other four were:

First, don't play the political opportunist's game by putting distance between yourself and the President when some White House decision or policy becomes unpopular. During the 1984 re-election campaign I was criticized by some political observers for not separating myself from the White House on certain issues. My feeling was and is that having become Vice President because of the popularity of the President, I owe him my loyalty and support.

The same observers argue that the only way a Vice President can get elected President in his own right is by splitting with the incumbent. I disagree. During the course of a presidential campaign, a Vice President can spell out in positive terms what his national agenda will be if he's elected President. But he can't have it both ways—going with the President in good times, then criticizing him at the first sign of trouble—and maintain the confidence of others.

Second, don't play the Washington news-leaking game. Not long after I became Vice President, I was approached by a well-known columnist, who said that he'd had a special arrangement with one of my predecessors. Every once in a while they'd get together for a background, not-for-attribution interview. The columnist would be filled in on what was going on around the White House–Executive Office Building complex. In return, he frequently gave favorable, complimentary treatment to his "high-level source." The question, submitted through a third party, was whether I'd be interested in a similar arrangement.

I'd been around Washington long enough to know that this sort of friendly accommodation between a journalist and a government official isn't unusual. In fact, it becomes a game in itself to read the morning papers and pinpoint the "high-level" leakers. But I also knew, from having worked in three administrations, that nothing inhibits free expression around a White House Cabinet or conference table more than a general feeling that "I'd better watch what I say, it may show up in the Washington *Post* or *The New York Times* tomorrow morning—or in some book three years from now."

That's why I sent word back to the inquiring columnist that while I'd be glad to talk to him any time, on the same open basis I'd talk to any other reporter, I wasn't interested in being an unidentified "high-level source." And it's why I regard all meetings and conversations about White House policy as confidential, not grist for the writing and sale of "insider" books.

This leads directly to the third rule, what I call the Stockman Rule: conduct all interviews on the record—even interviews with friends, especially if you want to keep them as friends. That way you're less likely to be surprised when you later read or hear yourself quoted in the press. Case in point: Dave Stockman and reporter Bill Greider.

One morning in late 1981, a forlorn, familiar figure in a dark blue suit showed up at my office seeking advice. It was Stockman, the Director of the Office of Management and Budget, to tell me that the December issue of *Atlantic Monthly* featured a piece entitled "The Education of David Stockman." The article, written by Greider, was based on interviews with Dave and gave a blow-by-blow account of the budget debate inside the Administration, with the OMB director portrayed as a disillusioned "Reaganaut" who no longer had faith in the President's fiscal program.

Since Stockman was one of the architects of that program, the Greider piece played into the hands of the President's Democratic critics on Capitol Hill. Dave seemed distraught. He said he had no idea he'd be quoted in that way.

Dave Stockman was one of the brightest young men I'd ever seen in Washington when it came to crunching numbers. His grasp of the most minute details of the federal budget was awesome. The President had placed complete trust in him. He was the cutting edge—literally—of the Administration's program to reduce government spending and bureaucratic waste. Other than the President himself, no White House spokesman was more closely identified with "Reaganomics" than the OMB director. The Greider article, therefore, had the potential of becoming a political, not just a public relations embarrassment. The question in my mind was how anyone as bright as David Stockman could have fallen into such a trap.

What Dave told me was that Bill Greider, though an Administration critic, was his old friend. From time to time he and Greider would get together for an early breakfast at the Hay-Adams Hotel, across Lafayette Park from the White House, and talk about Dave's work at OMB. The sessions were supposed to be "off the record," but Dave said they were tape-recorded by the reporter. That seemed a little naive—thinking you're talking "off the record" into an unconcealed tape recorder—but I let it pass. My thought was that everyone's entitled to one mistake.

When Dave finished telling his story, my advice was that he go down to the Oval Office as soon as possible, get an appointment with the President, and give him the same account he'd just given me. "Admit you've made a mistake and apologize," I advised him. "The President's a fair man and he thinks a lot of you. Let him know you're sorry, then let the chips fall."

The climax of the Stockman–*Atlantic Monthly* flap came when Dave had lunch with the President, apologized, and was let off the hook by an understanding Ronald Reagan.

Four years later, after Dave had left the Administration, a full-length book appeared that not only repeated and expanded on what he'd told Greider, but gave a detailed, direct-quote account of his lunch with the President. This time Dave couldn't claim he was misunderstood or thought he was talking off the record. He wrote the book himself.

The final rule has to do with what the Vice President owes the President along with loyalty—his best judgment, whether he and the President agree or differ on an issue.

Of course, it takes a certain kind of presidential personality to allow a Vice President to disagree, even privately, a personality strong enough not to resist or resent a contrary opinion. This is the sort of strength in a leader that comes from within and isn't reflected by bluster and bullying.

One of our strongest Presidents, Abraham Lincoln, was

a soft-spoken leader who had the inner self-confidence to include within his Cabinet headstrong, fractious personalities. Lincoln's consideration for the opinion of others was often mistaken for weakness. His penchant for telling jokes at Cabinet meetings and in public was seen by his critics as the mark of a frivolous, unconcentrated mind. But when the moment of truth came, the inner Lincoln always emerged, a leader in command.

Ronald Reagan's place in history won't be created by contemporary writers and historians but by those of the twenty-first century. In terms of leadership for the 1980s, however, the Reagan record is one of a President who had the will and found the way to move the country in a different direction than it was going the two previous decades. If, as his predecessor claimed, America suffered from a great "national malaise" in the last half of the 1970s, Reagan cured it. More likely he simply restored public faith in the country's basic health by imbuing an America which had come to doubt itself with his own unlimited optimism and self-confidence.

That self-confidence was reflected in the makeup of the Reagan Cabinet. Seated at the table during Cabinet meetings these past six and a half years have been strong-willed personalities that might have made a weaker President feel threatened. To name only a few: Al Haig, who wanted to influence the course of U.S. foreign policy the way Henry Kissinger had during the Nixon-Ford years; George Shultz, a Secretary of State who differed from Haig in temperament but not in tenacity; Secretary of Defense Cap Weinberger, an incisive, experienced administrator; Secretary of the Treasury Don Regan, tough-minded, not one to back away from controversy; Secretary of Commerce Mac Baldrige, a private-sector expert with a steel-trap mind; and Jim Baker, who brought the same resourcefulness to Treasury during the President's second term that he demonstrated as White House chief of staff during the first term.

None of these Cabinet members was or is a "yes man." On the contrary, the Reagan style of "collegial" management encouraged outspokenness at Cabinet meetings, with the President listening to a spectrum of opinion, then bringing the discussion back to fundamental principles.*

Cabinet meetings gave the President his only real chance to get a broad view of the operation of the executive branch, to stay in touch with its various departments. For many Cabinet members this was their only chance to communicate directly with the President over the course of a week. Knowing this, I saw the Vice President's role at these sessions as limited. With open, direct access to the Oval Office, there was ample opportunity to weigh in with my opinion on Administration policy and issues, without cutting into Cabinet time or putting the President in a position of having to decide "for" or "against" his Vice President.

The most productive sessions I had with the President came on Thursday of each week, when the two of us—alone, without staff—would get together for lunch, either in the Oval Office, a small adjoining office, or weather permitting, on the south lawn terrace. The menu seldom varied. We took advantage of the occasion to indulge our shared taste for Mexican food: tortilla chips and salsa for openers, then cheese soup and/or chili followed by sherbet unless a heavy state dinner was coming up that evening, in which case we'd opt for the soup and fruit served up by White House stewards.

There was no formal agenda. At times he'd ask me about a specific project I was working on, or if there was an upcoming overseas trip on my schedule, we'd discuss what message he wanted to deliver to my foreign hosts. The lunches were relaxed, the conversation wide-ranging, from affairs of state to small talk. And invariably I'd return to my

---

* One of the ironies of modern American political history was to be that one of our most conservative Presidents has patterned his approach to the office after one of our most liberal. While over the years President Reagan moved from being a liberal Democrat to a conservative Republican, his admiration for Franklin D. Roosevelt is undiminished. I've often suspected that except for the ideological furor it would have created, a portrait of Roosevelt might have been hanging on the wall of the Reagan Cabinet room these past seven years. Reagan views FDR as having saved the country's free institutions during the emergency years of the 1930s and '40s. Also, Roosevelt delegated responsibility to people he trusted, while keeping his eye on the big picture, a style of executive management Reagan admires.

office with some new joke he'd heard, sometimes two, that
he wanted to pass on.

    Walter Mondale had words of advice when I replaced
him as Vice President. "Be sure not to take any line respon-
sibilities," he warned. By that he meant permanent assignments covering specific areas of Administration policy.
    The general rule in taking on any executive project is:
never assume responsibility for something without the authority to carry it out successfully. The Vice President's authority in any executive area comes from the White House,
but the lines are sometimes blurred. Since Washington is a
turf-conscious environment—never more so than at or near
the center of power—a Vice President perceived to be stepping over a line could be on a collision course with the
White House staff or some Cabinet member.
    One of the best (or worst) examples of what can happen
when a Vice President takes on a job that threatens someone
else's turf occurred when Nelson Rockefeller held the office
in 1974–75. Because of Rockefeller's experience as governor
of New York, he hoped to play a major role in shaping the
Ford administration's domestic policy. But placed in charge
of the White House Domestic Council, he soon ran into
problems with the White House staff—despite the fact that
he had President Ford's blessing. Rockefeller's agenda for a
Ford administration domestic policy simply didn't mesh
with the staff's. Once, when I was CIA director, I visited
Rockefeller in the Executive Office Building and he spent a
full twenty minutes complaining about the White House
staff. "My relations with the President are good," he said,
"but that damned staff has cut me off at the knees."
    What Rockefeller learned was that being number one
man in Albany hadn't prepared him for being number two
man in Washington. He lost the turf battle, as any Vice
President is bound to when he steps over the invisible line.
    Still, given a clear line of authority as well as responsi-
bility, I felt there were important assignments I could and
should carry out in the domestic area, including:
  • *Federal Deregulation.* In one of his first official acts in

the domestic policy area, the President appointed me chairman of a special Task Force on Regulatory Relief. The OMB's Jim Miller worked with me on this assignment, along with my own staff aide, Boyden Gray. The task force submitted its report in August 1983, after setting policies and making specific recommendations to eliminate or revise hundreds of unnecessary federal rules and regulations. As chairman, I was able to follow through on one of our key 1980 campaign pledges—to cut red tape and get the federal government off the backs of the American people.

• *The South Florida Task Force.* In 1981 a delegation of private citizens came to Washington to appeal for increased federal activity to interdict drug traffic in Miami. Ed Meese (then a White House staff member) and I met with the delegation. Out of this meeting came the President's creation of a special task force directed against international drug smugglers. I headed this group as well as the broader-based National Narcotics Border Interdiction System created a year later. Dan Murphy, my chief of staff, played a key role in working with the Pentagon, Coast Guard, and civilian agencies to coordinate efforts to curb the flow of illegal drugs into the United States.

My own work with these groups led to a greater awareness of the scope of the drug threat to this country and the fact that we're involved in a war—not just figuratively, but literally—against illegal drug traffickers. The casualties are real: Little more than a year after the South Florida Task Force was formed, I presented posthumous medals to the families of Ariel Rios and Eduardo Benitez, two courageous young agents of the Bureau of Alcohol, Tobacco, and Firearms. Both had been brutally murdered in the course of arresting international drug pushers.

Representing the President overseas—not only at state funerals but on special missions—is another facet of the modern vice presidency. From 1981 through the spring of 1987 I traveled to seventy-three foreign countries on presidential assignments both ceremonial and substantive.

Among the most significant and memorable of these trips
were:

Moscow 1982/1984. Witnessing the passage of power in
the world's oldest totalitarian society—first, with the death
of Leonid Brezhnev in November 1982, then the death of his
successor, Yuri Andropov, in February 1984. From my personal notes taken during the Andropov trip:

> *Streets deserted, no cars, no people, as we go
> from airport into town. Same dreariness as 15
> months ago, when B. died. We arrived, same place
> B. lay in state, and again see the soldiers with the
> wreaths, people waiting in line outside. No appear-
> ance of grief, no tears . . . A protocol man rushes
> us in, we go up the stairs behind other delegations,
> our soldiers laboring under the wreath with AMER-
> ICA on it. . . . Howard* and I walk in front of
> bier, pay our respects. I walk over to Igor Andropov,
> the son, who thanks us for coming. . . . Curious
> eyes follow as we leave, move past the long line, into
> the icy Moscow air. . . . Strange feeling once
> again, a funeral without God . . .†*
>
> *Next morning before funeral march, go to see
> President Zia at the Pakistani embassy in the apart-
> ment building. Lots of Soviet soldiers in lobby. No
> bubble in embassy so we "talk" by holding up signs,
> figuring the place is bugged. Sign held up saying
> AFGHAN . . . "Oh yes, that situation is no better,
> no worse." . . . We don't get close to discussing
> sensitive matters, but using the signs still seems like
> a good idea. . . . On the reviewing stand [later]*

---

* Howard Baker, then Senate Majority Leader, who accompanied me on the Andropov trip.

† At the Brezhnev funeral, I was witness to a startling incident not noted in any of the
news reports. I was seated in the visitors' section, in a unique position to see a grieving
widow approach Brezhnev's coffin to say her last farewells. She looked down and
then, in an unmistakable gesture, leaned forward to make the sign of the cross over
her husband's body. I was stunned. In the midst of all the pomp and military ceremony of a state funeral, it was visible proof that despite official policy and dogma for
over six decades, God was still very much alive in the Soviet Union.

you see them all, the old and new leaders . . .
Gorbachev, a new one; Romanof a new one . . .
The visit with Chernenko . . . He seems more
robust than he appeared standing out in the cold.
Smiled now and then, but can't say he was friendly.
All in all, the President's decision not to come was
the right one. . . .

Saipan/China. En route to Beijing in mid-October 1985, we visited Saipan, bringing back memories of the last time I'd been there. Sitting in the governor's house, looking out toward the blue-green ocean, I could visualize the fleet —my carrier, the U.S.S. *Jacinto* and the battleships in the distance, shelling the high ground—while my squadron covered the landing at the beaches.

It had been the summer of 1944. I remembered the puffs of smoke, the scene on the beaches as we came in close to strafe enemy positions, somehow not feeling the battle, not the way they felt it down there on the beaches.

There were the stories told later about the Japanese families that threw themselves off the cliff at the end of the island, because they'd been told the Americans were going to murder them all. And even after that, of Japanese soldiers who went into the jungle and dug in, even though their country had surrendered. It was hard to believe there'd been a war on that beautiful, peaceful island forty-one years before and that I'd been part of it.

Four days later we were in Beijing, where I saw change of a different kind. As envoy to China ten years before, I used to wonder if China would ever really modernize. Now there were government officials, who'd been in Mao jackets in the 1970s, dressed in three-piece suits, driving Mercedes touring cars instead of their Red Flag autos.

There were other changes, more significant. Deng now talks about Taiwan differently. He says the island can keep its own government, as well as economic and military system, and talks about "one China, two systems." But some things don't change and I guess never will. He still works his way through several packs a day, smoking (I counted) eight cigarettes in the one hour twenty minutes we talked.

They put us up at the Guest House, the same suite used by President Reagan when he visited. On our last night there was a small dinner—small for formal state dinners, about thirty guests in all—of creamed snail soup, Beijing duck wrapped in seeded biscuits, beef, California wine. The Chinese adapt. Li Xianien was host. He got things off by saying this would be an evening of "true friendship—no speeches. All those speeches at dinners sound the same. They're tiresome." I said, "I couldn't agree more, thank you very much," and tore up my speech. It was all relaxed, probably the best formal dinner I've ever attended.

Different, all very different from the way it had been only ten years before. There were only thirty people in the U.S. liaison office then. Now there are three hundred in the U.S. embassy, recognition of the importance of our relationship to China, now and for the future.

El Salvador. The idea was to stop over on my way home from the inauguration of President Raúl Alfonsin in Buenos Aires. I told our ambassador in San Salvador, Tom Pickering, that I'd do it, and the stopover turned out to be one of those visits that stays with you years later.

El Salvador was trying to combat a guerrilla movement clearly sponsored by its Communist neighbor, Nicaragua. To survive, the Salvadoran government needed U.S. aid. But the country's death squads—extremists who'd murdered Archbishop Romero and four American churchwomen in 1981, then two U.S. labor advisers in 1981—were jeopardizing our ability to get support funds through Congress.

My job was to tell President Alvaro Magana and senior Salvadoran leaders (including the man who would be elected to succeed Magana, José Napoleon Duarte), and most important of all, the Commandantes who ran El Salvador's military, that the activity of the death squads would have to cease and human rights would have to be respected if they expected American aid to continue. The message had to be delivered forcefully, but in a way that wouldn't offend key allies in the fight against the spread of Marxist-Leninism in Central America.

Our arrival was like no formal state arrival I'd ever

seen. There were weapons all around, and not for any nine-teen-gun salutes. After Air Force Two touched down, we transferred to choppers that carried us to an open field a few miles away. There was scrub brush on the edge of the field. Men in camouflaged military garb could be seen, guns at the ready, guarding against any possible attack, either from left-wing guerrillas or right-wing death squads.

There was a hurried motorcade to a nearby location. Troops were everywhere. We held our series of meetings, and hours later a "state dinner" was held in a long, narrow, overcrowded room filled with just about every major political and military figure in the country. As I looked around the table, I could better understand the reason for the show of force outside. It wasn't just for the Vice President of the United States. One well-aimed rocket or bomb and the entire leadership of the country would have been wiped out.

My toast: I don't think I've ever given a formal toast more carefully phrased, to get America's message across.

"Mr. President," I said, "you and many other Salvadorans have demonstrated extraordinary personal courage in the struggle against tyranny and extremism." Then came the other half of the message. "But your cause is being undermined by the murderous violence of reactionary minorities. . . . These right-wing fanatics are the best friends the Soviets, the Cubans, the Sandinistas, and the Salvadoran guerrillas have. Every murderous act they commit poisons the well of friendship between our two countries and helps impose an alien dictatorship on the people of El Salvador. These cowardly death-squad terrorists are just as repugnant to me, to President Reagan, to the United States Congress, and to the American people as the terrorists of the Left."

I felt the words were having an impact, but it wasn't the kind of speech where success or failure is measured by whether you're cheered or applauded. The immediate response seemed to be good; but whether I'd succeeded could only be measured by what happened after we left.

More than four years later, the outcome in El Salvador is still in the balance, but the country has joined a growing list of Central and South American democracies that have replaced the old oligarchies and dictatorships. What part those tense seven hours in San Salvador played in that process is hard to gauge. But I know I delivered our message in December 1983.

Beirut. This was the most difficult foreign trip I'd made or would ever be called on to make as Vice President. There were 241 dead after a truck loaded with explosives crashed into the U.S. Marine barracks in Beirut, and all the old words—tragic, heinous, senseless—wouldn't bring them back, or prevent the terrorists from striking again, at some other time and place.

It was October 1983, seven years after the murder of the American ambassador to Lebanon that occurred while I was director of the CIA. I remembered my meeting with President Ford, Henry Kissinger, and Brent Scowcroft in the White House Situation Room. We were concerned about the extent of danger to U.S. citizens in the Beirut area and whether to evacuate them, at the risk of having it appear that we'd lost confidence in a moderate, pro-Western government.

Had anything changed in the past seven years? Surveying the damage at the Marine barracks and talking to some of the survivors, it didn't seem so. But the importance of this area of the world to the United States and the West was too great simply to throw up our hands and walk away.

We had sent the Marines into Lebanon as part of an international peace-keeping team. The question now was whether there was anything at all we could do to help bring peace to the area. President Reagan continued to hope there was, that despite setbacks some way could be found to break the cycle of terrorist violence and stabilize not only Lebanon but the entire Middle East.

The Iran initiative began with the idea that there were changes coming in one of the centers of world terrorism. When the Ayatollah Khomeini died, there would be a power struggle among various factions to succeed him. Our estimate was that the struggle had already begun, with some factions more inclined toward a policy less hostile to the "Great Satan," America, than others.

The idea wasn't ours alone. Other countries with vital interests in the area had begun "reach out" operations—not only Israel but at least one Arab state which quietly recommended that we do the same.

As far as most Americans were concerned, Iran was Khomeini, period. But we had reports that beyond Khomeini were other Iranians whose attention was focused on Soviet troops on their country's borders. They saw more than 100,000 Russian soldiers occupying their Islamic neighbor, Afghanistan. They harbored the historic Iranian fear and distrust of their neighbor to the north.

To these Iranians it was the Soviet Union, not the United States, that represented the "Great Satan." They weren't "moderates" by any means; but by cultivating this faction, the coming change in Tehran could be for the better. Our alternative was to do nothing, let the inevitable change take place, and hope for the best. The decision was to "reach out."

It would be risky, but in that unstable part of the world every policy initiative is a risk. Sometimes Presidents have to take risks where our national interests are concerned. Based on what we knew from our own intelligence sources and what we heard from friendly nations close to the scene, the President decided the risk in this case would be worth it.

As I write these words, in early May 1987, congressional investigators and a special prosecutor are looking into every facet of what ultimately grew into the Iran-Contra affair. Without knowing what new facts will come to light in the months ahead, I won't speculate on the role played in the affair by others.

But having said that, there are elements of the Iran-Contra affair that I know won't change tomorrow, six months, or six years from now. Some of these elements were brought to light by the Tower Commission Report published earlier this year. Others relate to lessons to be drawn on how future administrations can prevent similar fiascos.

. . .

Begin with what I knew and when I knew it.

What I knew was that, working through the Israelis, an effort had been made to "reach out" to one of the Iranian factions, that there had been a weapons sale, and that in some way the hostage issue had become part of the project.

After the fact I was asked by reporters why I didn't know more. The answer was and is that the people running the operation had it compartmentalized, like pieces of a puzzle. My first real chance to see the picture as a whole didn't come until December 1986, when Dave Durenberger, then chairman of the Senate Intelligence Committee, briefed me on his committee's preliminary investigation of the affair.

What Dave had to say left me with the feeling, expressed to my chief of staff, Craig Fuller, that I'd been deliberately excluded from key meetings involving details of the Iran operation. That was my initial reaction, but I was only partly right. It wasn't simply that the Vice President had been excluded. What had been excluded were the safeguards in the White House decision-making process, beginning with the key safeguard in dealing with foreign-policy matters, the National Security Council.

In the long term, "reaching out" meant preparing the way for a post-Khomeini Iran that would be a stabilizing, not a disruptive, force in the Middle East. It was an idea that was hard to argue against. But in the short term, this meant selling $12 million worth of TOW missiles to the Iranians. That was an idea that was hard to swallow, until it was put to the President in the context of the *$8 billion* total arms trade going on between Iran and other countries.

The question was whether selling weapons to a so-called "moderate" faction within one of the world's leading sponsors of international terrorism ran counter to the Administration's policy against dealing with terrorists. But as the President saw it, "reaching out" was separate and apart from that policy. To his mind we weren't selling arms to the kidnappers, so we weren't negotiating with terrorists.

It was a fine line, but consistent with what those inside the administration knew of the President's concern about the hostages. Though he didn't dwell on the subject publicly, it became an overriding issue inside the White House. He met and stayed in touch with the hostage families and felt a personal as well as official commitment to bring the American hostages home.

For my part, I agreed with the President that we needed to develop long-range plans for a less hostile relationship with post-Khomeini Iran. And I shared the President's concern for our American hostages. But what troubled me—and I expressed these misgivings—was that the United States was involved in a major foreign-policy initiative with only limited control over how it was carried out. True, we were working with a loyal ally, Israel; but at times even the Israelis indicated they were at a loss to understand the volatile political situation in Iran.

In August 1986, when I visited Jerusalem and was asked to meet with Amiram Nir, Israel's leading expert on counterterrorism. I was in Israel to talk with leaders there about overall U.S.-Israeli relations. Craig Fuller, my chief of staff, got a call from Nir, who said he wanted to brief me. Craig wasn't aware of our contacts with Iran, and I didn't really know who Nir was. An earlier request that I meet with Nir had come from Marine Lieutenant Colonel Oliver North of the NSC staff.

Nir's official title was Special Assistant on Counterterrorism to Israeli Prime Minister Shimon Peres. Still, something about the situation made me uneasy—so uneasy that I got up in the middle of the night and put in a secured call to NSC Director Vice Admiral John Poindexter to find out if he knew about the request. The operator couldn't reach Poindexter, and instead I got North, who reassured me about the meeting. He said the original request had come from Prime Minister Peres himself, our host for the visit, and it would simply be a "listening" session on my part, with Nir filling me in.

I met with Nir in my quarters at the King David Hotel,

with Fuller present to take notes. Nir was a man in his early to mid forties, one of those people—like Oliver North—who looked and talked as if he'd rather be in the field than sitting behind a desk. Our meeting lasted twenty-five minutes. He went into the background of what he called the "two layers" of our Iran initiative. The first layer was tactical ("freeing the hostages"), the second strategic ("building contact with Iran so that we're ready when a change takes place"). The original idea, as I understood it, was to "reach out" to those Iranian factions more likely to be friendly to the West. But Nir was talking about first working with one group ("moderates") and then making contact with another ("radicals"), because they had better leverage on getting the hostages freed. He didn't, however, spell out exactly who these individuals were, and when our meeting was over my feeling about our lack of control over the operation remained.

Nir was supplying pieces of a puzzle, but as the Tower Commission pointed out, only a few people had the big picture.

I knew, for example, about former NSC Director Bud McFarlane's secret trip to Iran in May 1986. Accompanied by Lieutenant Colonel North, McFarlane—on a mission approved by the President—had flown to Tehran aboard an Israeli Air Force 707 carrying TOW missile launchers. But along with the President, I didn't know until November 1986 that North and John Poindexter, the Navy vice admiral who succeeded McFarlane, had conducted other secret operations outside the NSC process.

When North's activities—including possible diversion of Iranian weapons funds to the Nicaraguan Contras—became known in the third week of November, they were reported by the press as NSC operations. But they weren't. Oliver North wasn't a member of the NSC. He was an NSC staffer, working under Poindexter.

I knew Ollie North as the Marine lieutenant colonel who had worked on the Grenada operation.* A decorated

* As chairman of the White House Special Situations Group, I helped coordinate plans to send American forces to Grenada after neighboring Caribbean countries

Vietnam veteran, he was respected around the White House as a prodigious worker who "gets things done." His activities took him from the Central American jungles to civic group lunches, where he addressed audiences on United States foreign policy. But North remained a staffer, not an NSC member—an important distinction for future Presidents who want to avoid runaway covert operations.

The statutory membership of the National Security Council is made up of the President, the Vice President, the Secretaries of State and Defense, the director of the CIA, and the chairman of the Joint Chiefs of Staff. As defined by the 1947 law creating it (the same law that created the CIA), the NSC's purpose is "to advise the President with respect to the integration of domestic, foreign, and military policies relating to the national security . . ."

That's clear enough. The NSC was created to advise the President, not to take on the job of the CIA in running covert operations. But while the NSC staff took on a covert operation it wasn't designed to conduct, at no point along the way, from its beginning to its end, was the NSC membership formally brought together to discuss the Iran initiative. Not one meeting of the National Security Council was ever held to consider all phases of the operation—not only its possible benefits, but the problems and pitfalls it might face.

Bryce Harlow, who served in the Eisenhower White House, once told the story of an NSC meeting that took place in 1958, when the decision was made to send Marines into Lebanon to shore up the shaky pro-Western government of President Camille Chamoun. As Bryce recalled, Eisenhower, after being briefed on preparations to insure the success of the action, turned to his Secretary of State, John Foster Dulles, and said, "Foster, I'm satisfied everything's been done to make things go right. Now tell me, what are our plans if things go *wrong*?"

In that instance the President himself, an expert on

---

called on the United States to prevent a Castro-inspired Marxist takeover of the island. The Special Situations Group operates only in the absence of the President. The group monitors foreign-policy crises and makes recommendations, but the final decision is always the President's.

high-risk military ventures, asked the key question. But normally the NSC's role is to raise questions—to examine the pros and cons the President needs to consider before giving the go-ahead on a foreign-policy venture—especially a high-risk venture in the Middle East.

President Reagan never had the benefit of that kind of comprehensive advice on Iran. The NSC advisory apparatus was there, but it wasn't used. Instead it was bypassed, and the information and advice the President received came to him piecemeal—only pieces of the puzzle, not the full picture.

What lesson can future Presidents learn from Iran-Contra? An old lesson that's all too often forgotten: Don't look for shortcuts and don't try to circumvent the process. Most important of all, follow the rules.

Rule one is that in planning and carrying out a covert operation, the law has to be followed to the letter.

Rule two is never try to strike a bargain with terrorists.

In retrospect there were signals along the way that gave fair warning that the Iran initiative was headed for trouble. As it turned out, George Shultz and Cap Weinberger had serious doubts, too. If I'd known that and asked the President to call a meeting of the NSC, he might have seen the project in a different light, as a gamble doomed to fail.

There were other questions as well that were asked by reporters after the story broke in mid-November—not only the question of what I'd known and when I'd known it but the inevitable questions I'd heard more than any others during my years as Vice President:

If I differed with the President, why didn't I spell out my differences? A Vice President can spell out his differences privately, but differing with the President publicly when an Administration policy is under attack would be the worst kind of cheap-shot opportunism. Would I have done the same thing in the same way if I were President? Second-guessing is a luxury best left to the political opposition and editorial commentators, not to members of the President's own team. And if I ever expected to become President myself, shouldn't I define George Bush's position on this and other issues, separate and apart from Ronald Reagan's? There's a time and a place for all things. A Vice President who puts his own agenda ahead of the President's at the wrong time and place—who places self-interest above all else—wouldn't deserve to be President in any case.

Finally, in the aftermath of Iran-Contra, there were questions raised about Ronald Reagan's executive management style: Does this President pay too little attention to detail, delegating too much authority to subordinates?

Every President has his own executive style. Franklin Roosevelt, the role model for the Reagan style, kept his eye on the horizon, leaving the details to others. Jimmy Carter, on the other hand, took time to check the names of people using the White House tennis courts.

The key question, then, isn't so much the style of executive management; it's the quality of presidential leadership. And the answer to how well Ronald Reagan runs the White House lies not in the style used in handling a single issue, but in his Administration's overall record since he first took office.

I recall sitting on the inaugural platform that clear, crisp day, January 20, 1981. The forecast had been for rain, but the sun broke through and the temperature was in the mid-fifties. The ceremonies took place for the first time in history, on the West Front of the Capitol, looking toward Pennsylvania Avenue. First, I took the oath of Vice President, administered by my friend, Justice Potter Stewart, while Barbara held the family bible; then there was a hymn, "Faith of our Fathers"; then Chief Justice Warren Burger administered the oath to the new President. There was a twenty-one-gun salute. A pause. Then Ronald Reagan spoke, pledging a stronger America, at peace, its economy revived, with renewed respect overseas and restored confidence here at home—"an era of national renewal."

Looking back, we've moved a long way in that direction. Looking forward, we still have miles to go.

Ten

LOOKING
FORWARD

When a candidate says, "I'm glad you asked me that question," political cynics immediately assume the opposite: that the question is one the candidate really didn't want to be asked. But the truth is that there are many questions you'd like to answer that never seem to come up. I've gone away from dozens of interviews asking myself why reporters didn't get around to some issue or subject I wanted to talk about. I've wondered why it didn't come up and even speculated how I would have raised it and other questions if I were a reporter.

Q: *Hearing your life story, one thing becomes pretty clear: you don't seem to hold a job very long.*

GB: You've been talking to Barbara. She says the same thing. We've moved twenty-eight times in forty years. As a matter of fact, we've lived in the Vice President's house longer than any other house since we were married.

Q: *All those jobs, though—Congress, the U.N., China, the CIA—any recommendations you'd make? Let's start with Congress.*

GB: The main thing I'd recommend there is a code of ethics for all members, the same standard currently applied to the executive branch. Full disclosure of assets, liabilities, outside income of members, as well as families and their staffs. A conflict-of-interest code. It's overdue.

Q: *Isn't that a lot easier for you to say? After all, you're not a member of Congress anymore.*

GB: I've been saying the same thing for twenty years, ever since I was a member of Congress. The first thing I did on coming to Washington in January 1967 was make a

full disclosure of everything we owned and owed. Then
I introduced an Ethics and Disclosure resolution in the
House.

Q: *What happened to it?*
GB: The same thing that happens to most bills introduced
by freshmen in Congress. It didn't get very far. But
ethics is a nonpartisan issue that won't go away—one
of the issues of the 1980s, more important than ever.
Scams on Wall Street, scams in government—it's up to
Washington to set the ethical standard for the country.
I'm a great believer in Grover Cleveland's maxim "a
public office is a public trust."

Q: *Your next job was at the U.N. Any recommendations
there?*
GB: I start with the idea that for all its shortcomings, the
U.N. serves a valuable purpose at the agency level,
working on problems like agriculture, the environment, and health. But because votes in the General
Assembly are influenced by regional grouping and bloc
voting, U.N. resolutions tend to be irrelevant. One recommendation, if the money were available, is for the
General Assembly meetings to be rotated to different
parts of the world, every so often first in New York
City, then, say, Moscow. Operating in the political environment of the Soviet Union at regular intervals
might be just the tonic needed for U.N. diplomats like
those who used to call me at all hours to criticize New
York.

Another recommendation: When I left that job, I
wrote a memorandum to President Nixon, advising
that the U.S. ambassador to the U.N. shouldn't have
full cabinet status. Let me explain why. President Eisenhower elevated the job to Cabinet level in order to
give his ambassador, Henry Cabot Lodge, greater stat-
ure. It looked like a good idea on paper. But in practice
this creates unnecessary tension with the Secretary of
State. As a full Cabinet member, a U.N. ambassador is
perceived as having equal status with the Secretary of

State—not working under him but directly under the President. The result was that on occasion I'd get one policy direction from the State Department; then a little while later Henry Kissinger, the NSC adviser, would call from the White House invoking the President's name, to tell me to ignore the State Department's instructions and do something else. Foreign policy is risky enough without having two conflicting voices in the Cabinet, talking to the world in two different ways. Our ambassador to the U.N. ought to report to the Secretary of State and the President, the way other ambassadors do.

Q: *You mentioned foreign policy. Let's get specific. Any recommendations or thoughts about U.S.-China relations, based on your experience there?*

GB: Yes, our relations with China are important in their own right, not in terms of what some have called a "card" in the U.S.-Soviet relations. There has to be a peaceful resolution to the Taiwan question, of course, but tensions in that area aren't as great now as they were in past years. Beyond that, there's every reason our relations with China should grow and prosper in the years ahead because it is important to both our countries, strategically, culturally, and economically.

Q: *Your last stop before the vice presidency was the CIA. Any added thoughts about covert actions, in light of Iran-Contra?*

GB: It's hard for people in a free society to accept the fact that covert action is often necessary for a world power to survive. An American President faced with a potential threat to national security should have some alternative between doing nothing and waiting for a crisis to blow up in our face. The answer is covert action— but it has to be conducted along strictly legal guidelines. When I was CIA director, I helped put President Ford's executive order governing covert actions into effect. That order provides for congressional oversight of covert activities. The order also makes clear that the

CIA—not the NSC—is the proper agency to conduct covert operations. The rules are spelled out. They cannot be ignored or bypassed.

The long-range effect of something like Iran-Contra is to put all covert actions under a cloud. I agree that Congress has a legitimate concern in this area, but at the same time, you can't run covert operations if everybody on Capitol Hill, members and staff alike, has access to all information about what the CIA's doing at any given time. There are bound to be leaks, and leaks jeopardize covert operations and the lives of the people conducting them. There has to be a balance —strict observance of the law by those who operate covert actions and an understanding by Congress and the press that there are intelligence secrets that have to be kept secret. I'm in favor of a single congressional oversight committee—a Joint Intelligence Committee modeled after the leak-proof Joint Committee on Atomic Energy that was so successful in the 1940s and '50s.

One more thought about the CIA—the same point I made about the U.N. ambassador. I don't think the director of the CIA ought to be part of the Cabinet. He's not supposed to be a policymaker, and getting the country's chief intelligence officer involved in policy— not to mention politics—is outside the CIA charter. When I was with the CIA, I made it a practice to attend only those Cabinet meetings where I was expected to report on something. When I finished my report, I'd leave. And no politics, either. There has to be a wall between the CIA and the two P's—policy and politics.

Q: *I want to ask you about a third P, the press. Are you satisfied with the way the media cover you?*

GB: Criticism goes with the territory when you're in politics. I've had good relations with the press over the years, though I'll admit that some of the things written about me since I became Vice President haven't made good breakfast-table reading. But my answer is that, on balance, I've been treated fairly.

Q: *But what about the 1984 campaign? I seem to recall there were some press problems back then. You didn't seem too happy with your coverage at times.*

GB: Let's put it this way. Geraldine Ferraro and I agreed on very few things in 1984, but we had a shared feeling that coverage of the vice presidential campaign lacked something. Still, I think the press does its job as well as it can, and I do mine as well as I can. I learned a great deal in that campaign. It's an adversarial relationship at times, but there's no reason it can't be between friendly adversaries.

Q: *It's a little early—the campaign's over a year away— but would you like to talk about your program for the decade of the 1990s?*

GB: You're right, it's early. But I'll have a lot to say about that after I become a formal candidate and the campaign progresses.

Q: *Okay, let's talk about the past seven years. You mentioned what you consider the Administration's achievements. Any disappointments?*

GB: There are always disappointments, projects I feel are unfinished. One that comes to mind traces back to my days as chairman of the Harris County, Texas Republican Party in the early 1960s. We worked overtime hoping to attract black voters. As a congressman, I tried to put my hopes into actions, but we didn't have much success breaking blacks away from voting the straight Democratic ticket. I'd still like to make that breakthrough on a national scale, and I've kept my door open not only to blacks but other minority groups. I believe both blacks and Hispanics have a home in the G.O.P. For example, I've stressed the fact that one-party voting, while it's bad for the Republican Party, is even worse for the black community. The democrats were taking black voters for granted twenty years ago, and they still are.

As Vice President I have tried to keep not only my door but my mind open to what other people think, even if I disagree. I always want to hear the other person's point of view—provided, of course, that I get a chance to express my own. Even if you don't change anybody's mind, it clears the air. It gets both sides seeing each other as human beings, not just in political or ideological terms. I think that's an element of leadership—not just talking but listening.

Q: *Speaking of leadership, even if you don't want to detail any programs, what do you think will be the issue of the 1988 presidential campaign?*

GB: There's plenty of time left for campaign speeches, but if you want a short answer, it's leadership itself, how the various candidates perceive it.

My own perception comes from experience—building a business, my work in government running various offices—seeing how both the private and public sectors operate. I've learned that leadership isn't just making decisions and giving orders. It's hearing all points of view before making the decision. That's the way leadership works in a free society, by keeping open doors and open minds. For that matter, it's important everywhere in American life—tolerance for the other person's point of view—understanding that as Americans the values we share are more important than any differences we have.

Q: *All right, the last two questions: When the Reagan-Bush ticket was selected in 1980, you asked the American people, "Are you better off now than you were four years ago?" Looking forward toward the last decade of the century, your thoughts: Are Americans going to be better off in the year 2000 than they are today?*

GB: Yes, definitely. I've seen our country go through Depression, World War II, Korea, Viet Nam, the days in the 1960s and 1970s when some people thought our society was coming apart. But instead we've come out of that as a better and stronger country.

Q: *Last question. Going back to 1948, the year you left college and went out to Texas. Out of all the things you've done since then—in business, Congress, the U.N., China, the CIA, the vice presidency—what single accomplishment are you proudest of?*

GB: The fact that our children still come home.

Index